微观中国
1-MINUTE CHINA

NINGXIA: QUIET AND QUICK

微观宁夏

（汉英版）

蒋文龄 主编

创于1897 商務印書館 The Commercial Press

2019年 · 北京

丛书策划　聂晓阳　周洪波

主　　编　蒋文龄
副 主 编　郝　彤　徐向红
撰　　写　（按音序排列）
黑小花　李光荣　李晓园　刘汉立　马　慧
马鹏丽　宋晓明　唐荣尧　田艳芳　田玉珍
王跃英　徐向红　许长礼　张　弘　张廷珍
张樱紫　张志翔

图片统筹　陶克图
英文翻译　梅　皓〔美〕
英文审订　魏令查　邢三洲　赵春燕
中文编辑　戴军明
英文编辑　刘　彤
中文审读　肖淼晨
书籍设计　东方美迪

Chief Producers　Nie Xiaoyang, Zhou Hongbo

Chief Compiler　Jiang Wenling
Deputy Compiler　Hao Tong, Xu Xianghong
Writers　(Surname in alphabetic order)
Hei Xiaohua, Li Guangrong, Li Xiaoyuan, Liu Hanli, Ma Hui,
Ma Pengli, Song Xiaoming, Tang Rongyao, Tian Yanfang,
Tian Yuzhen, Wang Yueying, Xu Xianghong, Xu Changli,
Zhang Hong, Zhang Tingzhen, Zhang Yingzi, Zhang Zhixiang

Photo Coordinator　Tao Ketu
English Translator　Mei Hao（USA）
English Reviewer　Wei Lingcha, Xing Sanzhou, Zhao Chunyan
Chinese Editor　Dai Junming
English Editor　Liu Tong
Chinese Reviewer　Xiao Miaochen
Art Design　EmDesign

把厚重而神奇的宁夏还给世人

世界上总有一些默默无闻不被人们特别关注的地方，宁夏就是其中一个。作为大西北面积最小的省份，宁夏实在太低调了，以至于许多人几乎忽略了它的存在。

一位宁夏老人给海外亲人准备了一份精致的中国地图作为礼物，不经意地发现，把地图四角折起来，宁夏恰好位于对折线上。仔细打量一下今天的中国地图，宁夏正位于中国陆疆的几何中心。宁夏地处黄河上游，沿黄河两岸是几百万亩肥沃土地的引黄灌区，素有“塞上江南”之称，是内陆沙漠地带的一片绿洲。《国家人文地理》总编辑李海洲说，那片地域更多地充满了马背上的较量，蹄印如雨之下其实是另一种江南，它叫作宁夏。

宁夏显然是藏着的，而且藏在中国地理和历史的双重腹地中。任何景物，如果不通过一种文化、一种文明来展现，是毫无意义的。宁夏回族自治区成立于 1958 年 10 月，成立发展至今，宁夏经济社会发展等取得长足进步，政通人和、环境优美、人民安居乐业，首府银川被评为宜居城市，银川平原被评为中国十大新天府。2016 年 7 月，习近平总书记在宁夏考察时强调，（宁夏）要认真落实党中央决策部署，贯彻新发展理念，主动融入国家发展战略，进一步解放思想、真抓实干、奋力前进，努力实现经济繁荣、民族团结、环境优美、人民富裕，确保与全国同步建成全面小康社会。2018 年，适逢宁夏回族自治区成立 60 周年，策划出版《微观宁夏》，旨在向中外读者还原一个真实而生动、兼具自然美和人文美的宁夏，展示一个藏在历史深处、厚重而神奇的宁夏。

一

宁夏不缺历史。宁夏灵武发现距今约 1.6 亿年前恐龙化石遗址，为展现史前生态景观，研究西北地区远古时期地理、气候，恐龙种属的繁衍、迁徙、灭亡，地球陆地板块漂移学说，提供了珍贵的实物资料和重要科学信息；宁夏水洞沟发现的旧石器时代晚期人类活动的遗址和遗物，记载了早在3万年前，人类就在宁夏这片土地上繁衍生息，表明宁夏是中华民族远古文明的发祥地之一；被国际灌排委员会列入世界灌溉工程遗产名录的“宁夏引黄古灌区”，是我国最古老的黄河水利工程之一。宁夏与黄河息息相关，黄河孕育了中华民族的历史，也哺育了宁夏的历史。2016年度全国十大考古新发现之一青铜峡鸽子山遗址、2017年度全国十大考古新发现之一彭阳姚河商周遗址，为中华文明不同历史时期的发展提供更久远的史料。宁夏有很多历史古城堡、古塔和烽火台，有战国、秦、明、清时期的长城，清楚地记载着中国不同历史时期的模样。秦始皇统一中国后，派兵在宁夏屯垦，修筑了闻名世界的秦长城。也许是因为有长城围起来的缘故，行旅作家唐荣尧认为，宁夏是藏着的、出乎意料的。他用了8年的时间，从新闻记者的角度，以诗人的笔调、学者的严谨以及田野考察者孤寂而坚韧的精神，用文学的语言向世人展示宁夏时光镜面上的人和事。他说，宁夏更像一个偏居中国腹地的散淡之人，在巷陌池边缓缓驻足，在草色烟光中兀自喃喃低语，安逸而恬淡。

二

奇特的地貌、多元的文化、神秘的历史，宁夏就是一片神奇的土地。宁夏有历史，更有人文、有情怀、有民俗、有生活、有故事。九曲黄河流经宁夏后，在腾格里沙漠、乌兰布和沙漠和毛乌素沙漠的重重包围中左冲右突，在半荒漠状态的自然环境中，拍打出田园似锦的宁夏平原，滋养出姹紫嫣红的塞上江南。张钦楠在《阅读城市》里说，城市是人类所创造的最美妙、最高级、最复杂又最深刻的产物。每个城市有着它独特的自然、人文和历史背景而各不相同。我们要阅读的是，它们不同在何处、又为何不同?

三

从没有来过宁夏的人，对宁夏的印象大都是典型的大西北，恶劣的气候、突兀的黄土高坡、干旱的荒漠、频繁的沙尘暴、空气里弥漫着干燥的泥土气息……和“塞上江南”是不沾边的。然而，银川“七十二连湖”，以水的温柔静静地撑起了“塞上江南”的美誉。

宁夏回族自治区党委书记石泰峰曾用三句诗向媒体介绍宁夏。他说，宁夏虽然面积不大，却具备了各种自然风情、地貌，有着深厚的历史积淀。如果不到银川，不到吴忠，不到石嘴山，就体验不到“贺兰山下果园成，塞北江南旧有名”的风情；如果不到中卫，不到沙坡头，就体会不到唐代大诗人王维描绘的“大漠孤烟直，长河落日圆”的雄浑；如果不上六盘山，就体会不到毛泽东同志所书“天高云淡，望断南飞雁。不到长城非好汉”的豪迈。宁夏的风情、雄浑、豪迈就是这么简单而诗意。

这个几乎被世人忽略的、被长城围着的、藏在历史深处的中国西北边地，被美国《纽约时报》评选为全球必去的 46 个最佳旅游地。

四

一个城市有了文化，城市才有温度，城市生活才更有内涵，人们对这座城市才有归属感和认同感。

在宁夏，每一个街道都有自己的故事，也都有自己神奇的传说，你知道或不知道，它都静静地沉淀在这个地方的血液里，在历史的沉淀中仔细享受着，因为它们是这个地方的灵魂担当。

认识宁夏，就要了解宁夏这个地方的灵魂。

作为《微观中国》系列丛书中的一册，我们尝试用真情微妙的笔端，在街头巷陌里、在细微末节处，讲好有历史厚度和有情怀温度的多味多彩有声响的宁夏故事。

宁夏地处北纬 38 度，是世界公认的葡萄酒酿造的黄金地带，宁夏贺兰山东麓葡萄酒产区被写入世界葡萄酒地图。每个人心中都有一座城，作为生于斯长于斯的宁夏人，这里，阳光正好、天蓝云白；这里，有故事、有葡萄酒。举起酒杯，浅饮慢斟，在一个惬意的午后，享受时光的穿梭，悦读《微观宁夏》，为你静候微醺时光。

蒋文龄

2018 年 7 月

Majestic and Magical Ningxia

There are a few places in this world that are unknown to most, that have no special attention paid to them. Ningxia is one of these places. As the smallest province by area in North-western China, Ningxia is very low-key, to the extent that some almost ignore its existence.

An old man of Ningxia prepared an exquisite map of China as a present for his relatives overseas. He discovered by accident that if one folds in the four corners of the map, Ningxia was at the intersection of the fold lines. A close look at a map of China reveals that Ningxia is at the geometric centre of the land of China. Ningxia is located in the upper reaches of the Yellow River, which irrigates thousands of square kilometres of fertile soil along its banks within the province. The province also has the fame of lush southern-style fields north of the Great Wall – it is an oasis in the inland desert. Editor-in-chief of *National Human Geography* Li Haizhou said, despite it's a place full of measures of strength, Ningxia is abundant in products and glamour.

Whilst Ningxia evidently is hidden, hidden in both Chinese geography and history. Any scene, if not viewed through the lens of culture and civilisation, is meaningless. Since October 1958 when the Ningxia Hui Autonomous Region was established, it has made great progress in many aspects. Things run well administratively, and people are content. The environment is beautiful, and people live peacefully and happily. The capital, Yinchuan, is considered one of the most livable cities, and the Ningxia plains one of the ten best regions of China. In July, 2016 when Chinese President Xi Jinping toured Ningxia, he emphasised that it should earnestly put into effect the policies of the Central Committee of the Party, implement new development concepts, and take the initiative to engage itself in the national development strategies. Carrying forward emancipation of the mind, working earnestly and hard as it moves forward, striving strenuously for economic prosperity, with ethnicities coming together in a beautiful environment where the people are prosperous, ensuring the creation of a moderately prosperous society in all aspects in line with the rest of the nation – this is the destiny of Ningxia. 2018 marks the 60th anniversary of the creation of the Ningxia Hui Autonomous Region, so we have planned and published *Ningxia: Quiet and Quick* as one of the *One-Minute China* series in the hope of providing to readers both in China and abroad a true and vibrant depiction of Ningxia: its natural and cultural beauty as well as its majestic and magical history.

Ningxia is full of history. In Lingwu, fossils of dinosaurs from approximately 160 million years ago have been discovered. They provide real material and important scientific information about ancient ecoscape, geography, climate, dinosaur and plate tectonics. At Shuidonggou there were discovered traces and articles of late Paleolithic human activities, showing that there were humans living here 30,000 years ago, and that Ningxia is one of the sites of the ancient cultures of the Chinese peoples. The irrigation projects that draw water from the Yellow River have been placed on the list of Heritage Irrigation Structures by the International Commission on Irrigation and Drainage, this is one of the oldest waterworks on the Yellow River in China. Ningxia is intimately connected to the Yellow River. The Yellow River gave birth to the history of the Chinese peoples, and also nourished the history of Ningxia. One of the ten greatest archaeological finds of 2016 was the site of ruins at Mount Gezi in Qingtong Gorge, and one of the ten greatest archaeological finds of 2017 were the Shang and Zhou dynasties remains at the Yao River in Pengyang, which provided very old historical material about the development of Chinese culture in different periods. Ningxia has many historical forts, pagodas and signal towers. There are sections of the Great Wall from the Warring States Period, Qin, Ming and Qing dynasties which clearly record how it was built at different periods in Chinese history. After the first emperor unified China, he sent troops to Ningxia to work the land, and build the world-famous Qin Great Wall. Writer Tang Rongyao believes, maybe because of the surrounding Wall, Ningxia became a hidden place of wonder. Over the course of eight years, from the angle of a news reporter, with the tone of a poet and seriousness of a scholar as well as the sharp and lonely spirit of a field researcher, he used literary language to display to the world the people and events over the years in Ningxia. He says that Ningxia is like a transcendentalist living in the remote hinterlands of China, slowly halting in thoroughfares, talking calmly in a low voice, relaxed and tranquil.

A peculiar landscape, various cultures, mysterious history – Ningxia is a magical place. Ningxia has history and culture, feelings and customs, life and stories. The Yellow River enters the Tengger, Ulan Buh and Mu Us Deserts, dashing about in these semi-desolate regions, forming a pastoral Ningxia plain, nourishing the colourful southern-style landscapes with its water. Zhang Qinnan in *City Reading* said that the city is the most wonderful, most exquisite, highest and deepest thing we humans create. Every city has its own distinctive nature, culture and history. What we are to read about is how and why they're different.

Nobody has ever come to Ningxia and gotten the impression that it's typical North-western China, with a harsh climate, with abrupt sharp loess slopes, dry and desolate deserts, frequent sandstorms, and air all full of dry dust. Instead, the 72 inter-related lakes in Yinchuan have given the beauty to Ningxia from which the epithet "lush southern-style fields north of the Great Wall" comes.

Secretary of the Party Committee of the Ningxia Hui Autonomous Region Shi Taifeng once described Ningxia to the media with citations from poems. He said that although Ningxia is small in area, it's full of gorgeous landscapes and amazing history. If one doesn't go to Yinchuan, Wuzhong and Shizuishan, one can't experience the breath-taking landscape of the orchards at the foot of Helan Mountains, and the famous southern-style landscapes in the northern frontier. If one doesn't go to Zhongwei and Shapotou, one misses out on the glorious scenes of a cloud of smoke rising upright on the vast desert and the magnificent sun setting over the long Yellow River as described by Tang dynasty poet Wang Wei. If one doesn't go to Liupan Mountains, one won't feel the magnificence described in Mao Zedong's poem about high skies, thin clouds, and geese flying to the south. The landscape of Ningxia is simple, poetic and magnificent. Though overlooked by many, surrounded by the Great Wall, and hidden in the depths of history, it's been listed as one of the 46 must-see places for travellers by *The New York Times*.

Only when a city has culture can it have warmth, and only then will life in the city be more interesting, will the people have a sense of belonging, and a sense of recognition.

In Ningxia, every street has its own story, and has its own magical legend. Whether or not you know it, these things will still accumulate in the blood of this place. Enjoy finely these accumulations of history, as they are the bearers of the soul of this place.

To know Ningxia, one must understand the soul of this place.

As a book in the *One-Minute China* series, we try to use these short stories contained within; in the streets and alleyways, in the smallest details, in the extensive history and warmest feelings, we hope you enjoy the symphony of sights and thoughts of Ningxia.

Ningxia is situated at a latitude of 38 degrees north, which is agreed to be the golden band for wine production. The vineyards at the eastern foot of Helan Mountains are now on the world's map for wine production. Everyone has a city in their heart. Born and bred locally, I assure you that the sunshine is perfect here. The sky is blue, and the clouds white. We have stories as well as wine. So it is advisable to read *Ningxia: Quiet and Quick*, while sipping at your wine on a pleasant afternoon.

Jiang Wenling
July 2018

Contents 目录

摄影：苏成远

自然 · 山水

Nature and Landscape

端坐在地图中心的雄鹰
An Eagle Sitting in the Centre of the Map

有人曾这样表述宁夏的地理位势，将一幅中国地图的陆疆四角对折后，宁夏恰好在折线相交的中心，也就是中国陆疆的几何中心，不高不低，不东不西。而且，在中国地图上审视宁夏的地域形状，会惊喜地发现，它就是一只端坐的雄鹰。

Some people have thus described Ningxia's geographic position: if you take a map of China and fold the four corners together, Ningxia is at the meeting point of these four lines. It's also China's geometric centre of land, neither high nor low, neither east nor west. Furthermore, if you look at the shape of Ningxia on a map, you'll be delighted to discover it's that of an eagle sitting straight there.

宁夏黄河流凌美
Ice-Run on the Yellow River

从银川平原起步，黄河开始向高纬度地区北流，冬季河面结冰，黄河进入冬眠。第二年春天，黄河开始冰融漫溢。为不让水淹农田、影响春耕，常用飞机投弹的方法炸开冰面，于是重重叠叠、相拥相撞的冰凌浮游于河上，形成壮观的河开冰走的“流凌”，河面上雾气缭绕，美不胜收。

Starting from the Ningxia Plain, the Yellow River flows north towards higher latitudes. In the winter the surface of the river freezes, and the Yellow River enters hibernation. In the spring of the second year, the river begins to slowly melt and flow. In order to prevent the water from flooding fields and influence spring agriculture, planes are used to drop projectiles on the surface of the ice to break it up. Thus numerous heavy blocks of ice float upon the river, colliding with each other, making for an impressive “ice run”. Mist floats all about in the beautiful scene.

供图：宁夏文化和旅游厅

供图：宁夏画报社

把诗意揽入怀中
Poem into Your Arms

宁夏含蓄而内敛。不到宁夏平原，你就很难理解唐诗“贺兰山下果园成，塞北江南旧有名”所描绘的瓜果飘香的江南风情；不到宁夏平原西段的中卫，你就无法体会“大漠孤烟直，长河落日圆”的雄浑；不到宁夏南部的六盘山，你就无法体会“天高云淡，望断南飞雁，不到长城非好汉”的豪迈。宁夏将自然风情、地貌及豪迈的地域性格，诗意般揽入怀中。

Ningxia is veiled and introverted. If you don’t visit the Ningxia Plain, you won’t understand the southern feeling with the fragrances of fruits, described in Tang Dynasty poem, “There are fruit orchards at the base of Helan Mountains; these lush southern-style fields north of the Great Wall have long been famous.” If you don’t visit Zhongwei at the western reaches of the Ningxia Plain, you won’t be able to experience the vigour and force Tang poet Wang Wei expressed when he wrote “A lonely trail of smoke rises on the desert, and the round sun sets over the vast Yellow River”. If you don’t visit Liupan Mountains in the south of Ningxia, you won’t experience the boldness of the scene thus described, “The sky is high and the clouds are thin, in the south swan geese fly, and one who fails to reach the Great Wall is not a true man.” Ningxia combines natural feelings and bold landscapes into a poem that you take into your arms.

供图：宁夏画报社

冲出长城天地宽
Breaking Out of the Great Wall

长城既是屏障，也是自我防御的心理体现。从南部的六盘山到中部的罗山再到北部的贺兰山，从先秦到明代，宁夏的长城是不断移动的。宁夏也是逐步在突破长城，才有了“冲出长城天地宽”的开拓与开放性格。

The Great Wall is a barrier, and the product of the psychological mind-set of self-defence. From Liupan Mountains in the south to Luoshan Mountains in the middle to Helan Mountains in the north, from the pre-Qin to the Ming Dynasty, the Great Wall in Ningxia moved continuously. Ningxia also gradually grew out of conflict, and thus has the open nature of “breaking out of heaven and earth”.

“塞北江南”旧有名
Southern-Style Fields North of the Great Wall

两汉时期，宁夏曾是“沃野千里，谷稼殷积”。唐代诗人韦蟾《送卢潘尚书之灵武》诗说：“贺兰山下果园成，塞北江南旧有名。”塞北就是塞上。南北朝时，北周打败了南朝陈将吴明彻，并把俘获的吴明彻部将迁到了宁夏灵州，这些从南朝迁来的人尚礼好学，将南方尊儒尚文之风以及先进的农业技术植入宁夏， 于是就逐渐形成了后来的“塞北江南”。

During the time of the two Han dynasties, Ningxia was a place of vast green fields and huge grain stores. Tang poet Wei Chan in his poem *Farewell to Minister Lu Pan Going to Lingwu* wrote, “There are fruit orchards at the base of Helan Mountains; these lush southern-style fields north of the Great Wall have long been famous.” During the Northern and Southern dynasties period, the Northern Zhou defeated the Southern Chen dynasty general Wu Mingche, and sent the captured officers who served under Wu to Lingzhou in Ningxia. These people from the Southern dynasty respected Confucian etiquette and valued education, and brought these traditions of honouring Confucianism and advanced agricultural techniques into Ningxia. It was in this way that these famous southern-style fields came into being in Ningxia.

穿越千年时光走廊
Millennium Corridor

公元1038年，党项族首领李元昊在贺兰山下称帝，建立大白高国。因在夏州以西，后人称其为“西夏”。元代忽必烈下令，在西夏故地设置“宁夏路”，寄意“宁静的夏地”。后来，马来西亚女歌手梁静茹演唱的《宁夏》，歌词就是在宁夏创作的。宁夏地名穿越千年时光走廊，把历史与现代、地理与艺术有机地连接了起来。

In the year 1038, Tangut leader Li Yuanhao named himself emperor at the base of Helan Mountains, establishing the Grand and High White Kingdom. As it was to the west of Xiazhou, it was called Xixia ("Western Xia") by later people. The first emperor of the Yuan dynasty, Kublai Khan, ordered the construction of a "Ningxia Lu (an administrative division below the level of provinces in the Yuan dynasty)" here, with the meaning of calm (ning) place in Xia. In modern times, Malaysian singer Fish Leong sings a song *Ningxia*, the words of which were written in Ningxia. The name Ningxia has travelled a corridor of a millennium, organically connecting history and modern times, geography and art.

躺在平原晒太阳的河
A River Lying on the Plain

黄河自黑山峡小观音进入宁夏境内，出青铜峡，黄河与各引黄干渠便在银川平原蔓延开来。尽管水往低处流，但黄河遇见银川平原，就是这么慵懒，平躺着、晒着太阳，哺育着宁夏人民，不问西东。

The Yellow River enters Ningxia at the Xiaoguanyin Ridge of Heishan Gorge, and exits at the Qingtong Gorge. The flow of the river and all the channels diverting water from it spread out over the Ningxia Plain. Although water flows towards lower ground, when the Yellow River meets the Ningxia Plain, it indolently lies down and suns itself, nurturing the people of Ningxia.

供图：宁夏画报社

袖珍里藏着大乾坤
Pocket-Sized World

宁夏不大，南北长约450公里、东西宽约250公里。开车行驰的话，一天的工夫就可以把宁夏从南到北、从东到西转一圈。和一些大省区相比，宁夏虽是袖珍的，但宁夏汇聚了各种地貌，高山、平原、盆地、台地、峡谷、湿地、黄土丘陵、沙漠、草原……这在全国各省区是罕见的，可谓袖珍里藏着大乾坤。难怪张贤亮称宁夏为“中国的微缩景观”。

Ningxia isn't large, being only 450 kilometres from north to south and 250 kilometres from east to west. If you drive, you can take a tour of all of Ningxia in a single day. Compared with other provinces, Ningxia is pocked-sized. However, it has all kinds of landscapes, from mountains, plains, basins, and mesas to valleys, wetlands, loess hills, deserts, and grasslands. This is rare in the other provinces of China. One can say that it's a pocket-sized world. It's no wonder the novelist Zhang Xianliang described Ningxia as "a micro-landscape of China".

刻在石头上的无字天书
A Book without Words

贺兰山岩石上有近6000幅神秘的岩画，生动地记录了一万年前远古人类生产、生活等场景。这些岩画充满着原始精神的张力和呐喊，体现着远古先民独特的崇拜和信仰，他们把对大自然的观察与理解、祈盼与情感，镌刻进了永恒的时空，成为一部刻在石头上的无字天书。

There are more than 6,000 rock paintings upon the stones of Helan Mountains which vibrantly record human production, life and other scenes 10,000 years ago. These rock paintings are full of the strains and shouts of primitive spirit, giving expression to the unique methods of worship and beliefs of ancient peoples. They engrave these people's views and understandings of nature, their prayers and feelings into eternity, forming a kind of "heavenly book", but one without words.

供图：宁夏文化和旅游厅

供图：宁夏画报社

宁夏“八达岭”
Ningxia's “Badaling”

北岔口长城位于青铜峡市以西约 40 公里处的贺兰山南麓的营子山，呈南北走向，西临内蒙古，南起青铜峡广武乡芦沟湖，北至邵岗乡磨石口，全长 40.6 公里，是迄今宁夏境内明代长城保存最完整的一段，被誉为宁夏“八达岭”。和北京八达岭的砖石长城相比，宁夏的土长城多了一份历史美、沧桑美。

The Beichakou Great Wall is situated about 40 kilometres west from Qingtongxia City at Mount Yingzi in the Helan mountains' south range. It runs north to south, and is near Inner Mongolia in the west. The southern section starts at Lugou Lake in Guangwu Town in Qingtongxia, and runs to Moshikou in Shaogang Town in the north, for a total length of 40.6 kilometres. It's the best-preserved Ming dynasty segment of the wall in Ningxia, and has been called Ningxia's “Badaling”, in reference to the famous Badaling Great Wall in Beijing. Compared with Badaling's stone Great Wall, Ningxia's earthen Great Wall has an extra component of beauty, one that reflects the vicissitudes of time.

“几”字起笔的地方
The Start of the Giant Character

黄河流出青铜峡后，改变了从西往东的走向，一路向北，浩荡而去。犹如一位大书法家，挥着狼毫，笔锋一转，在广袤的大地上写下了一个巨大的“几”字，宁夏就在“几”字起笔的地方。

After the Yellow River flows out of the Qingtong Gorge, it changes his west-to-east course, and flows northwards with a mighty current. Like a master calligrapher, it flicks its weasel-hair brush, and makes a turn, painting a giant Chinese character “几” on the landscape of China. So Ningxia is right at the start of this giant character.

自然中透着刚毅
Fortitude in Nature

一方水土养一方人。宁夏山水，既有“踏破贺兰山阙”的英雄气势，也有“天高云淡，望断南飞雁”的诗意画卷；既有黄河岸边七十二连湖滋养万亩稻田的温润，还有六盘山万亩山花的野性浪漫。宁夏山水，就像棱角分明的宁夏四季景观，多元且丰沛，在自然中透着刚毅，就像宁夏人。

Each area has its own way of supporting its inhabitants. One thinks of the heroic spirit of conquering the mighty Helan Mountains by footsteps, the poem describing high skies with thin clouds and swan geese flying, the warmth of the seventy-two linked lakes on the banks of the Yellow River nourishing countless fields of rice, and the savage romance of the mountain flowers on Liupan Mountains. The scenery of Ningxia is like its four sharply defined seasons, diverse and plentiful. Fortitude permeating nature is just like the character of the people of Ningxia.

沙漠魔方
Desert Magic Cube

宁夏西北部的腾格里沙漠边缘，治沙者掘开沙层，栽进麦草。一束束麦草齐齐的，形成了田字格——这是治沙人摸索出来的经验，这样的方格固沙是沙漠的咒语。一车一车的麦草卸下，一束束栽成一个个方格子；一车一车的树苗卸下，住进草方格。若有一架航拍仪，就可拍到延绵不绝的“草方格”，像一朵朵硕大的方形奇葩，盛开成一道沙漠奇观。

In the north-western Ningxia lies the edge of Tengger Desert. Sand controllers dig open layers of sand and plant ryegrass. Grids are formed by these rows of ryegrass plants. This is the result of the experience of the sand controllers; the way these grids hold the grass in place is the curse of the desert. Truckloads of ryegrass are unloaded, and bundles are planted in these grid patterns. Truckloads of small trees are discharged and planted into these grids. If one took an aerial photograph, the result would be an endless expanse of these “grass grids”. It’s definitely an interesting sight to behold.

摄影：陶克图

贺兰山的精灵
Spirit of Helan

岩羊是低跳“冠军”，每天清晨和黄昏，贺兰山上或三五成群、或成群结队的岩羊像一片片流动的云，在熹微的晨光和沉沉的暮霭中腾挪跳跃、竞相出没。跳跃在山间，抬头看蓝天，低头觅食草。这贺兰山自由奔放的灵性象征——岩壁上的精灵闯进了岩画，成为贺兰山千万岩画中生动的“活岩画”。

The blue sheep is the champion of the low jump. At dawn and dusk every day, groups of blue sheep make their way around the mountain, jumping about in dim morning light and soft semi-dark of dusk. They raise their heads to look at the sky, and lower them to forage for edible grasses. These animals are the symbols of the soul of Helan Mountains, and have been inscribed in the rock paintings there, now serving as “living paintings” reflecting depictions made of them ages ago.

摄影：陶克图

七十二连湖
The Seventy-Two Linked Lakes

银川城中有湖，湖中有城，连绵不断，大小七十二湖，湖湖相通。“连湖渔歌”还是乾隆年间“朔方八景”之一。阅海、小西湖、北塔湖、宝湖、三丁湖、官湖、高台寺湖、金波湖、连湖、鸣翠湖、鹤泉湖……一湾湾湖水，谁能想到塞北也有江南“落霞与孤鹜齐飞，秋水共长天一色”的美景？

The lakes in Yinchuan have settlements within them, one after another. There are 72 lakes, large and small, that flow into each other. The “Song of Fishing in the Linked Lakes” was one of the “eight sights of the north” during the Qianlong Emperor’s reign in the Qing dynasty. Yuehai, Small West Lake, Beita Lake, Baohu Lake, Sanding Lake, Guanhu Lake, Gaotaisi Lake, Jinbo Lake, Lianhu Lake, Mingcui Lake, Hequan Lake… who would have thought that north of the Great Wall there would be southern-style beauty such as described in the poems of Wang Bo in the Tang dynasty?

杏花的邀请
Invitation of the Flowers

杏花是春天发出的邀请函，一朵朵杏花，像赶考的举子，将各自的锦绣文章写出来，怒放于人间四月天，肆意向六盘山吐露着容颜和韵味，以各种姿态装点着干渴的黄土地，一任百里花香满山开放。诗人说，群山一夜听春雨，万人乘车赏花来。

Apricot blossoms are an invitation to the spring. Each flower is like a scholar on the way to the imperial examination, preparing to write his beautiful essay out. They burst out in April, revealing their looks and charm to Liupan Mountains. They decorate the dry loess in all manners, and their fragrance flows everywhere. Poets say that as soon as it rains in spring, myriads of people will ride to the mountains to appreciate the flowers.

供图：宁夏文化和旅游厅

父亲山，母亲河
Father Mountain, Mother River

贺兰山像一位 24 亿年的长者，以平均两千多米的海拔，阻隔了西伯利亚寒流和腾格里、乌兰布和沙漠的侵蚀，承担着守护宁夏平原的重任；黄河像一位慈祥的母亲，以自己宽大的臂弯，滋养着宁夏平原的一草一木。父亲山母亲河哺育出一个包容、富裕、文明、发展的新宁夏。

Helan Mountains is 2.4 billion years old, and has an average elevation of 2,000 metres above sea level. It blocks the cold flow of Siberia and the incursions of the Tengger and Ulan Buh deserts; it has the important role of protecting the Ningxia Plain. The Yellow River is like a caring mother, with its wide embrace nourishing the plain. The mother and father have nurtured a new Ningxia to grow up inclusive, prosperous, cultured and developed.

唐徕渠
Tanglai Canal

明万历《朔方新志》记载："唐徕渠亦汉故渠而复浚于唐者。"现干渠全长 314 公里，承担 120 多万亩农田灌溉及 20 多万亩湖泊湿地补水任务。诗人马乐群称道："唐徕渠水波金黄金黄的 / 比江南的稻浪还好看 / 比王之涣的诗句还响亮 / 每天 我沿着渠行走 / 水波 从唐朝走到今天……"唐徕渠流淌了两千多年，是一条真正意义上的宁夏平原血脉通道。

In *The New Chronicles of the North*, written in the Wanli Emperor's reign in the Ming dynasty, it is written: "The Tanglai Canal, originally built in the Han dynasty, was dredged by the Tang." The canal is currently 314 kilometres long, and irrigates over 80,000 hectares of fields whilst at the same time providing extra water to over 133 square kilometres of lakes and wetlands. Poet Ma Lequn said, "The waves on the water of the Tanglai are bright and golden, even lovelier than the rippling waves of rice plants in the south. They're even more resonating than the poetry of the Tang poet Wang Zhihuan. Every day, I walk along the canal. Waves flow from the Tang dynasty until today." Water has flown in the Tanglai Canal for two millennia. It is in the truest sense a vein for the Ningxia plain.

镶嵌在黄土高原上的璀璨明珠
Pearl in the Loess Highland

红色、紫色的山崖、山峰、山脊、怪石，突兀于黄土高原之上，丹霞地貌景观奇特，四季景色各异，春有漫山野花开放，夏有成片绿草染坡，秋有红叶似火，冬有白雪压顶。不管四季如何变迁，不变的永远是那如烈焰朱唇的暗红色的丹霞风情。

Red and purple cliffs, peaks, ridges, and queer stones rise abruptly from the loess highland. The Danxia landform (a landscape of red sandstone mainly existing in China, characterised by sharp cliffs) is a peculiar sight, with different scenes in each season. In the spring the mountains are covered with flowers, in the summer green grasses colour the slopes, in the autumn red leaves are aflame all about, and in the winter the peaks are covered with snow. No matter how the seasons change, the burning crimson base of the Danxia landscape always remain.

摄影：师庆和

在梦里看见的自然
Nature in Dreams

诗人雷抒雁看到宁夏六盘山野荷谷情不自禁大发感慨，野荷谷，就是他梦里大自然的样子。山泉水叮咚奔跃小溪，阳光斑斑点点在碧绿的草地上嬉戏，各色小花儿贴着草地羞羞地开着，惊鸿一瞥间，一株一株静谧的花儿在微风中等待有缘人。

Poet Lei Shuyan was moved when he saw the Yehe Valley at Liupan Mountains. Yehe Valley is as he envisions nature in his dreams. Springs create small streams, and sunlight plays over the lush green grass. Flowers in all colours bloom gently, and for a sudden brief moment a breeze blows over the flowers, making them tremble in anticipation of meeting that special someone.

相守千年的“鸳鸯”
Yuanyang Lake

鸳鸯湖并没有鸳鸯，而是新石器时代居民在毛乌素沙漠边缘生活所依靠的两个湖，仿若一对鸳鸯安居于此。北湖湖水淡甜可饮，周围芦苇、蒿草丛生，水草丰美。南湖为季节湖，有雨则盈，无雨则涸。南北两湖相依相伴守望千年。如今，人们来这里不是寻找鸳鸯，而是寻找一种忠贞的坚守。

Yuanyang Lake doesn't have any Mandarin ducks (yuanyang, a symbol of affectionate couples in China), but rather is the site where Neolithic peoples lived at the border of the Mu Us Desert, next to two bodies of water that resembled a pair of Mandarin ducks living together. The north lake has clear, sweet water that is potable, and is surrounded by reeds, wormwood and aquatic grasses. The south lake is seasonal, full when it rains, and dry when it does not. The two lakes have faced each other for thousands of years. When people visit now, they aren't looking for ducks, but rather a symbol of loyalty and steadfastness.

不住龙的老龙潭
Old Dragon Pool

2001 年，中国邮政发行了一套四枚“峰、林、潭、谷”六盘山主题的特种邮票，其中的“潭”就是老龙潭。老龙潭位于泾源县城南 22 公里处，是泾河的源头，泾河水从老龙潭出发，流经宁、甘、陕三省区 28 市县，蜿蜒 530 公里，以湍湍清澈之态、百泉汇流之势而闻名，于陕西高陵县汇入渭河，由此留下了“泾清渭浊”的自然佳景。

In 2001, China Post issued a series of stamps themed around Liupan Mountains titled “peak, forest, pool and valley”. The “pool” referenced is Laolongtan, or “Old Dragon Pool”. Located 22 kilometres south of the town of Jing County, it is the source of the Jinghe River. Clear water flows out of the lake, through 28 counties and cities in Ningxia, Gansu and Shaanxi. It winds and grinds for 530 kilometres, limpid and turbulent, famous as the confluence of hundreds of springs. It enters the Weihe River in Gaoling County in Shaanxi, where its clear water mixes with the muddy flow of the Weihe River, making for an amazing natural sight.

供图：宁夏文化和旅游厅

供图：宁夏画报社

流淌千年的水文化史
A Millennium of Water Culture

宁夏引黄古灌区是我国最古老的黄河水利工程之一，它是一部流淌千年的水文化史，秦渠、汉渠、汉延渠、唐徕渠等古渠都是它的兄弟。2017 年在墨西哥召开的国际灌排大会上被列入世界灌溉工程遗产名录。这是黄河流域主干道上第一处世界灌溉工程遗产。

The diversions of water from the Yellow River in Ningxia is one of the first irrigation projects of the Yellow River in China, representing more than a millennium of water culture – the Qin Canal, Han Canal, Hanyan Canal, Tanglai Canal and other ancient canals are all its brothers. In 2017 in Mexico it was listed as a World Heritage Irrigation Structure by the International Commission on Irrigation and Drainage, the first project on the Yellow River to be recognised as such.

没有风景却有尊严的清水河
A Dignified River

宁夏中南部地区的清水河是一条 300 公里长的河，是宁夏境内流入黄河最大、最长的支流，有着从“苦水河”的乳名到如今“清水河”的官名的变化，矿化度比较高的本色却千年不变，是一条没有风景却有尊严的河流。作家李进祥说，她无法代表宁夏的外在之美，却代表宁夏的内在之美。清浅而又厚重，苦涩而又甘饴，细小而又壮阔，清水河的面貌也是宁夏的内在面貌。

The Qingshui (“clear water”) River is situated in the south-central portion of Ningxia, and runs for 300 kilometres. It’s the longest and largest branch of the Yellow River in Ningxia. It was originally called the Kushui (“bitter water”) River. It has a relatively high mineral concentration which is consistent for thousands of years; it’s a river without scenery, but a dignified one. Author Li Jinxiang said the river represents Ningxia’s interior beauty instead of exterior one. The flow is clear and shallow yet massive, bitter yet sweet, narrow yet broad. The river is the inherent appearance of Ningxia.

幸运小鸟红嘴鸥
Lucky Bird

摄影师的镜头聚焦银川北塔湖，发现“一家三口”在北塔湖上休憩觅食的和谐画面，这幸福的小东西名叫红嘴鸥。每年春天，成群的红嘴鸥从昆明北迁至西伯利亚，在漫长的迁徙之路上，银川成了它们休憩觅食的中转站，于是热情的银川人与红嘴鸥互动的和谐画面就在从全国各地赶来的摄影师的镜头里定格。

A photographer focusing his lens at Beita Lake in Yinchuan discovered a “family of three” resting and foraging upon the lake. These lucky birds are called black-headed gulls. Every year in spring, flocks of these birds migrate north from Kunming to Siberia. On the course of their long journey, Yinchuan has become a stopover for them to rest and forage, thus the harmonious scenes of the interactions between them and the people of Ningxia have become a subject for photographers from all over China to come and capture.

一部立着的史诗
Mount Helan, a Standing Epic

贺兰山是一部立着的史诗。人文学者说，这是北方游牧部族历史的长廊；地理学者说，这是温带荒漠与温带草原的分界线；地貌学者说，这是划开宁夏平原绿洲和阿拉善荒漠的山脉；气象学者说，这是西伯利亚寒流和太平洋暖流抵达尽头的地方……贺兰山以亘古不变的身躯见证着历史。

Helan Mountains is a standing epic. Humanists say that this place is a long historical corridor for northern nomadic tribes; geologists say this place is a demarcation line between temperate desert and temperate grassland; geographers say that it is a mountain range that divides Ningxia’s plain oases from the Alxa Desert; climate scientists say that this is where the Siberian cold current and Pacific warm current meet. The body of Helan Mountains has lain here from ancient times until now unchanged, a witness to history.

黄河的“小棉袄”
Favourite Daughter

如果将黄河流经的九省区，比作黄河的九个儿女，“天下黄河富宁夏”，不难看出黄河对宁夏的偏爱。宁夏就是黄河的小女儿、“小棉袄”。黄河伸出母亲的臂弯，呵护着宁夏平原，流淌在平原中的黄河享受着女儿的依恋，舒缓从容，如歌行板。

If one divides the Yellow River into nine sections for the nine provinces it flows through, and thinks of them as nine children, it’s not hard to see that the river favours Ningxia. There is a famous phrase, “The Yellow River makes Ningxia rich.” Ningxia is the river’s favourite daughter. The river extends its arm to protect the Ningxia Plain, flowing through the plain as it enjoys her love and reluctance to part. Leisurely and calm, it’s a song with an andante tempo.

文身之山

Tattooed Mountain

“贺兰山岩画，它保留了几千年甚至上万年的古老文明信息，见证了生活在这里的古先民的生活勇气以及他们和自然的关系。”作家冯骥才参观贺兰山岩画后如是感叹，并欣然题词“岁月失语，惟石能言”。数以万计的远古岩画，使贺兰山变成了一座文身之山。观赏岩画，就是和古人对话，就是一趟心灵研修之旅。

“The rock paintings of Helan Mountains preserve cultural information from thousands of years ago to more than ten thousand years ago. They are evidence of the brave lives and relationship with nature that the ancient residents had.” Author Feng Jicai was taken with awe after seeing these rock paintings, and joyfully wrote an inscription “Words are lost over time, and then only stones can speak”. Numerous ancient rock paintings make Helan Mountains tattooed. Appreciating these rock paintings is having a dialogue with the ancients, a spiritual journey.

“太阳神”是岩画中的太阳

The Rock Painting of “Sun God”

“太阳神”岩画是贺兰山岩画中的“太阳”，磨刻在距地面 40 余米处的石壁上。岩画头部有放射形线条，面部呈圆形，重环双眼，长有睫毛，炯炯有神，非常威武。这是古代游牧民族心中的“太阳神”。这幅岩画曾多次作为世界岩画研讨会的会徽使用。

The “sun god” is the sun in the rock paintings of Helan Mountains, carved into a rock cliff more than 40 metres high. On top of the rock, rays are carved, and on the face there is a circle with two fiery round eyes and long eyelashes which make for a very powerful appearance. This is the “sun god” in the hearts of the ancient nomadic people. This rock painting has been used many times in the emblem of the World Rock Art Symposium.

摄影：陶克图

摄影：辛怡丽

地球裂变出的一滴眼泪
Tear of the Earth

1920年海原大地震留下了亚洲第一大、世界第二大堰塞湖——党家岔震湖。一场地质灾害后，震湖就像上天的一滴眼泪留在人间，成就了黄土高原上独特的地震景观，成为地球裂变的样板秘境。如果你是带着思念而来，没准儿就会想起歌手齐秦的《一面湖水》来："高山上的湖水，是躺在地球表面上的一颗眼泪；我枕畔的眼泪，就是挂在你心间的一面湖水。"

The 1920 Haiyuan earthquake created Asia's largest and the world's second largest quake lake – the Dangjiacha Earthquake Lake. After the quake this lake looks like a drop of tear from the heaven, and is a unique earthquake feature upon the loess highlands, the evidence of the change an earthquake can bring about. It may make you think of Chyi Chin's song *Surface of the Lake*, "The water of the mountain lake lies there like a tear upon the surface of the earth; the tears on my pillow lie in your heart like the surface of a lake."

睁着千万年的眼睛
Eyes Open for Countless Years

先民以慧为笔、以石为纸，在贺兰山巍峨的山体上镌刻下神秘的图画，千百年无人能清晰解析。诗人形容它是刻在石头上的史诗，画家说它是人类最早铺给大地的画布，政治家说它是政治较量的隐喻，文字学家说它是中国古文字的源头。岩画是睁着千万年的眼睛，默默地注视着山里山外自然和历史的变迁。

The ancient people used wisdom as their brush, and rocks as their canvas, carving mysterious images into the stones of towering Helan Mountains, ones that later visitors are unable to decipher. Poets say that these are poems upon the rocks, painters say that stone was the earliest canvas, politicians say they are metaphors for measuring political strength, philologists say they are the origins of ancient characters in China. These rock paintings are eyes that have been open for countless years, quietly watching the natural and historical developments within and without the mountains.

风带走了模样，却留下了味道

What the Wind Leaves Behind

甘盐池是唐宋时期十八大盐湖之一，也是海原大地震的极震区。诗人曾用“东海碧波水倒流”的诗句，描写碧波荡漾的盐湖美景。1920 年的海原大地震中，盐池的“碧波”悄无声息地潜入地下，湖水向北移动了约 1000 米，宛若一盆水被倾斜着放置在了深沉而苍凉的甘盐池滩里，水蒸发完了，味道却没被风带走。

Lake Ganyan (“sweet salt”) was one of the 18 major salt lakes in the Tang and Song dynasties, and is also the epicentre of the Haiyuan Earthquake. A poet used the words “the azure waters of the East Sea flow backwards” to describe the beautiful rippling surface of the salt lake. In the Haiyuan Earthquake of 1920, these “azure waves” suddenly disappeared into the earth, and the waters of the lake were moved a kilometre north. It seems like a bowl of water tipped onto this deep and desolate floodplain; it would evaporate, but leaves behind its own flavour.

摄影：田玉珍

绕地球转了两圈

The 1920 Haiyuan Earthquake

“山峰在夜幕下移动，山崩如瀑布般一泻而下，巨大的地裂吞没了房屋、驼队，村庄在起伏的土海中如庞贝城般消失得无影无踪……”美国《国家地理杂志》如此描述 1920 年被全球 96 个地震台记录的海原“环球大地震”。这次地震震级 8.5 级，烈度 12 度，死亡人数 27 万，地震震波约等于绕地球转了两圈。

“Mountains move in the night, landslides crash down like waterfalls, the ground splits swallow houses and camels, villages on the shaking ground disappear like Pompeii...” This is how the USA’s *National Geographic* described the 1920 Haiyuan Earthquake, which registered on 96 seismographic stations around the world. The quake had a magnitude of 8.5 and intensity of 12, killed 270,000 people, and created a seismic wave that circled the earth twice.

供图：宁夏文化和旅游厅

太极沙坡头
Shapotou

黄河离开中卫孟家湾进入沙坡头时，腾格里沙漠戛然而止，与黄河温情相拥，勾勒出一幅曲线优美的阴阳“太极图”。这幅图的南侧是香山向北蜿蜒的末端，北侧则是广袤的腾格里沙漠，山是河衣，沙为河骨，河为沙魂，相依相偎，勾勒出山、水、沙相遇的奇迹。

When the Yellow River leaves Mengjiawan of Zhongwei City and enters Shapotou, the Tengger Desert suddenly stops. The desert area and the Yellow River embrace each other with warm feelings, outline-drawing “diagram of the universe”. The southern portion of this painting is the northern limit of Zhongwei's Mount Xiangshan Hills, and the northern portion is the vast Tengger Desert. The mountain is the clothing of the river, the sand is the bones of the river, and the river is the soul of the sand. They depend on and comfort each other, meeting to form a miracle.

山水“维密秀”
Landscape Show

六盘山里，不少山石缝隙是雨水冲刷出的裂痕，雨水带来的草籽和一些植物的根在这缝隙间落地生根，它们一捋一捋地疏疏密密攀在山腰上。这些攀在山腰上的草木，像一位手艺高超的民间老裁缝，一针一线把裂开的山缝在一起，缝制成一场场山水“维密秀”。

At Liupan Mountains, many mountain crevices are the vestiges of rainfall erosion. The rains bring seeds and small plants which land in these crevices and take root, forming bands upon the mountains. These mountain climbers seem like the work of a highly skilled tailor, with needle and thread mending the cracks on the mountain's face stich by stitch, making for a wonderful landscape show.

供图：宁夏文化和旅游厅

最不矜持的市花
Least Restrained City Flower

每逢五月初，宁夏的沙枣花搭乘春风的末班车，野性地盛开，给大地送来缕缕浓香。一株株沙枣花，就是一个个风中的女王。它的花米粒那么大，密密实实开满一树。作为银川市的市花，沙枣花盛开时，银川就成了一个有特殊香味的巨大香包。黄河岸边、小区院内、街头巷尾……在全世界的城市市花中，沙枣花恐怕是最朴素、最不矜持的了。

Every May, Ningxia's oleaster rides the last train of the spring wind, and blooms wildly, adding a thick fragrance to the landscape. Each flower is a queen in the wind. Trees are covered with big clusters of flowers. This is the city flower of Yinchuan, and when they bloom, the city is covered in their special fragrance. On the banks of the Yellow River, within the communities here, in the streets and alleyways… Of all the city flowers of the world, the oleaster may be the plainest, lest restrained of them all.

沙枣花香
Fragrance of Oleaster

“沙枣花开哎，香天下；塞上江南哎，好宁夏……”半夏时光，从南到北，城市乡村，沙枣花开遍塞上大地，芳香四溢。整个宁夏大地就像谁打翻了蜜罐，空气中悠悠弥漫着香甜醇厚的味道。那一刻，置身宁夏大地，就只是满满地嗅着花香、享受着宁静。

“The flowers of the oleaster bloom, covering the land with their fragrance. The southern-style landscapes in Ningxia make it beautiful.” From north to south, from cities to villages, the flowers of the oleaster are everywhere, releasing their strong fragrance. It smells as if someone has dumped a large jar of honey all over Ningxia, the thick scent permeating the air all about. At that time, if you’re in Ningxia, you’ll find yourself enjoying and relaxing as the perfumed air is all about you.

好水川
Haoshui River

《走进隆德》一书说，好水川，位于隆德县北，与县城隔山相距8华里。川源于六盘山主峰西麓山根下，川水自东而西，全长60余里。源头好水镇附近有一泉眼，水涌甘洌，经久不涸，俗称“好水泉”，川因泉而得名。历史上西夏和宋朝的“好水川之战”，一定程度上是牧场的争夺，对马匹有着绝对依赖心理的党项人是无法忽视六盘山这一天然牧场的。

The book *Entering Longde* says the Haoshui (“good water”) River is located north of Longde County, 4 kilometres from the county town. The source of the river is at the base of the western reaches of the main peak of Liupan Mountains. The Haoshui River runs from east to west, with a total length of more than 30 kilometres. There is a spring near Haoshui Town that flows consistently with sweet water. It’s known as the “Haoshui Spring”, which is where the river got its name from. In historical times, the Western Xia and Song dynasty’s “Haoshui River War” was to a definite extent a fight over pasture. For the Tangut people, heavily reliant on horses, there was no way they could ignore this pasture at Liupan Mountains.

摄影：陶克图

摄影：强继周

坐在云端里的田地
Field in the Clouds

绿从田中来，田在云上飘，远山之上。宁夏南部山区的人民，在黄土高原上应山势而创造出梯田，使山坡、小村、梯田巧妙结合，以汗水与劳作，向人们解读了天人合一、如诗如画的和谐篇章，体现了一种生存智慧、一种生命坚持。

Green comes from the fields, and the fields float in the clouds and on the distant mountains. The people of the mountainous area of southern Ningxia create terraced fields on the sides of the mountains, combining the mountain slopes, small villages and terraced fields in a beautiful combination. Through sweat and hard work, they've understood the theory that humans are integral to nature. Like a poem or a painting, they've formed a harmonious composition that evidences survival wisdom and tenacity for life.

喜鹊之乡
The Home of Magpies

喜鹊是报喜之鸟，也是银川的市鸟。银川人喜悦度很高，每天都是听着喜鹊欢快的叫声出门，听着喜鹊欢快的叫声回家。银川市水多树多，气候好，喜鹊非常多。它们毛色发亮，在枝头上晒着幸福的时光，在草地上踱着自信的方步。银川人喜欢喜鹊，人鹊和谐。银川市被中国野生动物保护协会授予“中国喜鹊之乡”。

The magpie is a bird whose arrival signals joy in China, and is also the city bird of Yinchuan. The people of Yinchuan are quite joyous, and hear the sounds of the magpie every day as they leave home, as they return. As Yinchuan is a city with lots of water, many trees, and a nice climate, the magpies are very numerous. Their feathers are shiny, and they enjoy spending time in trees and walking upon the grass. The people of Yinchuan like magpies, and live harmoniously with them. Yinchuan has been designated as "The Home of Magpies" by the China Wildlife Conservation Association.

岩羊一家亲
Blue Sheep Family

冬天的贺兰山，大概在天气晴朗的下午四五点钟的时候，岩羊就会出来，它们到沟里找水喝。岩羊长着和山体一样深枯黄色的皮毛，不移动时像是山中的石头。一般岩羊都是一家三口一起行动，喝水的时候，小岩羊低头喝水，岩羊夫妻轮流站在水边四处张望，一旦发现丝毫的动静，它们就箭一般消失了。

During winter on Helan Mountains, when the weather is clear, around four or five in the afternoon, the blue sheep will come out, looking for water in the ditches. The sheep are the same colour as the mountain, deep withered yellow, and are indistinguishable from the rocks when they don't move. They usually travel as single-child families. They take turns drinking water as the others look out over their surroundings. If they see any movement at all, they'll shoot off like arrows, disappearing.

摄影：陶克图

泥土里的哲学

Philosophy in the Soil

作家肖彭说，有人说彭阳梯田像一首田园诗、一幅水彩画，不仅丝毫不过分，在他看来还远远不够。因为彭阳梯田不仅是一道风景，而且是一方人生命的基石，一个时代的文化映象。他建议在北京读哲学的儿子去看看，儿子说，梯田是泥土里生长起来的哲学，是劳动人民对人类的智慧贡献。

Author Xiao Peng says that some people say that the terraced fields of Pengyang County are like a pastoral poem, a watercolour painting, not excessive in the slightest degree, but to him it isn't enough. The terraced fields of Pengyang aren't just a landscape, but rather a foundation for life, a reflection of an era. He recommended his son in Beijing studying philosophy to come here to have a look. In the eyes of his son, these terraced fields are philosophy that's grown out of the earth here, a wise contribution of these workers to humanity.

供图：宁夏文化和旅游厅

色调与平和

Colour and Calm

北京媒体人李雁津说，宁夏大地的总体色调是黄色和绿色的，厚实的黄土，漫漫黄沙，以及到处可见的赏心悦目的绿。在这样的基调中，黄河于宁静中掀起黄色的微澜，挟裹着千年历史缓缓流过，一切似乎又都归于平和。

Beijing media personality Li Yanjin says Ningxia is green and yellow everywhere, with thick loess, lots of yellow sand, and greenery to enjoy all about. Amidst these base colours, the Yellow River flows through with its little ripples, slowly carrying thousands of years of history; everything seems to return to peace and calm.

城市·记忆
City and Memories

摄影：范毅强

历史文化名城
A Famous City of History and Culture

银川是历史悠久的塞上古城，民间传说中又称“凤凰城”。西倚贺兰山、东临黄河，利用黄河水进行自流引灌已有2000多年的历史。物产丰富，大米品质优良，有“塞北江南、鱼米之乡”之称。1986年被评为“国家历史文化名城”。了解银川、欣赏银川，留在记忆中的，不仅仅是西北风情，更多的是对自然山川的爱恋。

Yinchuan is a famous city north to the Great Wall with a long history. It has been traditionally called the “Phoenix City”. At its west is Helan Mountains, and at its east is the Yellow River. It has used the water of the Yellow River to irrigate fields for more than two millennia. It is a city of plenty, which produces rice of excellent quality, as well as fish. In 1986, it was named as a “Nation-level Historical and Cultural City”. To understand and appreciate Yinchuan is not just a matter of familiarising oneself with the North-western China, but also one of appreciating the beauty of the nature.

城在湖中，湖在城中
City and Water

大大小小的湿地保护区、景观水道和水上公园散落成星罗棋布的明珠，让银川这座城市充满了灵性，形成了独有的美丽。自小在银川长大的蒯陟文说，站在湖边，带着感谢，我想，幸好，我也还有这么一个安静的地方，可以整理自己的生活，感悟自己的生命。

Wetland reserves, scenic canals and water parks dot the landscape like pearls strewn upon a path. These aquatic areas give a special character to Yinchuan, a special kind of beauty. Kuai Zhiwen, who grew up in Yinchuan says that when one stands at the side of a lake, one feels thankful, and blessed to have such a quiet and nice place. It’s a place to reflect upon one’s life.

摄影：孙国才

摄影：强幼德

一个移民城市
City of Migration

石嘴山市自古以来就是移民地区。从秦、汉至清代，中原或南方各族人民不断前来戍边、屯垦、经商、开矿，设置的郡、县、堡、寨基本上都是移民城。1949年后，来自五湖四海、南腔北调的开拓者，演绎和谱写出了这个城市的主旋律。50%以上的人口由移民和移民后裔构成，千百年来的民族交融，多种文化的碰撞，塑造了石嘴山各方风俗交织、多方文化共存、开放包容的移民文化特点。

The city of Shizuishan is inhabited by those that came from elsewhere. Since the time of the Qin and Han until the Qing dynasty, people from the central China as well as the south of China have continually come here to pioneer, garrison the frontiers, conduct business, mine, and establish all manner of communities, counties, forts and fortresses. After 1949, people have come from all over, bringing great changes to the area. More than a half of the population of the city either is from or has roots from other places. Over more than a millennium, with all kinds of cultures coming in contact with each other, Shizuishan becomes a tapestry woven out of the threads of so many places, where multiple cultures coexist, and everyone comes together.

洁白如银之城
A City Made of Silver

银川平原七十二湖连片，是名副其实的“塞上江南”。湖与湖相望，水与水相连，银川成了塞上湖城、水上世界。水上有鸟，鸟鸣中传递着绿色，微风荡漾，湖面波光粼粼，远远看上去这座城市如同银子铺就。加上黄河流经，在千年时光的灌溉中，带来了“米粮川”式的富裕。银川名如其城。

The seventy-two lakes in Yinchuan are quite famous. Where they meet each other, wonderful landscapes reminiscent of scenes much further south are formed, with birds making their calls all about, within the seas of green foliage. Waters ripple in the gentle breeze and being watched from far away it seems made of silver. The Yellow River flows year after year, and the prosperity of the city has grown with it. This's where the name of Yinchuan ("silver river") came from.

凤凰城
Phoenix City

传说远古有一只幸福鸟凤凰，从江南飞到塞北，给愁云笼罩的六盘山换上翠绿的衣衫，把满头白发的贺兰山化成青丝少年，将宁夏川变作肥田沃土、牛羊遍地的塞上江南。为了抵御外来侵略者，凤凰将自己化为一座城，将宁夏的苍生全都装进城里，紧闭城门，保护了这里的人民。为了怀念凤凰，人们把银川城称为“凤凰城”。

In legends, there was a lucky phoenix which flew from the south of China to the north of the Great Wall, that covered Liupan Mountains in greenery and changed the white-haired old man of Helan Mountains into a young full of green, transforming Ningxia into a fertile area, with cows and sheep roaming all about. In order to keep out of invaders, a city was formed, and all of the common people of Ningxia were put inside the city. The gate of the city was closed to protect them. In order to remember the phoenix, Yinchuan was named the “Phoenix City”.

黄河水韵的诗画
Poems of the Yellow River

黄河穿吴忠城而过，吴忠顺势而依，以黄河为轴心，在黄河两岸建造“路、水、绿、特”相互融合，融入“河畅、水清、岸绿、景美”风情和“塞上江南”特色的滨河生态水韵城市。“一城黄河水韵，千年诗画吴忠。”城市空间格局塑造了吴忠的温婉与灵秀。

The Yellow River passes through Wuzhong City, which forms the centre of the urban area. Roads, a river, greenery and uniqueness are the aspects that make the place special. A fast flowing river, clear water, green coasts and beautiful scenes make for a unique and harmonious scene north to the Great Wall. As water flows through so do more than a thousand years of history. Just like the flow of the waterway, the character of the city is gentle and delicately beautiful.

摄影：苏成远

供图：宁夏画报社

丝绸之路上的文化重镇
A Spot on the Silk Road

固原于公元前 114 年建城，秦始皇时期，作为边陲重镇纳入了统一的版图，秦与汉初属北地郡。固原是明代九边重镇之一，是丝绸之路必经之地。随着丝绸之路的畅通，从北魏到隋唐时期，固原境内出现了大量的石窟及石、铜佛造像，如鎏金铜佛、玉菩萨等造像的出现，标志着丝绸之路东段北道的繁荣与发达，同样也展示了固原地域文明的进程和悠久的历史文化。

Originating in the year 114 BC, in the reign of the first emperor of the Qin dynasty, Guyuan was a major site on the border of China. Guyuan was one of the nine major border fortifications of the Ming dynasty, and an important location upon the Silk Road. As the Silk Road opened up, from the time of the Northern Wei dynasty to that of the Sui and Tang dynasties, the Guyuan border became witness to many rock Buddhist grottoes and stones, copper or gilded Buddhist sculptures, as well as jade bodhisattvas and the like. These are all testaments to its position on the eastern portion of the Silk Road, and also are markers to the progression of culture in this area.

绿色爬上山半腰
National Forest City

石嘴山市是诞生在宁夏北部的一座工业城市，位于寸草不长的贺兰山坡地戈壁滩上。后来，这个城市却摘取了“国家森林城市”的桂冠。桂冠来之不易。人工挖石背土，种下一株又一株树苗，让绿树一直生长到贺兰山半腰。石嘴山人的坚韧让绿色爬满坡，也深深震撼着来到这里的游人。

Shizuishan is an industrial city that sprung up in the north of Ningxia, one that is located in a desolate area at the reaches of Helan Mountains. Later, it was recognised as a “National Forest City”. Earth and stones were moved, and trees were planted to create a nice place on the middle reaches of the mountain. The people of the city made green extend everywhere, to form a wonderful sight for visitors.

摄影：马力

西夏王陵
Imperial Mausoleum of Western Xia

西夏王陵是西夏历代帝王陵以及皇家陵墓。王陵位于银川市西，贺兰山东麓，东西约 5 公里，南北约 10 公里，在 50 余平方公里的范围内分布着 9 座帝王陵墓和 200 多座王侯勋戚的陪葬墓。“贺兰山下古冢稠，高下有如浮水沤。”西夏王陵是现存最大的一处西夏文化遗址，已成为人们了解西夏历史遗存的一处胜地。

This is a site of the Imperial Mausoleum of Western Xia. They're situated to the west of Yinchuan City, on the eastern reaches of Helan Mountains. The site stretches about 5 kilometres from east to west, and 10 kilometres from north to south. In an area of more than 50 square kilometres, nine kings are buried with more than 200 nobles. This is a famous site for the burial of nobility and one of the most important sites for the history of the Tangut culture.

百年旱柳的如烟往事
Dryland Willows

唐徕渠边柳树成行。一棵树干大部分腐朽而又几乎成为“空心”的柳树，粗大的树干仰天裸露，仅剩的躯干旁新生的枝叶无畏地抽条吐绿。百年旱柳，注定是有记忆的画面、有故事的风景。据史料记载，贞观年间，唐太宗李世民曾传旨天下，“驿道栽柳树以荫行旅”。从此，所有大唐国土的驿道柳树成荫。

The sides of the Tanglai Canal are lined with willows. Most of the trunk of a tree has rotted away, leaving it empty on the inside. The thick branches of the tree extend to the sky, with only a few branches on the sides of the trunk sprouting leaves. These dryland willows have grown for a long time, recording the passing of time in their landscape, a scene of stories. According to historical records, during the Zhenguan Period of the Tang dynasty, Li Shimin, the emperor, made an order to have willow trees planted along courier roads to provide shade for those who travelled upon them. For this reason, all these routes of the Tang dynasty are lined with willows.

红军长征纪念馆
Liupanshan Red Army Long March Memorial Hall

六盘山红军长征纪念馆，由馆（纪念馆）、碑（纪念碑）、广场（纪念广场）、亭（纪念亭）和台（吟诗台）五部分组成。馆内有四个展厅，分为“红军不怕远征难”“红旗漫卷西风”“三军过后尽开颜”“不到长城非好汉”，展示了红军长征中的上百件遗物、文物、图片资料，再现了中国工农红军长征三次经过六盘山区时的斗争历史以及六盘山儿女在长征精神鼓舞下建设家园的情景。

The Liupanshan Red Army Long March Memorial Hall comprises five elements: the Memorial Hall, the Memorial Stele, the Memorial Square, and the Memorial Pavilion, and the Recitation Platform. A large amount of items, documents, and pictures are on display that reflect the brave journey of the Red Army on its Long March, unafraid of difficulty. The exhibits recreate the arduous and lengthy journey that the Red Army made, passing through the Liupan Mountains area three times in total, and intensity of the course that the people of the Liupan Mountains area showed in creating this scene.

供图：宁夏画报社

最有文化的地方
The Most Cultured Area

在银川兴庆区西南部有一座著名的寺院叫承天寺，寺内中间一座耸立云端的古塔，就是承天寺塔，也称“西塔”。承天寺塔是宁夏现存一百多座古塔中最高的一座砖塔。承天寺塔周围有三“多”，古玩市场多、书画装裱店铺多、文房用品多。这里承袭着老银川的历史文化遗韵，成了最有文化的地方。

There's a temple in the Xingqing District of Yinchuan City called Chengtian Temple; within there is a tall tower which is known as the Chengtian Tower, or just the “West Tower”. The Chengtian Tower is the tallest of the more than one hundred brick towers in Ningxia. It holds the forefront in three categories: there are the most antique markets nearby, the most painting shops nearby, and the most stationery stores nearby. The tower is an organ that carries the traditions of Yinchuan, and is the place most steeped in culture there.

摄影：陶克图

“西海固”的华丽转身

“Xihaigu”

“苦甲天下”，苦难让西海固更期待美好。他们饱含沉痛、忧思、奋发和希望地把文学当成庄稼，把书法当成生活。移民搬迁，人们陆续迁入新区，生活不再缺水，不再缺衣少食，孩子们可以上学读书，接触外面的世界，窑洞、水窖、干裂的土地……已悄然远去。如今的“西海固”，已是精神和文化的代名词。

“Xihaigu” is a general reference to the six most poverty-stricken counties in Ningxia, which includes Xiji, Haiyuan, Guyuan, Longde, Jingyuan and Pengyang. This is an area in which life isn’t always easy, but there is beauty to look forward to. Bitterness, anxiousness, thought, and hope come together to form a whole. People move about and migrate, conditions improve, and children attend school and contact the outside world. Caves, cisterns and parched earth become things of the past. “Xihaigu” becomes a symbol for the culture which remains in the place where an era has passed.

破译远古农业生产密码

Clues to the Origins of Agriculture

2017 年，考古界将目光聚焦在了宁夏青铜峡鸽子山，在这里发现了磨盘、磨棒等对植物种子进行加工的磨器。这里发现的磨盘数量之大，在中国考古领域绝无仅有。这一考古发现在某种程度上揭开了距今 1.2 万年到 1 万年之间这一地区远古先民在原始农业萌生期的生产图景。考古专家赵志军说，鸽子山遗址为人们探讨农业起源提供了重要线索。

In 2017, archaeologists turned their sights to Mount Gezi (or Dove Mountain) in Qingtongxia, Ningxia. Here, they discovered millstones, pestles, and other instruments for processing plant matter. This was the largest discovery of millstones in China, second to no other. The artefacts unearthed here were between 10,000 and 12,000 years old, and paint a picture of prehistoric life in the region. According to archaeologist Zhao Zhijun, the ruins at Mount Gezi provide important clues to the origins of agriculture amongst humans.

彭阳姚河塬遗址
Yaoheyuan Ruins

宁夏彭阳姚河塬遗址是2017年全国十大考古新发现之一，也是已发掘的西周遗址中，唯一一处城墙、诸侯级别大墓、铸铜作坊、甲骨文四要素俱全的诸侯国遗址。考古专家刘绪说，这里是周人最西边的大后方，像这样既有遗址又有墓葬的发现，是非常罕见的。这一考古新发现把六盘山地区的建制史从西汉提前至西周早期，提前了近1000年。

The ruins at the Yaoheyuan in Pengyang County of Ningxia were one of the ten greatest archaeological finds of 2017, and are the only find from the Western Zhou dynasty that includes a city wall, royal tombs, copper works, and oracle bones. Archaeologist Liu Xu says that this is the westernmost site for the Zhou dynasty, and that for tombs to be found here is quite rare. The discovery of this site in Liupan Mountains area pushes the history of this region back from the Western Han to the early Western Zhou dynasty, an entire millennium.

中华黄河坛
The Yellow River Altar of China

常言道：饮水思源。作为华夏新天府的塞上江南宁夏，从黄河母亲那里得到的太多太多……为礼敬黄河、祭拜黄河、感恩黄河而建的中华黄河坛，位于青铜峡市小坝镇，背靠贺兰山脉，隔河屹立牛首山，左傍万里黄河臂弯，右依青铜峡峡口，是黄河金岸的标志性建筑，也是宁夏人对自然的一种敬畏。

It's often said that you should be thankful to the spring when drinking water. Resources come in such plenty from the Yellow River. In order to respect the waterway, an altar was built to it in Xiaoba Town in Qingtongxia City, up against Helan Mountains, across the river from Mount Niushou, at the mouth of the Qingtong Gorge. This is a landmark upon the gold coast of the Yellow River, and is a sign of respect for nature from the people of Ningxia.

摄影：李继辉

红军西征指挥部
To the West

红军西征期间，曾将西方野战军总部设在同心县的豫旺堡，西方野战军司令员兼政委彭德怀在这里先后指挥了王家团庄进攻战、红城水阻击战、七营反击战等战斗，把陕甘革命根据地拓展为陕甘宁革命根据地，为党中央把中国革命的大本营放在西北奠定了坚实的基础。西征红军贯彻党的民族宗教政策，维护了抗日民族统一战线。

As the Red Army made its march westwards, the headquarters of the Western Field Army was placed at Yuwangbu in Tongxin County. The Western Field Army's commander and commissar Peng Dehua conducted multiple important campaigns based here, expanding the base area from Shaanxi and Gansu to also included Ningxia, laying a major foundation stone for the stronghold of Chinese revolution. The Red Army of the West implemented the Party's policy on ethnic groups and religions, which united people of different religions and maintained a united front against Japanese invasion.

《诗经》与固原
***Book of Songs* and Guyuan**

固原是一座文化底蕴深厚的历史古城。《诗经·小雅·六月》"薄伐猃狁，至于大原"揭开了固原历史文化记载的篇章。《出车》是一位武士自叙他随统帅南仲出征猃狁凯旋的情景，"天子命我，城彼朔方"记载了西周在包括固原在内的北方游牧区筑城设防的史实。数千年来，有关固原的诗词歌赋有数百首之多，道尽了边塞的固原、历史的固原、文化的固原、丝路的固原。

Guyuan is a place steeped in culture and history. It is mentioned in the *Book of Songs*, the first anthology of poetry in ancient China. Guyuan was first mentioned in the poem of "June". In the poem of "Dispatch", it's described by a soldier recounting his return after a successful expedition against the Xianyun people. This work from the Western Zhou dynasty describes Guyuan's role in the construction of border defences for the area inhabited by nomads. Over the course of many centuries, hundreds of songs and poems have been written about the area, talking about defence, history, culture and the Silk Road.

摄影：白云鹏

摄影：张晓磊

“飞黄腾达”
Fly across the Yellow River

中卫市地处腾格里沙漠和黄河缠绕的地方，是典型的沙漠之都。沙坡头是中卫著名的风景区之一，在沙坡头除了赏景，还有两个主要的“节目”——滑沙和“飞黄腾达”。从沙堤最高处坐溜索，靠个人的动能就会“飞”越黄河，回头到“达”脚下的腾格里沙漠，“飞黄腾达”名副其实。

Zhongwei City is situated between the Tengger Desert and the Yellow River; it's a typical desert city. Shapotou is one of the major attractions here. Aside from sights, there are also two “activities”: sand-skiing and flying across the Yellow River. Riding a rope from the highest area of the sand bank, one can “fly” down the slope, then across the Yellow River, and arrive at the bottom in the Tengger Desert. This is a popular activity here.

供图：宁夏文化和旅游厅

古钱币收藏第一县
Xiji County Coinage Museum

西吉县钱币博物馆古币藏品达 20 万枚，现陈列展品 3500 余枚，上至商周贝币，下至新中国成立初期第一套人民币，被誉为“华夏古钱币收藏第一县”。钱币馆创始人李怀仁，20 世纪 80 年代，他经常骑着自行车下乡寻宝，曾花五分钱买到了国内唯一的乾隆母钱。

The Xiji County Coinage Museum has more than 200,000 specimens, with more than 3,500 on display, from coins of the Shang and Zhou dynasties to the first set of Renminbi issued by the People's Republic of China. This county has been recognised as the numismatic capital of China. The museum was started by Li Huairen. In the 1980s, he rode around on his bicycle searching for specimens, and once spent 0.05 yuan to buy the only extant master coin from the Qianlong Emperor's reign in the Qing dynasty.

吹起来的羊皮筏子
Sheepskin Rafts

20 世纪 40 年代，黄河边上的老筏客，13 岁便开始吹筏子。筏子俗称排子，是用羊皮吹出来的。范长江在《中国西北角》里说，西北水上运输皮筏比木船更为普遍。皮筏漂流黄河迄今至少有 2000 年或更久远的历史，是当时黄河主要运输工具之一，而现在则成了文化记忆和游客的拍摄定格画面。

In the 1940s, sheepskin rafts were a common sight on the banks of the Yellow River here. In *North-western Corner of China*, Fan Changjiang recounts how they were more common than wooden skiffs. This is a kind of craft with more than 2,000 years of history on this waterway, and one of the major transport vessels on the water. Now they serve as vestiges of culture as well as photographic subjects for tourists.

彭德怀与斯诺
Peng Dehuai and Edgar Snow

美国著名记者斯诺于 1936 年 8 月来到红军西征的前沿——豫旺堡，与彭德怀等有了亲密接触。彭德怀向斯诺介绍了红军的生活情况、游击战的战略战术、红军的抗日统战工作等。采访中，斯诺了解了彭德怀的革命经历，对彭德怀留下了深刻印象，说彭德怀是自己见过的最简朴的高级指挥官，而且很有才智，善于驰骋，又能吃苦耐劳，是个很活泼的人。

American author Edgar Snow came to the front of the Red Army's western expedition at Yuwangbu in August 1936, and met with Peng Dehuai, forming a close connection. Peng introduced the living conditions of the Red Army to Snow, how they employed guerrilla tactics and fought against the Japanese occupation. During the course of his interviews Snow came to understand Peng's revolutionary experience, which left him with a deep impression. He said that he was the simplest and most unadorned high-level military commander he'd met, clever and capable, able to endure hardship, and very full of vigour.

你的姓氏，我的名字

Names Imprinted into the Land

明初的宁夏平原，成了大明王朝疆域的边界，大批将士驻守这里，一些地方的名字，因驻守这里的将官姓名而得名，人名便是地名。吴忠、杨和、金贵、叶盛、潘昶、李俊……人名与地名重叠成了宁夏平原上地名的一大特色。“王洪”演绎成了“望洪”，“吴忠”从军营成了城市的名字，“叶盛”不仅是一个镇的名字，还成了横跨在黄河上的一座桥的名字。许多地名也烙下了深深的边塞印记。

The Ningxia Plain was a border region at the start of the Ming dynasty. A large number of military men were stationed here, and a number of place names come from the personal names of officials, ones that originated then and have persisted until the present day. Wuzhong, Yanghe, Jingui, Yesheng, Panchang, Lijun… these are all commonplace names in Ningxia. Wang Hong's name exists in a different form, Wu Zhong had a city named after him, Ye Sheng isn't just the name of a single town, but also that of a bridge on the Yellow River. A number of these names have become imprinted into the land itself.

巨大的兵营

Giant Camp

宁夏在明初变成了边防之地，一些地名便有了浓厚的军事色彩，中卫、平虏、头营、三营、七营、八营、洪广营、兴武营……有些是军事管理机构的名称，有些是驻军首长的名字，“卫、营、堡、寨”让这一时期的宁夏，几乎变成了一个巨大的兵营。安宁对于历史上的宁夏非常重要，也就有了镇北堡、平吉堡、宁安堡、惠安堡等带有期望和平的地名。如今，“昔日的兵营”变成了人民安居乐业的地方。

Ningxia became an area for border defence during the early Ming dynasty. A number of places here have names full of military flair: Zhongwei ("central guard"), Pinglu ("pacifying savages"), Touying ("head camp"), Sanying, Qiying and Baying ("third, seventh and eighth camps"), Hongguangying ("Hongguang camp"), Xingwuying ("camp of strength"). Some are the names of military administrative organs, and some are the names of heads of garrisons. Wei ("guard"), Ying ("camp"), Bu ("fortress"), Zhai ("stockade") all appear commonly in place names that originated at this time, making the names on the map of Ningxia read like a directory of a giant cantonment. Peace was very important to Ningxia throughout history, and there are names that reflect this, too, such as Zhenbeibu ("fort of north"), Pingjibu ("fort of peace and luck"), Ning'anbu ("fort of tranquillity and safety"), and Hui'anbu ("fort of benefit and safety"). In modern times, these cantonments of days past have become places where people live happily and peacefully.

消失的仁存渡口
Rencun Ferry Crossing

老船工张嘎子十多岁时就在渡口戏水摆船。他说，这是当年旧银川黄河宁夏段黄金水道最大的一个渡口，连接着灵武和永宁之间的水面，运输从这里南来北往的人或货物。著名的如晋商八大家，有几百条船，每年从宁夏各地收购来甘草、枸杞、羊毛等从渡口运到包头，辗转再到北京、天津和全国各地。1970 年底叶盛黄河大桥建成通车，代替了渡口。

When he was a young child, Mr. Zhang began to work at the Rencun ferry crossing where the boats were. He says that in those days it was the largest ferry crossing on the golden watercourse in Ningxia, connecting Lingwu and Yongning, transporting people and goods travelling north to south. Hundreds of boats were involved, with Shanxi merchants coming each year to buy herbal medicines, goji berries, wool and other goods from all over Ningxia, and then transporting them first to Baotou and then to Beijing, Tianjin and other places around the country. At the end of 1970, the Yesheng Yellow River Bridge was completed and opened to traffic, replacing the ferry crossing.

想想也只有银川了
Only Yinchuan

一位外地游客在银川逛了几天，有感于银川独特的地理风貌、悠久的文化积淀和改革开放的日新月异，感慨地说："在古老博大的中国，有哪座城市能集塞上江南的富饶、婉丽，和西北人的粗犷、豪放、热情、时尚于一身？想想也只有银川了。"

A tourist came to Yinchuan and walked around the city for a few days, taking in the local geographical features, long historical accretion and rapid changes after opening up and reform, and remarked with awe, "In a country so ancient and broad, it's amazing to see a city like Yinchuan, which combines the beautiful and fertile southern-style fields with the bold and unconstrained passion of the people of the Northwest. It's a fascinating combination you can only find here."

摄影：李靖

固原，历史的纽扣
Button of History

无论是先秦时期的长城还是汉代开凿的丝绸之路，无论是宋夏交界的前沿地带还是明代设置于此的九边重镇，固原在漫漫长河中，像一枚钉在胡服和汉裳纽结处的纽扣，而一支支载着茶叶、丝绸或西域珍宝的驼队，一个个扮演着文化交流角色的商队、使者，便是在金戈和弓角的缝隙中穿针引线。

Whether talking about the pre-Qin Great Wall or the Silk Road in the Han dynasty, whether talking about a frontier region during the time of the Song or one of the nine important towns for border defence in the Ming dynasty, Guyuan has sat along the river of time, like a button that binds the clothes of the northern tribes and the Han people. The trade caravans and the camels carried tea, silk to the west and gems to the east, serving a role as a central actor in the interchange between various peoples and civilisations.

"盐环定"扬黄灌溉工程
"Yanhuanding"

由宁夏盐池、甘肃环县、陕西定边组成的"盐环定革命老区"像一块拼图，把三省区最干旱缺水的地带剪贴在中国西北大地上。喝上甘甜的黄河水，成为老区人民心心念念的一个梦。从1990年开工到现在，"盐环定"扬黄灌溉工程犹如一条生命的血脉，圆了几代人几十万人的盼水梦，结束了和牛羊共喝苦咸水的历史。

The "Yanhuanding Revolutionary Area" is formed like a jigsaw puzzle from Yanchi County in Ningxia, Huanxian County in Gansu and Dingbian County in Shaanxi. All three of these areas are poor in terms of water resources. To be able to drink the sweet water of the Yellow River was long a dream of the people there. With work initiated in 1990, the Yanhuanding Irrigation Project is like a lifeline for the area which turned the dreams of tens of thousands of people into reality, bringing an end to the situation that persisted in this region throughout history.

摄影：王占生

摄影：王立洲

我在老巷子等你
I'll Await You in the Lane

隆德县红崖村巷子，是一个装着故事的老箱子，轻轻打开这个箱子，老树、古钟、枯井、红灯笼……从箱子飞出的一件件古物件，还有那古朴悠长的街巷，构成了一幅远离现代喧嚣的乡野画卷。斑驳的石砖、精美的墙雕、古老的水井、陆离的壁画、悠长的碎石路……静静地躺在那里，向南来北往的游客诉说时光的故事。斑驳的土墙木板上一句“我在老巷子等你”，打开了过往者的情感闸门。

The lanes of Hongya ("red cliff") Village in Longde County are like an old case full of stories. If you open the case carefully you'll see old trees, old bells, dry wells, red lanterns… All the things that fly out of this case, as well as these old and simple streets and lanes form a painting of rural live far removed from the clamour of modern society. Mottled bricks, beautiful walls carved in relief, old wells, oddly colourful wall paintings, long cobblestone roads… They lie here quietly, telling stories of times past to travellers. Upon the flecked wall there is a wooden board inscribed with the sentence "I'll await you in the lane". It's a moving sight to passers-by.

摄影：李东海

一座胜利之山
A Victorious Range

20 世纪 30 年代，红二十五军，红一、二、四方面军长征都曾先后经过六盘山地区。1935 年 10 月 5 日至 9 日，毛泽东、张闻天等率中央红军进入宁夏，途经西吉、隆德、固原、彭阳四县，历时五天四夜。与前来围追堵截的国民党军进行过大小战斗五次，在毛泽东的指挥下，取得了青石嘴战斗的胜利。毛泽东豪情满怀，写下“天高云淡，望断南飞雁，不到长城非好汉”的壮丽诗篇。六盘山是红军长征翻越的最后一座高山，是一座胜利之山。

In the 1930s, the Twenty-Fifth, First, Second and Fourth Red Armies made expeditions crossing through the Liupan Mountains area. From October 5 to 9, 1935, Mao Zedong, Zhang Wentian and other commanders of the Central Red Army entered Ningxia, travelling through the four counties of Xiji, Longde, Guyuan and Pengyang for five days and four nights. There were five engagements, large and small, with the encircling KMT, but under the direction of Mao Zedong, victory was obtained at the battle of Qingshizui. Full of passion and pride, upon this occasion, Mao Zedong penned a poem that begins thusly, “As thin clouds float in the high sky, to the south swan geese fly. Visiting the Great Wall makes a true man.” This poem, *Liupan Mountains to the Tune of Qingping*, is very well known in China today. Liupan Mountains is the last high range the Red Army crossed in the Long March, and a site of victory.

“振兴宁夏”
“Prosperous Development of Ningxia”

1994 年，灵武矿务局职工韩志洲的妻子李芳洲生了四胞胎，三男一女。当时《宁夏日报》记者田春林及他的同事们正好做了采访，并为四胞胎起名“振、兴、宁、夏”，从此也结下了 20 多年超越血缘的亲情缘分。“振兴宁夏”也成了时代记忆。

In 1994, the wife of Lingwu Mining Bureau employee Han Zhizhou, Li Fangzhou gave birth to quadruplets: three sons and one daughter. The *Ningxia Daily* reporter Tian Chunlin and his colleagues came to interview them, and named their children, Zhen, Xing, Ning and Xia. *Zhenxing Ningxia* means “prosperous development of Ningxia”. More than two decades later, this is a memory for the people of the province, an interesting moment in time.

北半球第一龙
Dragon of the North

2005 年 4 月 26 日在中国西部宁夏灵武出土了“灵武龙”恐龙化石的脊椎，挖掘坑道里专家们无法抑制喜悦而惊呼，这是“最美脊椎”。经中科院古脊椎动物与古人类研究所研究员、恐龙专家徐星鉴定，灵武恐龙化石属梁龙类中一个罕见的分支——叉背龙类，距今约 1.6 亿年，某些数据如背椎长度甚至超过目前已知所有恐龙属种。梁龙在赤道以北首次发现，堪称“北半球第一龙”，属国宝级恐龙化石。

On April 26, 2005, the vertebrae of a dinosaur termed the “Lingwu Dragon” were unearthed in Lingwu, Ningxia. This was an amazing find which delighted archaeologists as the bones were in excellent condition. Researcher at the Institute of Vertebrate Paleontology and Paleoanthropology of the Chinese Academy of Sciences and dinosaur expert Xu Xing determined that the Lingwu dinosaur was a part of a rare branch of the Diplodocidae, a *Dicraeosaurus*. They lived 160 million years ago, and some data shows that their spines may have been longer than any other known dinosaur. This was the first Diplodocus to be discovered above the equator. This dragon of the north was listed as a national-treasure level dinosaur fossil.

摄影：彭文润

改写历史的发现

Rewriting History

1990年，宁夏贺兰山拜寺口方塔出土了西夏文佛经《吉祥遍至口合本续》，这是迄今为止中国境内发现的最早的木活字印本。它的出现，使人类发明活字印刷术有实物证据的时间整整提前了一个世纪，改写了世界印刷史。

In 1990, a Tangut Buddhist scripture was discovered at the Square Pagoda at Helan Mountains, making it the earliest woodblock printing discovered in China. After it was found, it proved that woodblock printing existed more than a century earlier than previously thought, changing the understanding of the history of printing in the world.

西北的咽喉

Throat of the Northwest

学者李敬泽到固原，充满豪气地写下这样的话："如果我是几百年前的将军，我会久久地凝视固原，血与剑与风的固原，马群汹涌的固原。在广大帝国版图上，固原是一个微小的点，但两千年间，任何一个目光锐利的战略家都会一眼盯住这个点。"是的，如果突破固原，整个甘肃就成了被切断的臂膀，而通向西安的门就轰然洞开，固原曾如同西北的咽喉。

When scholar Li Jingze visited Guyuan, he wrote the following words, "If I were a general centuries ago, I would keep an eye on Guyuan, this place of blood and swords and wind, where herds of horses pound the earth. On the map of the wide empire, Guyuan is just a small speck, but during the past two thousand years any military strategist making a plan would give it heed." This is true; if one broke through Guyuan, all of Gansu Province would be like a broken arm, with the gate to Xi'an wide open, because this area was the throat of the Northwest.

程子华赠锦旗

A Gift of Silk Banner from Cheng Zihua

1936年，红军二十五军团西征抵达豫旺堡，得到洪家岗子洪寿林对红军开展革命工作的理解和支持。洪寿林宣传："红军是仁义之师，必定胜利。"还动员群众给红军送粮送物，为革命做了很多有益的工作。红军与洪寿林同善相济，真诚合作，时任红军二十五军军长的程子华为洪寿林送去题有"爱民如天"的红绸大锦旗，留下千古佳话。

In 1936, when the Twenty-Fifth Red Army made its expedition west to arrive at Yuwangbu, they received the support of Hong Shoulin of the Hongmen Sect. He told said, "The Red Army is an upholder of kindheartedness and justice, and must be victorious." He mobilized his followers to deliver grain and useful items to the army, making a great contribution to the revolution. The Red Army had continued good relations and cooperation with Hong, and the commander of the Twenty-Fifth Red Army at the time, Cheng Zihua bestowed upon Hong the gift of a red silk banner inscribed with the words "love the people like heaven".

供图：宁夏画报社

以石为嘴、依山而兴的传奇
Shizuishan

因“山石突出如嘴”而衍生的石嘴山市，依煤而兴，成为享誉西北的“塞上煤城”。诗人马萧萧在《中国地名手记》中这样描述：“太西煤，被它说出了滚滚烈焰；在南来的书生意气里，一匹为朔方修辞的马，只需一张石嘴；以石为嘴的山，方可称山，方可问雷电之心而无乌云之愧。”煤炭开采也留下无数的煤灰山，为覆土治理粉煤灰山，这座城市云集了天南地北的奇石异卉，将昔日的粉煤灰山孕育成了美轮美奂的中华奇石山城。

Shizuishan (“mount rock mouth”) City has long flourished on the basis of coal, and is known as one of the famous coal cities north to the Great Wall. Poet Ma Xiaoxiao wrote in *Notes of Chinese Place Names*, “Taixi coal burns with bright fire. In the feelings of scholars that come from the south, using a horse as a metaphor for the dreary north, all that’s needed is this place, Shizuishan. The mountain with a rock mouth is energetic as thunder, yet no clouds are needed.” Coal extraction has left its traces all about, and in order to earth up these sites full of flyash, all manner of stones have been brought from all over, forming bizarre landscapes that are a testament to the persistence of the industry here.

将台堡红军会师
Meeting at Jiangtaibu

1936 年 10 月 22 日，红二方面军总指挥部及二军团与一军团二师在西吉县将台堡会师，宣告红军长征三大主力胜利会师，结束了伟大的长征，将台堡也从此闻名于世。2017 年 3 月，将台堡成为“全国爱国主义教育示范基地”。将台堡红军长征会师纪念碑的建成，是对英勇牺牲的红军将士的缅怀，更是对今人及后人的一种激励。

On October 22, 1936, the three main forces of the Red Army met at Jiangtaibu in Xiji County, and it was announced that the grand Long March was concluded. From here Jiangtaibu became famous. In March of 2017, Jiangtaibu was listed as a “National Patriotic Education Demonstration Base”. A stele was erected to commemorate the Long March of the Red Army, and immortalise the bravery and sacrifice of the soldiers that made the march.

街道记忆
Thoroughfares

银川的街巷，横的叫路，竖的叫街，但新华街和解放街叫街是例外。解放街因宁夏解放而得名，记载着旧时银川“一条街上两栋楼、一个警察看两头”的情景，是宁夏第一条柏油马路、第一条通公交车的城市马路。如今，路边的鼓楼、玉皇阁、邮政大楼、百货大楼、凤凰碑等，依然是银川的标志性建筑。如果街道有记忆，它无疑是这座城市里阅历最丰富的老者，装满了这个城市成长的记忆。

With regard to the thoroughfares in Ningxia, the horizontal ones are called roads and the vertical ones streets, but Xinhua Street and Jiefang Street are exceptions. Jiefang (“liberation”) Street is named for the liberation of Ningxia, and is Ningxia’s first asphalt-paved road, as well as the first one to have a public bus. Today, the Drum Tower, Pavilion of the Jade Emperor, Postal Building, Department Store and Phoenix Stele all stand alongside this road, and remain architectural landmarks. If the street had a memory, it doubtlessly would be the elder with the most knowledge of the city, full of memories of the metropolis’ growth.

五十里长街
50-Li Long Street

银川的北京路俗称“五十里长街”，是宁夏第一条八车道街道，既宽又长，像一条绸缎连接东西。北京路成为银川最主要的干道。宽阔平坦的路面、移步换景的街衢，东到黄河边，西连贺兰山……每一位从外地来银川的客人，无论去哪儿都会走到宽敞气派的北京路上。

Yinchuan’s Beijing Road is known colloquially as the “50-li long street”. It’s Ningxia’s first eight-lane thoroughfare, wide and long, connecting the east and west like a silk cord. Beijing Road is the main artery of Yinchuan. As one traverses the wide and flat surface, various scenes come into view. With the bank of the Yellow River in the east, and Helan Mountains in the west… everyone who comes to visit Yinchuan will come by the grand Beijing Road.

摄影：陶克图

神奇的四棵树
Four Trees

永宁县李俊镇郭家湾村有四棵一样粗的古老银白杨，它们都已经存活 370 多年了，依然挺立在边长 8 米的正方形四个角上，高 20 余米，树冠遮地面积 1 亩左右。每棵树四个大人手拉手都抱不过来，枝头上长年栖息着现在已经很少见的珍禽“苍鹭”。当地村民已经习惯在这里祈求风调雨顺、吉祥安康，表达对大自然的敬畏。

Guojiawan Village in Lijun Town, Yongning County has a group of four old white poplars, more than 370 years in age. They stand at the corners of a square with a eight-metre side length and are more than 20 metres tall. They cover an area of almost 700 square metres. The four trees are quite thick, extend their branches out to each other, and provide roosting places for rare herons. The people of the village are accustomed to praying for favourable weather and good fortune here, expressing their respect for nature.

菜园里长出的文化庄稼
Cultural Village

海原县南华山北麓的新石器时期菜园文化遗址，沉睡了五千年后破土而出。这是一支农牧并重、崇尚简朴、自成体系的原始土著文化，距今约 5000 年，是古人类生息、繁衍、生产劳动的场所和墓葬地，处于母系氏族向父系氏族过渡期。“菜园遗存”是 20 世纪 80 年代宁夏考古的重大发现之一。

In the northern reaches of Mount Nanhua in Haiyuan County there are the remains of a Neolithic farming culture, evidence of human life five millennia old. This was a place where people farmed and kept livestock, maintaining a simple lifestyle, forming an aboriginal culture. This is the site of evidence for a people that lived 5,000 years ago, a place where they grew, worked, and produced, when there was a transition from matriarchy to patriarchy in their society. The remains of this “vegetable garden” culture were one of the great finds of the 1980s in Ningxia.

走进《诗经》的乡愁
Nostalgia for the *Book of Songs*

两千多年前的一个晚秋，一位再次从中原奉命前往六盘山下的周朝战士，在一场引起乡愁的秋雨里，写下了“昔我往矣，杨柳依依。今我来思，雨雪霏霏”的诗句。诗句后来被收入《诗经》。那时的六盘山下，依依杨柳覆盖，生态良好；那时的六盘山，是周朝的军事力量伸及最远的地方。

In the late autumn of a year more than two millennia ago, a warrior of the Zhou dynasty came from the central China to Liupan Mountains for the second time, and wrote a short poem in the rains of the late autumn in which he reflected on his longing for his home as he rode amongst the falling precipitation and willows. The most famous line of the poem reads, “When I think about my last expedition, I remember the wind blowing in the leaves of the willow trees. Now, as I am on my route, heavy snow fills the sky.” This poem was collected in the *Book of Songs*. At that time, willows grew all around the lower reaches of Liupan Mountains. This area marked the furthest extent of Zhou military power.

供图：固原市博物馆

从波斯远道而来的鎏金银壶

The Gilded Silver Pot from Persia

鎏金银壶是波斯萨珊王朝的一件金属手工艺品，距今已有 1500 年的历史，其工艺具有典型的波斯萨珊王朝风格，主题图案描绘的是古希腊神话故事。它经由丝绸之路来到中国，仅此一件，留在了固原李贤墓，如今是固原博物馆镇馆之宝，也是中外历史文化交流的见证和丝绸之路商贸频繁的缩影。借用诺贝尔奖得主马尔克斯的一句名言：任何物品都有灵性。

The gilded silver pot is a metal craft from the Sassanid Empire of Persia, dating back 1,500 years in history. Its workmanship is full of the flavour of the Sassanid era, and usually depicts ancient Greek myths. It came to China via the Silk Road. Found at the Li Xian Tomb in Guyuan, it is the only one extant. It's now kept as a treasure of the Guyuan Museum, and functions as a representation of the frequent trade between China and the outside world upon the Silk Road. As Nobel Prize laureate Gabriel García Márquez said, "Every object has a soul."

震柳是本活的教科书

Earthquake Willow

海原县西安镇哨马营村有一棵柳树，据说是当年杨六郎的拴马桩，从裂开处的年轮推算大概有 500 年的历史了。1920 年大地震时，将这棵古柳劈成两半。古柳历经“一劈”之劫并没有倒下，没有枯萎。《人民日报》原副总编梁衡说，这是个人间奇迹，地震能摧毁一座山，却不能折断一株柳。“震柳”不倒，精神绵长。这种撼世的存在，再一次诠释了生命的深邃与博大。

There's a willow in Shaomaying Village, Xi'an Town in Haiyuan County. It is said that Yang Yanzhao, a famous ancient general once used it as a hitching post for his horse. According to its growth rings, it must be more than five centuries old. During the great earthquake of 1920, this old tree was split in half, but neither toppled nor withered. The former deputy editor-in-chief of *People's Daily*, Liang Heng says that it's a miracle, that an earthquake could topple a mountain but not a willow tree. The "earthquake willow" still stands as a testament to the profundity of life.

摄影：田玉珍

摄影：吴宏林

二十三棵左公柳

Twenty-Three Commander Zuo's Willows

清朝同治年间，左宗棠率领湘兵来到西北。西北气候干燥，寥无生气，喝一口水就有半口被蒸发。于是，左宗棠命令军队沿途遍栽柳树，名曰"道柳"，现称"左公柳"。但当年少水干旱，栽种的柳树大多枯死。虽然左宗棠下了死命令，但存活下来的还是少得可怜，目前只有隆德县保存了二十三棵。

During the reign of the Tongzhi Emperor in the Qing dynasty, commander Zuo Zongtang led troops from Hunan on an expedition northwest. The climate of the northwest was dry, with a rather desert atmosphere. Therefore, the commander had his troops plant willow trees, calling it the "route willow". Now it is known as "Commander Zuo's Willows". As there was a drought in the year, many of the willows died. The commander made his orders, but very few trees survived, and now only twenty-three remain in Longde County.

长城塬上的"乔家大院"

The Courtyard of Family Qiao

1935年10月8日傍晚，毛泽东率红军到达固原彭阳长城塬乔家渠。乔生魁妻女见有部队进庄，便躲藏到家中案板底下，警卫人员向她们说明了红军是老百姓自己的队伍，消除了她们的恐惧心理。乔妻拿出从娘家带回的羊腿，给红军战士们做了晚饭。晚上，毛泽东就睡在用案板支起的简易床铺上。几十年过去了，乔生魁三代76人一直义务守护着这个院子。

In the evening of October 8, 1935, Mao Zedong led the Red Army to the courtyard of family Qiao in Changchengyuan Village, Pengyang County. When Qiao Shengkui's wife and daughters saw the army enter the village, they hurried to hide under the chopping boards. The guard personnel explained to them that the Red Army was the army of the people, allaying their fears. Qiao's wife took out a lamb leg and cooked for the soldiers of the army. At night, Mao Zedong slept on a simple bed propped up by chopping boards. Decades have now passed, and the third-generation descendants of Mr. Qiao still watch over this courtyard.

中国长城博物馆

Great Wall Museum

从战国时期开始，历代王朝几乎都在宁夏修筑过长城，沙石构筑的秦长城、黄土夯筑的隋长城、片石堆砌的宋壕堑、烽堠相接的明长城，不同建筑材料修筑的古长城，在宁夏境内累计绵延3000多里，跨山过塬，蜿蜒盘旋，状若游龙，连接着历史与现在。宁夏成了中国长城的博物馆。

Since the time of the Warring States Period, almost all historical dynasties had built segments of the Great Wall in Ningxia. Gravel was used for building the Great Wall in Qin dynasty, loess was suitable for ramming to construct fortifications in Sui dynasty, and stone fragments formed Song trenches and Ming watchtowers. As different methods of construction were successively used to build segments of the wall, Ningxia became a museum of the Great Wall in China. More than 1,500 kilometres of the wall extend within the province, crossing mountains and tablelands, winding about like a great long dragon, connecting past and present.

供图：宁夏文化和旅游厅

南长滩梨花白
White Pear Flowers in Nanchangtan

南长滩村有黄河、水车、梨花、古长城遗址以及一群世代生活在这里的西夏党项族后裔……群山环绕使得南滩村几乎与世隔绝。据说，党项族崇尚白色，当年为躲避蒙古兵而逃难至南长滩，希望通过雪白的梨花寄托对故国的哀思。一树梨花一段风月，悄悄地定格在这里。

Nanchangtan has the Yellow River, waterwheels, pear flowers, remains of the old Great Wall and the descendants of the Tangut people. However the mountains which encircle the village almost completely cut it off from the world. It's said that the Tangut people revered the colour white, and fled to Nanchangtan to avoid the Mongol army. The white flowers of the pear trees made them think of their original homeland. Each blossom is a piece of scenery in its own right. As they bloom here, you'll find yourself drawn to admire them thoughtlessly.

世外桃源 南长滩村
Nanchangtan Village

南长滩，是黄河流经宁夏的第一个村庄，民风淳朴。村民大多复姓拓拔，20 世纪 80 年代，西夏学泰斗李范文考察认定这个村庄居住的是西夏人的后裔。南长滩四面靠山，一河环流，有史前岩画、古代水车、古长城，有奔腾咆哮、左冲右突的黄河，有壁立千仞、怪石嶙峋的高山峡谷，有千万年黄河冲积形成的狭长绿洲滩地，有阡陌良田和百年果树，俨然就是世外桃源。

Nanchangtan is the first village on the Yellow River in Ningxia, and is simple in character. Most of the residents have the two-character surname "Tuoba". In the 1980s, Tangut culture expert Li Fanwen determined that the residents of this village are the descendants of the people of Western Xia. Nanchangtan is surrounded by mountains and encircled by a river. It has pre-historic rock paintings, an ancient waterwheel, and old parts of the Great Wall. Steep mountains and strange rocks are all about this place of green where the Yellow River has flown for thousands of years. Footpaths crisscross between fields as old trees grow. It's a kind of paradise.

舌尖·寻味
Food and Flavour

摄影：陶克图

拉面早茶
Noodles for Breakfast

每天早晨到吴忠拉面馆，泡上一壶盖碗茶，切上三两牛肉，拼上一盘豆芽韭菜、豆腐皮。一人一碗拉面，拉拉家常，谈谈国内外大事……还有人在这里打打扑克牌，从一早能“泡”到中午，既满足了口福，又饱了耳欲。在一喝一聊中，生意人谈妥了一单生意。放慢脚步，踱进拉面馆“泡一泡”，成了一种文化品位和生活方式。

Every morning at the noodle restaurant in Wuzhong, customers will order a pot of tea, a plate of beef, and an assorted dish. Everyone has a bowl of hand-stretched noodles as they talk about whatever is on their minds. Some people play cards, and stay until the noon. While drinking and chatting, businessmen may make a deal… A slow pace of life makes for a nice atmosphere in the noodle house. This is a way of life and a style of culture.

九碗十三花
Flowers on the Table

在宁夏，享用“九碗十三花”不仅是一种口福，还是一种身份的象征。宴席上的热菜全用九只大小一样的碗来盛，把九只碗摆成每边三碗的正方形，像是花蕊。再在正方形的四边摆放四碟素菜或两荤两素，像是花瓣。一桌菜，看上去像是盛开的花，被称为“九碗十三花”，用来招待最尊贵的客人。

In Ningxia, enjoying the “Nine Bowls and Thirteen Flowers” isn’t just a culinary experience, but also a symbol of nobility. At banquets, nine bowls of equal size are arranged with various foods in a 3×3 square, just like the stamen of a flower. Around them are four more plates like the petals of a flower, either four vegetable dishes, or two vegetable and two meat dishes, for a total of thirteen. The table is like a blooming flower, hence the name: “Nine Bowls and Thirteen Flowers”. This is a token of respect for distinguished guests.

供图：宁夏画报社

摄影：徐向红

一筷子到宁夏
Travel with Chopsticks

“宁味夏语”，就是以纯正美食代言地方文化，是北京一家宁夏清真美食餐厅。所用食材均来自宁夏各地，无论是辣爆羊羔肉、手抓滩羊肉、烤肉串、泉水煮大块黑山羊，还是野生黄河鱼汤泡饭、六盘小炒面等，都能让人“一筷子到宁夏”。因为宁味夏语，京城内更多的食客品味舌尖上宁夏美食时，也开始向往真正的宁夏之旅。

Ningwei-Xiayu, literally the taste of Ningxia, is an authentic location for Ningxia cuisine in Beijing. Here you'll have a glimpse of Ningxia culture. The ingredients for the food are imported from Ningxia. Each of the dishes such as spicy mutton, mutton eaten with hands, skewers, springwater-boiled lamb, rice with fish soup, and fried noodles will transport you to Ningxia with a touch of your chopsticks. Thanks to the restaurant, more people of the capital are able to sample the flavors of Ningxia, and therefore motivated to take a trip to this north-western province.

消暑解渴浆水面
Thick Soup Noodles

浆水面相传始于秦朝末年，民间用包菜、芹菜等在沸水里烫过后，拌以少量面粉，加温水发酵而成。汤汁淡白色，微酸。把浆水用辣椒和葱油炝过，再加进手工面条，就是一碗地道的浆水面。老张说，浆水面吃起来酸甜可口、消暑解渴，而且对高血压、肠胃病和泌尿病有一定的疗效。

These noodles originated towards the end of the Qin dynasty. When round cabbage, celery and other vegetables are boiled, a bit of flour is added. Then they are left in lukewarm water for fermentation. The soup is white and slightly sour. This soup is fried with chilies and spring onion oil, and then hand-prepared noodles are added to complete the dish. Mr. Zhang says this sweet-and-sour dish is good for combatting the summer heat and thirst, and has benefits in treating high blood pressure, gastrointestinal problems, and urinary diseases.

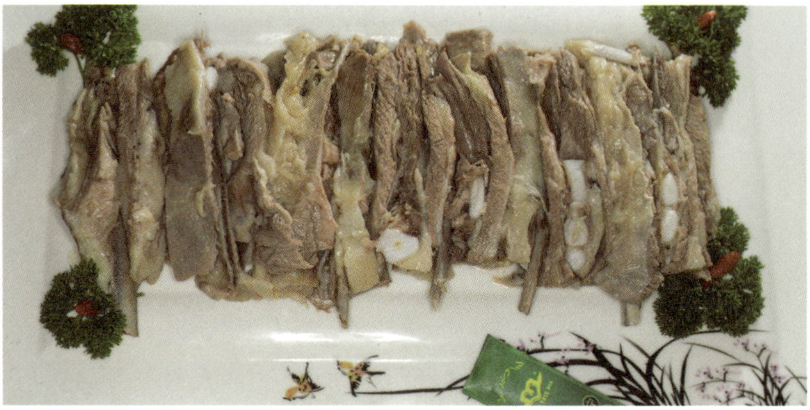

摄影：陈峰

吴忠手抓羊肉
Wuzhong's Mutton

手抓羊肉是吴忠人待客必备的传统菜肴。在宁夏，“老毛手抓”和“国强手抓”最为有名。《舌尖上的中国》到吴忠拍摄手抓羊肉时，“国强手抓”当家人马国强亲自出镜。他说，店里选用的羊肉必须是盐池滩羊，而且必须是羯羊，羊的年龄一般在1—2岁，重量控制在30斤左右。配上独家调味品，煮出来的羊肉软、嫩、鲜、香，肥而不腻、无膻味。

Mutton eaten with hands is a traditional dish in Wuzhong. In Ningxia, “Mao's Mutton” and “Guoqiang's Mutton” are the most famous. When the TV show *A Bite of China* visited Wuzhong for the dish, Ma Guoqiang gave an interview. He said that the store insists on using lamb from Yanchi County, and that it must be from a wether aged 1–2 years. The animal's weight should be around 15 kilos. He adds his special seasonings and boils the meat until it's tender, fragrant, and fatty without being oily, with the goaty taste being boiled away.

羊肉和馍的相遇
Mutton and Cake

羊肉和馍，当这两种西北典型的食材相遇时，中间的那个“泡”字就显示出了时间感。《环球人文地理》总编辑李海洲在银川品尝过羊肉泡馍后赞叹：“宁夏的羊肉和馍被时间之汤泡过后，汤清肉烂馍香，有酸中带辣、辣里透酸的味道；吃了这碗羊肉泡馍，才知道来到银川的理由——图的就是这口有解酒功效的羊肉泡馍。”

When mutton meets cake, either steamed or baked, the word “stew” pops up and points to the importance of time. Having savoured the shredded cake in mutton stew, Editor-in-chief of *Cultural Geography* magazine Li Haizhou remarked, “When Ningxia mutton and cake are stewed in soup, the meat becomes very tender and the cake delicious. The entire food tastes somewhere between spicy and sour. I didn't know why I came to Yinchuan until I had the *paomo*: a bite of the *paomo* that has a sobering effect.”

一碗洋芋面
Potato Noodles

洋芋面是宁夏最普通的一种面食，除了面就是洋芋，食料再简单不过。有时想，那么清爽好吃的一碗面食，是怎样的一双手做出来的呢？仔细打量，那是一双劈柴、割草，哪里的苦重就在哪里的手。当这样一双手把那碗面以一份深挚的感情端到你的面前，朴素而珍贵，心灵唯有感动。

Potato noodles are an ordinary dish in Ningxia. Aside from noodles, there is only potato in the bowl. Unbelievably simple! When enjoying the tasty noodles, you may wonder who made it. It turned out to be made by the hands of one who swings an axe to chop firewood, a sickle to harvest hay. Those hands are always ready to reach out to bear the heaviest burden. When such a pair of hands deliver to you a bowl of noodles, you'll be impressed by the simple but hospitable deed.

咕嘟嘟隆德土暖锅
Hot Pot

暖锅是隆德县的一道煲仔菜肴，用砂锅或是铜质的空心锅，里面一圈炭火，外面一圈是萝卜、豆芽、粉条、豆腐等家常底菜，倒入香浓的肉汤，表面铺满肥瘦相间的过油五花肉，文火咕嘟嘟边吃边煮。三九寒冬，室外冰封雪飘，一家人围锅而坐，一边吃着热气腾腾的暖锅，一边欣赏美丽的雪景，许下来年丰收与幸福的美好愿望，脸上和心里都暖暖的。

Hot pot is a stew dish from Longde County. It's made in a marmite or steel pot that has an open-ended column in the centre, fuelled by charcoal. Carrots, bean sprouts, noodles, tofu and other basic foods are put in, and then thick meat broth is added as well as oil-boiled pork both lean and fatty. It's continuously boiled as it's eaten. During the coldest days of winter, when snow flies through the sky outside, a family sits around the pot, eating and absorbing its warmth, appreciating the snowy view outside, wishing for a plentiful harvest and good fortune in the next year. Both faces and hearts are warm at this time.

撸串撸掉的是烦忧
Barbecue

有人说过，只有天才、音乐和烧烤这三样东西能超越国界。穿好的肉串整齐地排放在灼热的炭火上，听火烤肉吱吱作响，油脂的香气混合着辣椒孜然味儿一起迸发，这种诱惑让人无法抵抗。在寒冷的冬夜，抑或炎热的夏夜，邀三五好友，顺着舌尖来点烤串，将生活的沉重托付出去，一口一口撸掉烦恼。

It is said only genius, music and barbecue transcend national borders. Meat is placed on skewers above the burning charcoals. Then comes the sizzling. The fragrance of the fat mixes with that of cumin, making for an irresistible temptation. On either the cold winter nights or on the hot summer nights, invite a few friends out to enjoy barbecue together. Escape the heavy parts of life and eat away your worries.

供图：宁夏画报社

盐池滩羊

Yanchi Sheep

盐池滩羊肉之所以成为羊肉中的精品，是因为其肉质细嫩，脂肪少而分布均匀，胆固醇含量低，无膻味，营养丰富。美食家董克平到宁夏品尝过盐池滩羊肉后，在博客中这样写道："在柳杨堡村，我们见到了正宗的滩羊，用水加盐煮熟，煮好的羊肉盛在脸盆里，未上桌香味就飘过来了。香口饱腹，一不留神就吃多了。"

The mutton from the Tan sheep in Yanchi County is of excellent quality. Its fat, if any, is evenly distributed. It is low in cholesterol but high in nutrition. Meanwhile, it is devoid of that characteristic "goaty" flavour. Food expert Dong Keping wrote the following in his blog after sampling Yanchi mutton, "We saw real Yanchi sheep in Liuyangbu Village. The meat was boiled with salt and then put into a little basin; we could smell it even before it was served. It was so tasty and filling that I ended up overeating."

鱼汤 +N 在银川
Fish Plus

在《舌尖上的中国》里，有一种美食跨越了两季舌尖，那就是北京的鱼头泡饼。鱼汤 +N 的模式，似乎已经成为食江湖的万金良方。诗人王西平说，黄河鱼汤泡饭，为宁夏传统美食扳回一股正气。可贵的是，鱼汤里还泡有未经打磨的宁夏原米，保留了大米更多的营养成分，吃一口鱼肉软糯，入口即化。

On the programme *A Bite of China,* there was a dish covered by both seasons, the Beijing bread in fish stew. The Fish Plus format is quite popular. Poet Wang Xiping said that rice in fish soup – fish from the Yellow River is a classic dish in Ningxia. More importantly, this dish has the local unpolished primary rice as an ingredient, making the dish all the more nutritious. The fish and the rice melts instantly into tasty flavour in your mouth.

最好吃的羊肉在麻黄山
The Best Mutton

宁夏最好吃的羊肉在盐池，盐池最好吃的羊肉在麻黄山。麻黄山上多麻黄、甘草等草药植物，这里的羊常年吃的就是这些中草药植物。羊还吃一种叫百里香的香料植物，当地人称地椒。加上麻黄山常年地表无水，羊只能喝深井苦咸水。特殊的饮食习惯造就了这里的羊的良好肉质。当然了，这里海拔落差大，羊在这里是运动型的，走向餐桌，肥而不腻。

Ningxia's best mutton comes from Yanchi County, and Yanchi's best mutton comes from Mount Mahuang. Mount Mahuang has a lot of ephedra (*mahuang*, thus the mountain's name), liquorice and other plants which the goats there eat year-round. They also eat a lot of thyme. There's no water on the ground, so the goats only drink the brackish water from deep wells. The special diet makes for excellent quality meat. Of course, at this relatively high altitude the goats get plenty of exercise. When their meat reaches the table it's got a good fat content, but doesn't taste oily.

摄影：陶克图

炸油香
Oil Fried Foods

油香就是油炸面食，是宁夏回族人独特的食品，以油饼最为常见。在回族人所有的节日里，油香不可或缺。因场合的不同，人们以油香来表达祝福、庆贺、纪念或哀悼，这也使油香在每个回族人的生命中具有了“迎来送往”和“生死与共”的意义。当你吃到回族人送上的油香时，你能感受到他们的真诚。

This is a dish unique to Ningxia, a kind of fried cake. They're usually seen as cakes of deep-fried dough, and are an essential component to celebrations among the Hui people. They symbolise wishes for prosperity, felicitations, remembrance or mourning. For the Hui, they are often served on occasions of reception or departure. They also have the connotation of living together through thick and thin. You'll feel these peoples' sincerity when you try this dish.

供图：宁夏文化和旅游厅

别有滋味蒿子面
Artemisia Noodle

蒿子面在中宁县有着360多年的历史。因为野生的蒿子具有健胃、清热的功效，和面时，掺和磨细的野生蒿籽，配以羊肉臊子，吃出另一番滋味。大年初七，吃蒿子面，叫“拉魂面”；新婚夫妇结婚第二天，吃蒿子面，叫“喜庆面”；给小孩过满月和百日，吃蒿子面，叫“吉利面”；老人过生日吃蒿子面，作为长寿面。

Artemisia noodles have more than 360 years of history in Zhongning County. Wild Artemisia is good for the stomach and helps clear internal heat. When ground up and mixed mutton, it adds much to the flavour of noodles. On the seventh day of the Lunar New Year, eating Artemisia noodles implies an invitation for the dead to return. On the day after a wedding, they're meant to celebrate the conjugal life. On the occasions that a child turns one month or 100 days old, they are a token of good luck. The elderly eat them on birthdays as "longevity noodles".

深夜遇汆
Quick Boil

夜深人静，独坐掩卷，最爱的是遇到生汆面。肉丸子下到面里，面是揪的，汤是羊肉汤，还要有固原特产的粉条，腌韭菜，滴点辣油。拿起勺子，面和丸子同食，用勺子舀着，吹着热气，吃起来是哗啦啦地溜……夜遇生汆，夜色如汆，心情也汆夜而过。

Deep in the quiet night, when I finish reading, I'll have my greatest love: noodles and meat balls in mutton soup. Besides, there are starch noodles of Guyuan, pickled leeks, and a little bit of spicy oil. I pick up some noodles and a meatball in my spoon, and blow a little on them. I eat noisily, taking in the flavour nice and slowly. This is the perfect food for the midnight when I'm in a perfect mood.

小茴香大菜包
Fennel Buns

海原的茴香很有名，茴香大菜包是我的最爱。将茴香摘去老叶，洗净晾干，切成细末，拌入适量香油。鸡蛋打成蛋液，放入洗干净的虾皮、少许葱、姜末、盐，炒熟、晾凉，拌入馅中……开锅上汽 20 分钟，包子面皮暄腾，馅儿绿得养眼，味道好极了。那股香气成为挡不住的诱惑，哪一样也比不上茴香大菜包好吃。

The fennel of Haiyuan is renowned, and fennel buns are my favourite. One strips the dry leaves off the plant, washes and dries the rest, chops them finely and mixes in some fragrant oil. Beat some eggs, add washed and dried small shrimps, a bit of spring onions, ginger powder, and salt, cook it, and cool it off… After steaming them for 20 minutes, the skin will be soft and fluffy, and the filling a pleasing green colour. The taste is excellent, and the scent enticing – this is truly first-rate food.

摄影：徐向红

茶水里满含尊敬
Respect in the Tea

在宁夏，回族人喜欢用盖碗饮茶，饮茶是他们生活中的一件大事，也是待客的礼仪。客人远至，盖碗先上。主人将碗盖轻轻揭开，放入新鲜的茶料，然后盛水加盖，双手奉上。那香甜清醇的茶在盖碗里熠熠生辉，茶香四溢，映射出回族人的热情好客。要不都说，回族人的“茶水里满含尊敬”呢。

The Hui people of Ningxia enjoy drinking tea out of a covered bowl. Drinking tea is a big part of life as well as ritual. One sets out the bowls before the guests arrive. The host gently opens the bowls, puts in fresh tea, adds water, and covers the bowl, holding it up with two hands. The clear and sweet tea takes shape in the bowl, and the fragrance of tea drifts about. This little ceremony reflects the hospitality of the Hui people. You can say their tea is full of respect.

碗蒸羊羔肉
Mutton in the Bowl

吃了宁夏同心的碗蒸羊羔肉，也许会颠覆你对吃羊肉的感受。要选细嫩鲜美、没有膻味的羔肉，带骨剁成小块，用精盐、味精、花椒、大料和适量面粉拌匀入味后放在小碗里，上面再放上大葱、鲜姜，上笼蒸熟。当你闻到那满屋缭绕的香味，肚子会情不自禁地咕咕叫。对于本地人来说，每次吃碗蒸羊羔肉的日子，都像是过节。

Eating the mutton of Tongxin in Ningxia may change your feelings about mutton entirely. The meat is delicate and tender, without that goaty taste. It's chopped into small chunks with the bone still on it, and seasoned with salt, MSG, Chinese prickly ash, and aniseeds, before a suitable amount of flour is added. The result is mixed evenly in a small bowl, and then topped with spring onions and fresh ginger before being steamed. When you smell the scent wafting throughout the house, your hunger will be sparked. For the locals, every day you have this dish is like a holiday.

供图：宁夏文化和旅游厅

摄影：陈峰

把“0952”邮戳盖到全国
0952 Postmark

石嘴山大街小巷凉皮店很多，其中大武口区注册的凉皮店就有300多家。最有名的当属三住宅、一棵树、三棵树、刘红梅等店，凉皮跟这里的人一样，热情、泼辣、实在，成为人们抹不去的记忆。几位上了大学的年轻人，干脆在北京、深圳和美国开起了凉皮店，店名就叫“0952”，把石嘴山的邮戳盖到了全国甚至全球。

There are many restaurants that serve cold rice noodles in Shizuishan City; there are more than 300 registered in Dawukou District alone. The most famous have names like Three Homes, One Tree, Three Trees, Liu Hongmei, and so on. The cold noodles are like the people here: passionate, spicy, and sincere. They're hard to forget. Some people have started cold noodle shops in Beijing, Shenzhen, and even the USA called “0952”, taking the postcode for Shizuishan all over the world.

辣糊糊，辣乎？
Spicy Soup?

银川辣糊糊是本土生活味儿的香辣，每一家的味儿都不同。从名字也能感受一二，从街边一角的“姐妹辣糊糊”“文娣阿婆辣糊糊”，到全国加盟连锁的“小厨娘辣糊糊”，三五好友围坐在一锅咕嘟嘟冒着香辣热气的糊糊四周，一边吸溜着，一边感慨着人生的三五小事儿，五味杂陈的喜怒哀乐与这一锅锅浓稠温暖的辣糊糊，一起煮成了银川人生活的味道。

The spicy soup of Yinchuan is a specialty there, and each restaurant's is different. The name itself tells you what it's all about. From little shops like “Spicy Sisters” and “Auntie Wen's” to the national chain “Xiao Chu Niang”, groups of friends pack these stores all over the city, eating together and enjoying each others' company. Mixed flavours and emotions come together in the warm pots here, reflecting the lives of the local people.

舌尖化开的清蒸羊羔肉
Steamed Mutton

吃了宁夏同心、海原一带的清蒸羊羔肉，会颠覆你对吃羊肉的感受。宁夏羊羔肉细嫩鲜美，没有膻味。羊羔肉最好选用胸叉、上脊骨部位，剁成长方形条，用清凉水洗净，码在碗内，放上生姜、大葱、大蒜。再放上几粒生花椒，上笼蒸30分钟左右，然后扣至汤盘内上桌，配以醋、蒜汁、盐等调料佐食。从南方来的小青说，第一次吃清蒸羊羔肉就被惊艳到了，肉质软烂，不用使劲咀嚼，肉就在舌尖化开。

Eating the mutton of Tongxin and Haiyuan, steamed in clear soup, will change your view on the meat. The mutton of Ningxia is fine and delicate, and lacks the characteristic "goaty" flavour. The best lamb meat is from the thoracic fork and upper spine. Cut into long strips and washed in clear cool water, it's stacked up in a bowl, covered with fresh ginger, spring onions, garlic, and some prickly ash. Steam it for about 30 minutes, and then place it upside down on a dish. Now it is ready to serve with vinegar, garlic, salt, and other condiments. Xiaoqing, who came from the South said she was amazed by the dish the first time she ate it. The meat was soft and pliable, and it didn't take much effort to chew up. It just falls apart as soon as you took a bite.

摄影：陶克图

野菜变脸成名菜
Claim to Fame

“艾呛，榆钱呛，槐花呛。”每到四月间，银川大街小巷里总会听到提着野菜篮子叫卖的老乡们的声音。记得小时候，地里的艾草长到巴掌大的时候摘回来，洗净、控干水、拌上面，上蒸笼蒸十五分钟出锅，撒上盐面儿，拌些蒜末儿，淋上胡麻油，就是一道香喷喷的美味。这些野菜原本是过去饥饿时粮食的替代品，当下，这些野菜稀罕地成了星级酒店的一道野味名菜。

Wormwood, elm seeds, and flowers of the pagoda tree. In April, there will be hawkers crying their wild vegetables along the streets. In my childhood, when the wormwood grew to the size of a palm, we picked it, washed it, rung the water out, mixed it with flour, and steamed it for fifteen minutes. Then we sprinkled it with salt, ground garlic, and some sesame oil. It was fragrant and delicious. This wild vegetable was used as a substitute for grain in years of famine, and now is an ingredient used as a famous wild vegetable dish in starred hotels.

一场秋雨紫蘑来
Purple Mushroom

只要一场秋雨，贺兰山上的紫蘑菇便一夜间舒展身体，个个头上撑着一顶黑紫色的小伞，噌噌噌跑下山来。它有着丁香一样的香味，含有丰富的微量元素。当“丁香菇”邂逅土鸡，邂逅羊肉，那就是一道人间珍馐，让神仙也乐不思蜀。

Upon an autumn rain, purple mushrooms will pop up overnight on the Helan Mountains, like so many little parasols. They smell like lilac and abound in trace elements. When cooked with chicken or mutton, they are a rare delicacy, irresistible and addictive.

香得让人打喷嚏
Make you Sneeze

诗人有时说话容易夸张，有时候夸张得也恰如其分。北岛来宁夏参加诗歌朗诵会，热情的宁夏诗人们陪着他吃遍了银川大大小小的馆子，尝遍了形形色色的小吃，无论吃什么，北岛都说香，说好吃，吃不够，短短几天北岛说自己长胖了。离开宁夏时，北岛说，宁夏各种吃食香得特别嚣张，远远地闻到就香得让人打喷嚏。

Poets tend to exaggerate, but sometimes to an appropriate extent. When Bei Dao, a famous poet, came to Ningxia to participate in a poetry reading, the passionate locals took him to all manner of restaurants around Yinchuan, where he tried all kinds of food. No matter what he ate, he said it was delicious, and that he wanted more. In just a few days he said he felt he gained weight. When he left Ningxia, he said that the food there was clamorous, with such a fragrance that one would sneeze even if the aroma drifted from far away.

盐池羊肉
Yanchi Mutton

一炉火、一把盐，就是天上人间美味——盐池羊肉。曾经有位上海作家来宁夏采风，他说，十几年过去了，宁夏羊肉的香味好像一直还在嘴边。盐池羊肉好吃，固然和这里的自然环境有关，但更重要的，大概是因为这里的草鲜水美，羊吃得更是心无旁骛。

In Yanchi, it takes merely a stove and a sprinkle of salt to prepare the most wonderful mutton. An author in Shanghai, who visited Ningxia over a decade ago, said that, the flavour of the mutton still lingered in his mouth. The mutton here is of excellent quality because of the natural environment, where clear water and fresh grass make for a carefree setting for the lambs.

羊肉搓面
Rubbed Noodles

宁夏人对面食有一种情怀，一天不吃面就会觉得心里缺点儿什么。羊肉搓面更是让宁夏人割舍不下的一种风味面食。将面粉揉成面团，醒好后将面搓成筷子般粗细，然后下锅煮熟，再放入羊肉块，浇上用羊肉原汁、豆腐和新鲜蔬菜烩成的汤汁，再淋上一点儿辣椒红油，一碗羊肉搓面就成了。一道道搓面，就是拴住宁夏人的一道道细绳。

Noodles are quite popular in Ningxia; one feels somehow unsatisfied if a day goes by without noodles. Rubbed noodles with mutton soup are a staple for the local people. Dough is rolled into little balls and kept for a while, then rubbed into strips as thick as a chopstick. It's boiled and added chunks of mutton, and then mutton broth, tofu and fresh vegetables are cooked together to form the soup. Some chili oil is added to complete the dish. Each noodle is like a string that ties the people of Ningxia to their home.

供图：宁夏文化和旅游厅

摄影：陈峰

因为清纯，所以清炖
Simple and Plain

盐池滩羊肉天生丽质，所以大多时候都是清炖，因为清炖肉鲜味美。往往只用一把盐便可，无须再加任何佐料，不用烹、不用炒。若把美食比美人，烹调和化妆都是技术活，羊肉没味，调料佐之，女人不美，脂粉涂之。因为清纯所以清炖。清水出芙蓉，清水出美味。

The mutton of Yanchi County is of excellent quality, so it's often boiled plain to show off its flavour. Salt is the only seasoning needed, and there's no need to fry it. There is similarity between good food and a beautiful lady: cooking and makeup both involves skills. Whereas the mutton is bland, one adds seasonings; if a lady looks plain, she wears makeup. This is pure meat, so it's cooked in a pure manner.

封印的初恋味道
First Love

周末，常常看到情侣一对对或朋友三五成群聚在公园的一处绿伞下，手捧着白底蓝字颇有年代感的平吉堡瓷瓶酸奶，一边畅聊一边满足地吮吸这夏日清醇的味道，瓶底呼噜噜跳动的回响，拨动了彼此快乐的心弦。夏日乐悠悠的故事就这样被封印在了一个个平吉堡的小瓷瓶中。

On the weekend you'll frequently see couples and groups of friends under the green umbrellas in a park, holding white ceramic jars with blue characters upon them – this is Pingjibu yoghurt. They chat and drink in the air of the summer, and enjoy being with each other. The leisurely story of the summer is thus imprinted on this Pingjibu bottles.

酸汤细长面
Thin Noodles

过年过节，来了亲戚，抑或是农忙之际，母亲总会在灶房里忙得不亦乐乎，不停地擀，擀好几张，折叠后用快刀切细即成。醋炝汤，配以适量调料，撒上细丝葱花。酸汤舀到碗里，捞少许煮好的面条入碗，香味荡溢，美不胜言。一首诗说得很形象：“煮在锅里团团颤，捞在碗里莲花转，筷子挑起条条线，吃在嘴里吸不断。”

When relatives come over during the Spring Festivel or during the busy harvest season, my mother will hustle merrily around in the kitchen and keeps rolling out sheets of dough. After they're rolled and trimmed, she cuts them into thin long noodles with a sharp knife. When boiled, a small bundle of the noodles are put into a bowl of soup with vinegar, seasoning, and spring onions. Then the finished noodles with pleasant aroma. There has even been a poem about these noodles: "Boiled in the pot, the noodles spin like a top. In a bowl, they turn like a lotus. When picked up with chopsticks, the long lines bounce and hop. Once into the mouth, so chewy are the noodles that we savour each drop."

到黄渠桥吃个爆炒羊羔肉
Stir Fried Lamb

外地人来宁夏之后，回家时少不了带枸杞“神果”；外地人逛宁夏吃美食，当地人少不了用一道“黄渠桥爆炒羊羔肉”招牌菜来宴请远道而来的客人——似乎唯有这道酥嫩爽口、肥而不腻、色香俱佳的美味才能表达出宁夏人的好客、热情、实诚。也难怪每逢周末节假日平罗黄渠桥镇上停满了许多“宁 B”之外的车辆。

When visitors return from Ningxia they have to bring goji berries with them. In Ningxia, "Huangqu bridge fried lamb", a signature dish is often served to visitors at banquets. Tender, crispy, and fatty but not oily, this specialty looks nice and tastes good. Nothing can better convey the hospitality, passion and sincerity of the local people. It's no wonder why at weekends and holidays there are so many cars from other cities.

摄影：陈峰

荞面搅团，母亲的味道
Flour Jelly

小时候，母亲炒好酸菜肉臊子，然后另外在锅里熬好小米粥，再将荞面倒进去搅，“搅团要好，三百六十搅”。用擀杖快搅，再用勺背用力往锅底研揉，使其柔韧。吃搅团的汤汁很多，也可以配点儿咸韭菜，或在有蒜泥、辣汁的醋里蘸着吃。今年春节，在堂兄家又吃到一回荞面搅团。回来后，女儿念念不忘，几次提起。儿时母亲的味道并未消失。

When I was young my mother would take minced meat that had been fried with pickled vegetables and then add millet congee to the pot, and last buckwheat flour. She would stir it sort of 360 times. Stirring quickly with a rolling rod, grinding and kneading with the back of a spoon, she would make it pliable and tough. There are many broths that can accompany this dish, and one can add some salted leeks, garlic paste or spicy dipping sauce. Last spring festival, I had the dish at my cousin's house. After we came back, my daughter was thinking of it all the time, and kept bringing it up. The taste of mother's cooking from my childhood still lingers at the tip of tongue.

心肝宝贝羊杂碎
Lamb Entrails

宁夏到底有多少家羊杂碎店铺，谁也说不清。羊的这些五脏六腑的零碎，本是些上不了桌面的物什，却让宁夏人三天不吃心里闹得慌。小火将羊杂碎慢炖到酥烂绵软、汤汁浓稠如油，撒上香菜末儿，淋上特有的羊油辣椒，再就上一口新蒜，挑一筷子，香味在舌尖流连。羊杂碎就是那种你肚子饱了眼睛还在饿的小吃。

It's hard to say how many mutton tripe restaurants Ningxia has. The lamb's internal organs are chopped into small pieces to form dishes which are eaten frequently by the local people. Cooking slowly at low heat, the lamb's organs break apart and soften, and the broth becomes as thick as oil. Sprinkle on some chopped coriander, a few chilies that have been coated in mutton oil, and a bit of fresh garlic and its ready to eat. This is the kind of food you feel hungry looking at even if you're full.

手抓羊肉细细品
Savoring Mutton

手抓羊肉首选羯羊稚嫩的肋条。煮制时，整块入锅，仅需些许大料。盛盘时，点缀芫荽，辅以陈醋和大蒜。还有一种手抓，乃是羯羊的脖颈，出锅后，顺颈骨横刀裁切，外圆内方。品味手抓，还可分季节，夏天溽热，吃凉手抓，却不必担心肉会腥膻。细细品咂，入口的便不仅是一块手抓，还有对富贵美满的向往和期待。

The best part of mutton comes from the ribs of a young wether. The entire rib is placed in the pot to boil, with just a bit of aniseed for seasoning. It's served with coriander, vinegar and garlic. There is another type of this dish made from a wether's neck, which is cut broadwise after boiling. When it's oppressively hot in the summer, eating cold mutton in this style helps cool off. Each bite of this delicious dish is a step towards happiness and satisfaction.

唱出来的“羊肉面”
Mutton Noodles

布衣乐队主唱吴宁越说，每当想家的时候，他就会听到妈妈的呼唤：“你回家吧，在你最困难的时候，回家妈妈给你做最喜欢的羊肉面呀……”布衣乐队的《羊肉面》好听，宁夏的羊肉面更好吃。许多人听了《羊肉面》，因歌而不远千里跑来宁夏，只为品尝西北汉子歌中唱到的“羊肉面”。

The Buyi Band's lead singer Wu Ningyue says that every time he misses home, he hears his mother's words: "Come home if you aren't feeling well, and mother will make your favourite mutton noodles for you." The song *Mutton Noodles* by the band is a great one, and the mutton noodles of Ningxia are great food. Many people came to visit Ningxia after hearing the song, just to try the dish it was about.

一生追求只因一杯酒
Wine Life

宁夏农垦玉泉国际葡萄酒庄，可以说是宁夏葡萄酒的摇篮，贺兰山东麓产区一些酒庄的酿酒师与种植专家都是从这里走出来的。宁夏第一瓶红酒是这里的水泥槽酿出的，简单的设备、简单的工艺，却透着农垦酿酒人的执着与热爱。历史的变迁中，从农垦人变成酒庄人，有些人，因一杯酒而找到一生的追求。

The Ningxia Yuquan International Winery is considered the cradle of winemaking in Ningxia. All the winemakers and planters on the eastern reaches of the Helan Mountains started here. The first bottle of wine in Ningxia was produced here. Simple as they are, the facilities techniques are infused with the passion and love of the winemakers. Things change over time, and farmers become winemakers. Some people spend their lives in the wine realm.

供图：李光荣

摄影：陈峰

解腻养生八宝盖碗茶
Eight-treasure Tea

“八宝茶”是古丝绸之路流传下来招待亲友宾客的传统茶饮。盖碗，又称三泡台，上有盖，下有托盘，盛水的花碗口大底小，里面装着枸杞、桂圆、葡萄干、红枣、芝麻、沙枣、果干、玫瑰酱、冰糖、茶叶等各家秘制配料。炎热的夏天，喝盖碗茶比吃西瓜还要解渴。冬天早晨起来，一碗茶就点儿油香馓子，神清气爽。现在宴请宾客，吃完手抓或羊杂，“刮”几盅盖碗茶解腻又养生。

The “eight-treasure tea” originated on the ancient Silk Road as a drink for guests from afar. The container of the tea consists of a lid, a saucer, and a bowl. Inside the porcelain bowl are goji berries, longans, dried grapes, jujubes, sesame seeds, oleaster, dried fruit, rose jam, rock candy, and tea leaves. On a hot summer day, a cup of this tea is even more quenching than a watermelon. Waking up on a winter day, a bowl of the tea along with fried dough twists make for a fresh start to the morning. When entertaining guests, some mutton or mutton tripe along with a few cups of this tea make for a delicious and healthy combination.

诗人争抢韭菜合子
Chives Pocket Pie

诗人舒婷来到宁夏彭阳，吃第一口就喜欢上了彭阳的韭菜合子。看似十分普通但又十分讲究的韭菜合子，整整齐齐地码放在盘子中，摆上桌子，主妇笑盈盈地看着你，吃的人心里便盈满温暖和感动。舒婷开玩笑说，雷抒雁老师老跟她抢那韭菜合子，自己都要“怀恨在心”了呢。

When poet Shu Ting came to Pengyang in Ningxia, she tried *Jiucai Hezi*, the “chive pocket pie” of Pengyang, which is a bit like a fried panino or empanada. They look very ordinary, but actually a lot of work goes into them. They’re arranged carefully on a plate, and brought to you by the smiling hostess. One can hardly resist the savoury pies and the hospitality. She nursed a sort of grievance against professor Lei Shuyan because the latter stole one off her plate.

供图：宁夏文化和旅游厅

烩小吃
Braised Snack

当你看到厨师把夹板、豆腐、粉条、面筋、丸子等放到一个锅里，不要讶异，这是中卫“烩小吃”最朴素的做法。清莹的汤里融汇了各样配料，看一眼，就难以自禁。入口，质地软嫩，滋味鲜香，总会忍不住吃多。无论是宁夏本地人，还是外地人，吃烩小吃的时候，都能感受到宁夏也像这融汇各种食材的烩小吃一样有着包容和谐的精气神。

When you see the chef put a “pressing board”, tofu, noodles, gluten, and meatballs in the pot, don’t be afraid; this is how the “braised snack” of Zhongwei is made. Clear and glistening, the soup combines these ingredients into a hard-to-resist dish. It’s soft and tender, with a smooth, fresh taste, and you can never have enough of it. Whether you’re a Ningxia local or a visitor, when you eat the braised snack you’ll feel the spirit that blends these foods in a combination: inclusive and harmonious.

炒糊饽
Fried Paste Cakes

炒糊饽是吴忠流行多年的传统风味小吃。当地人用白面烙成薄饼，切成条状，再把羊肉切片加入红葱、花椒面、酱油、醋、辣椒等佐料上油锅爆炒，炒熟后续上适量肉汤烧开，倒入烙饼条翻炒或加盖焖至汤汁收干。白面烙饼滑韧适口，嚼之有劲，传统面食和当地的味道一起被炒进锅中，融为一体。

The fried paste cake has long been a popular traditional snack in Wuzhong. The local people bake wheat flour into a cake on a pan, cut it into strips, and then add slices of mutton, as well as red onions, prickly ash, soy sauce, vinegar, chilies and other ingredients along with oil and fry them. Some meat broth is then boiled and poured into a pan to fry with the cake strips, or be covered to boil down. These cakes are slippery, tough, and a litlle bit chewy. A traditional starch and local flavours are thus fried together to form a whole.

羊肉泡馍
Mutton and Cake

提到银川，很多人的第一印象就是羊肉泡馍，肉嫩馍韧，汤清肉烂。煮汤是最重要的，骨汤和肉汤分开煮，料重味醇、绵韧适口、肥而不腻，泡馍多切成条状，是大多数人喜欢吃的快餐。羊肉泡馍虽然外在豪爽简单，但内在却精致复杂，吃的就是那种连汤带水的过瘾。

Many people say that their first major impression of Yinchuan is the cuisine of mutton and cake, called *paomo*, with clear soup and well-cooked meat. The preparation of the soup is most important, with the bone soup and meat soup separately brewed. The condiments are dense in flavour, and make an impression on the palette. The meat is fatty but doesn't cloy one's tastes, and the cakes are usually cut into strips, which can please everyone's preferences. Although *paomo* appears simple and rough, it is exquisite and complicated in content. The mutton, together with the broth, makes for an addictive, irresistible flavour.

摄影：何春风

摄影：张涛

老板，来个饹饹
Order by Mistake

荞麦磨成面粉，有很多种做法，荞面搅团、荞面揉揉、荞面凉粉等。最具本地特色的是一种用“饸饹床子”把荞面压成条状的“饸饹”，像粉条儿一样，或蒸或煮熟后柔韧而滑润，拌以葱花、肉丝、辣椒等作料，吃起来清香可口，别有风味。一天，一位外地姑娘到餐馆，把菜单上的“饸饹”看成“饹饹”，便大声喊：“老板，来个饹饹。”

One can make a number of things with buckwheat flour, such as jelly, paste, and cold noodles. One of the most distinct is a “heluo” made with a special device. Buckwheat dough is pressed into strips, like noodles, and steamed or boiled until it’s pliant, tough and smooth. It’s mixed with chopped spring onions, meat strips, chilies and other ingredients to make a delicately savoury dish. One day, a visitor who was unfamiliar with the characters as both are only used in this specific compound, mistook “heluo” for “luoluo”, and called out in a loud voice, “One ‘luoluo’, please!”

葡萄酒的情与色
Wine of Nature

好葡萄酒是种出来的。贺兰山东麓产区的葡萄酒最本质的是接地气。独特的自然风土条件，“迎春展藤，冬藏埋土”，以“一座挡风的山、一河可控的水、三面环绕的沙”的独具优势，酿造出人文情怀与自然风土相融的“情与色”皆具的葡萄酒。微醺在老世界与新世界的门槛中间，让世界从这里发现中国葡萄酒。

The quality of wine depends on the grape plantation. On the eastern reaches of the Helan Mountains are a number of vineyards which enjoy the special natural conditions. The vines sprout in spring and take a rest in winter. The mountain blocks the wind and the river provides good irrigation, while sand flanks the area on three sides. The unique benefits of this region make for cultured feelings that blend with the natural landscape, yielding excellent wine.

供图：宁夏葡萄产业发展局

摄影：张治军

行旅·地标
Travel and Landmarks

藏着的宁夏
Hidden Ningxia

宁夏是藏着的，而且是藏在中国的地理和历史的双重腹地中。秦始皇统一中国后，筑起长城万余里，于是宁夏就这么被藏了起来，不被外人所熟知，甚至常常会有人误把宁夏的首府银川当作甘肃的一个市。美国《纽约时报》2013 年评选的全球必去的 46 个最佳旅游地，宁夏和巴黎等世界著名旅游景区一起名列其中。

Ningxia is hidden in both history and geology. After the first emperor of the Qin dynasty unified China and built the Great Wall, Ningxia was hidden from the outside. Many people even thought that Ningxia's capital, Yinchuan, was part of Gansu. When *The New York Times* selected 46 must-visit destinations, Ningxia was on the list, just like Paris.

给心灵放个假
Vacation for the Soul

“旅客朋友们，欢迎来到宁夏，我们的飞机已安全抵达距离银川约 20 公里的河东机场。”走出机场，拉着行李箱，抬头映入眼帘的是塞上江南图景上“来宁夏，给心灵放个假”的标语，少了些摩肩接踵，多了份闲暇惬意。仿若瞬间化作丝路驿站上的行者，向前迈出的每一步就像踢走心头的一个石块，天朗气清，长河落日，适宜放牧自己的心灵。

“Dear passengers, welcome to Ningxia; our plane has safely landed at Hedong Airport, approximately 20 kilometres from Yinchuan.” When one walks out of the arrivals hall, luggage in hand, one will see a mural of gardens upon the wall, with the words “Come to Ningxia to give your soul a vacation”. One gets a break from the crowding, and a chance to relax. It's as if one has become a traveller upon the Silk Road, lightening up with each step upon the path. The sky is clear and bright as the sun sets over the river, and one feels free.

供图：宁夏画报社

摄影：连伯亭

中国宜居新天府
Nice Place to Live

银川是一座热情的城市，得黄河之水、历史年轮、多元文化在这里积淀，贺兰山、六盘山一干一湿两座山的庇佑。有山有水，刚柔相济，地理位置不东不西，海拔不高不低，气候不冷不热，出则繁华，入则安静，大街小巷映衬在绿色和水色下，天蓝云白。2017 年，银川被《中国国家地理》评为“中国十大新天府之一”。

Yinchuan is a passionate city, which has the features of the Yellow River, history, and diverse culture. It has the contrasting wet and dry mountain ranges of Helan and Liupan, excellent scenery with all manner of contrasts, a central location, medium elevation, temperate climate, and a character that is both resplendent and calm. The wide thoroughfares and narrow alleyways have the green of foliage and water, and white clouds float in the blue sky. In 2017, Yinchuan was listed as one of the ten most livable cities in China by the magazine *Chinese National Geography*.

全域旅游景区
Tourist Attraction

宁夏是继海南之后，全国第二个全域旅游示范省区。无论线上线下，凡是来宁夏的游客都能够穿越千年前的西夏古国，感受贺兰山下金戈铁马的雄浑壮阔，欣赏戈壁大漠中长河落日的辽阔苍茫，体会六盘山上红旗漫卷西风的豪情壮志……沉浸式体验带来了更多更美妙的享受。

Ningxia is the second most popular province for tourism in China after Hainan. Whether on- or off-line, those curious about Ningxia can view the traces of the ancient Western Xia kingdom, the traces of ancient wars at the Helan Mountains, the sunsets over the river in the Gobi desert, the red banners furling at Liupan Mountains… an immersive journey will bring all kinds of beauty for you to enjoy.

供图：宁夏画报社

三沙源的今昔
Sanshayuan

十几年前，位于银川南二十里的三沙源还是个沙魔肆意横行的地方。每到春季银川人牙缝里塞的都是黄沙，这个占地两万多亩的沙漠随着连年的沙尘暴肆虐，快要堵住银川的南大门了。自 20 世纪 90 年代开始，治沙英雄张宝军开始在沙漠里植树、种草，养殖牛羊鸡鸭；如今的三沙源变成了绿洲，鸟儿翔集，水波荡漾，成了绿色天然氧吧。

More than ten years ago, this place 10 kilometres south to Yinchuan was still a wild expanse of desert. Every spring the locals found mouth full of sand, as the ever encroaching desert crept closer to the city. In the 1990s, sand management hero Zhang Baojun started to plant trees in the desert, as well as grasses. He brought cows, sheep, chickens and ducks. Sanshayuan today is an oasis, where birds fly, water ripples, and green and oxygen are in plentiful supply.

宁夏印象大逆转
Image Setback

一位网友说：原来印象里的宁夏是典型的大西北感觉，比如恶劣的气候，寸草不生的黄土高坡，空气里都会弥漫着干燥的泥土气息……但几天宁夏之行让他彻底改变了这种印象。植被交错，天总是蓝蓝的，几乎没有一丝云彩。宁夏虽小，却有着奇特的地貌、多元的文化、神秘的历史……这位网友不禁感叹：好一片神奇的土地。

Someone on the Internet said: I originally assumed that Ningxia was typical of the Northwestern China: crappy air, barren loess slopes, and a dry feeling all throughout the atmosphere. However, after I travelled around a few days, my view was completely changed. There's dense vegetative cover, and a sky that's always blue with few clouds. Although Ningxia is small, it has wonderful landscapes, diverse culture, fantastic history… The commentator couldn't help but remark, "What an amazing place!"

明朗纯净是银川
Clear and Clean

老子说，五色令人目盲。纷繁的色彩容易使人产生视觉疲劳。银川有着中国西北城市共有的单纯、干净和疏朗，但她更为明朗、更为纯净。文化学者余秋雨曾经惊奇于银川带给他的印象——色调单纯，视野开阔，非常干净，这是其他城市中不容易见到的。这样现代和整齐的城市风格，令人羡慕。

It's said that an overload of colour can make you colourblind. The different hues all about can prove tiring to one's sense of vision. Ningxia has the characteristics of a pure, clean and bright place in North-western China. Cultural scholar Yu Qiuyu once marvelled at the impression Ningxia gave to him – pure colours, a wide field of view, vast cleanliness – all of which are hard to find in a city. The modern and orderly nature of the city is enviable.

须弥山
Mount Sumeru

仓央嘉措在《若能在一滴眼泪中闭关》一诗中说："我独坐须弥山巅，将万里浮云一眼看开。"这个须弥山不单单指宁夏。宁夏须弥山石窟是我国开凿最早的石窟之一，位于六盘山北端，拥有大大小小的石窟162处，远远望去，石窟层层叠架，状如蜂房一般。须弥山石窟所处的位置是"丝绸之路"由长安到西域的最短的必经之地。

Tsangyang Gyatso wrote in the poem *If One Could Close with a Single Tear*, "I sit on the peak of Mount Sumeru(Xumi Mountains), and open my eyes to the myriad clouds." Ningxia also has a mountain called Xumi, and it has one of the earliest carved rock grottoes in China. Situated in the northern reaches of Liupan Mountains, there are in total 162 grottoes large and small. They look far out, one after another, almost like a beehive. Mount Xumi was a stop one must visit on the Silk Road when heading from Chang'an to the Western Regions.

供图：宁夏文化和旅游厅

供图：宁夏文化和旅游厅

最有意思的地方 Most Interesting Place

电影人凌峰说，镇北堡华夏西部影视城是宁夏最有意思的拍摄地，既有狂野的沙漠又有灵动的水乡，既有雄浑的黄河又有原始森林，既有清澈的湖泊又有开阔的古战场，既有沧桑长城又有崇山峻岭……古堡土墙，颓垣断壁，历史感厚重。这里拍摄的电影电视剧，像《红高粱》《大话西游》，要么明星红了，要么票房大卖。

Ling Feng, a celebrity from Taiwan, says the Zhenbeibu China West Film Studio is the best place to film in Ningxia. There are wild deserts and enticing water villages, the waters of the Yellow River and primeval forests. Clear lakes and wide ancient battlefields are both about. There are the long stretches of the Great Wall, old fortifications and earthen walls, barren ruins, and history everywhere. Films shot here such as *Red Sorghum* and *A Chinese Odyssey* have become quite famous.

沙与湖的珠联璧合 Sand and Lake

万亩水域环绕千顷沙丘，沙与湖珠联璧合——这就是沙湖。金沙、碧水、翠苇、飞鸟、游鱼、远山、彩荷七大景观融为一体，自然天成，凭借独特的自然风光，沙湖成为中国十大“魅力湿地”之一，成为鸟的天堂、鱼的世界、游人的乐园。

Vast waters encircle thousands of hills – Sha Lake, or “Sand Lake” is where sands and lakes come together, thus the name. Golden sands, blue waters, verdant reeds, flying birds, swimming fish, distant mountains and coloured lotuses form the seven major sights. What a gorgeous landscape! This is one of the ten top wetlands in China. It’s a paradise for birds, a world for fish, and an amusement park for tourists.

沙湖芦苇
Reeds at Sand Lake

沙湖芦苇是沙湖美景不可或缺的组成，没有了芦苇，沙湖也就没有了生机和朝气。这里的芦苇分布在沙湖的角角落落，恰到好处地散布在湖面，湖苇相映，如诗如画。芦苇丛更是各类动物，特别是鸟类栖息的理想家园。湖水清澈如海，苇丛点缀如画，沙湖芦苇如影相随，交相辉映，沙湖因为有芦苇而充满活力，越发灵动；芦苇因为在沙包围中、散落沙湖中而更显旖旎、靓丽。

The reeds at Sand Lake are an essential component of the scenic spot. Without the reeds, there wouldn't be a source of vitality here. These reeds are distributed around the outer reaches of the lake, and within it when there is sufficient ground. They form a scene like a poetic painting. They are also the habitat for a number of animals, especially for birds. The water of the lake is limpid like a small ocean, and the reeds grow thickly. The reeds and the lake form a symbiotic relationship and image. The reeds make the lake dynamic and bright. They are part of the charm and grace of the entire system.

摄影：贾民湖

宁夏归来不看沙
Sand in Ningxia

宁夏归来不看沙。沙漠遇到湖水，碰撞出一半金黄一半碧绿的沙湖；腾格里沙漠依偎在黄河臂弯，放弃了洒脱与不羁，化作阴阳绕指柔的沙坡头；黄沙古渡边古老的水车静静流淌，吟诵着“大漠孤烟直，长河落日圆”的千古美景。流沙痴恋指间的缠绵与温柔，河水不舍手心里的珍惜与温度。水与沙的厮守化作不离不弃的魂，繁衍出这片土地不息的生命。

A stark contrast between blue-greens and yellows exists at Sand Lake, where the desert meets the water. The Yellow River winds through the sands of the Tengger Desert, it meanders through the lands of Shapotou. A water wheel turns quietly on the banks where the old ferry port is. It evokes thoughts of the famous poem by Tang-dynasty poet Wang Wei in which he describes smoke rising and the sun setting over the river. The sands are touching and moving, and the waters precious and warm. The yellow and blue are inseparable, interconnected, essential to each other. Together, they form the soul of the land.

一场盛会
一份纪念
Gathering and Commemoration

“蓝蓝的湖水清澈见底，灿烂的阳光照射在湖面上，湖面闪闪发光。一阵秋风吹来，岸边的树叶沙沙作响，好像在给我们唱歌……一处风景一片天，走进花博园让人流连忘返。”一名小学生在作文中这样描绘银川花博园。一场盛会一份纪念，银川市花博园是第九届中国花卉博览会留给宁夏人的美好纪念，更成了人们“给心灵放个假”的好去处。

“The water of the lake is clear to the bottom as the brilliant sunlight shines over its surface, flickering with the ripples. An autumn wind blows and the leaves on the trees of the banks rustle, as if they’re singing for us… Walking here, you don’t want to leave.” An elementary school student thus described the Yinchuan Flower Expo Garden. A gathering and a commemoration, the site is a memorialisation of the 9th China Flower Expo for the people of Ningxia to enjoy, yet another place to relax yourself, heart and soul.

供图：宁夏画报社

“一盘散沙”
雕成的王国
Plate of Sand

一座城需要一个王，一个王要守护一座城。沙湖有这么一座城，不用钢铁筑成，无须巨石垒就。世界沙雕艺术家从四面八方来到沙湖，将“散沙一盘”的细沙雕刻成不同的形状，形成了一座城，只是这座城里住的不是一位王，而是向世人呈现东方与西方、古代与现代艺术的交汇，呈现一种不可思议，让人叹为观止的美和震撼。

A city needs a king, and a king needs to protect his city. Sand Lake has a city like this; one not built of steel and iron, with no need for fortifications. The sculptures come from all over, to make all kinds of designs out of the sand, forming a city. There isn’t just one king in this city where east and west meet to form an incredible, breath-taking view that moves the observer.

进一步是江南，退一步是大漠
South China Here, Desert There

电影《大话西游》有这样一幅画面：紫霞仙子撑着竹篙从芦苇荡中缓缓行来，袅袅婷婷，人美，景美。而这美景就是沙湖。进一步是江南，退一步是大漠。独特的自然风貌使沙湖成为极佳的拍摄取景地，不少电影、电视剧都曾在此取景。置身其间总让人有似是剧中人的感觉。

There's a scene in the film *A Chinese Odyssey*: Zixia floats through the reed marsh with a bamboo spar in hand, delicate and graceful. It's a beautiful person against a beautiful backdrop, which is that of Sand Lake. Here there are scenes that resemble South China, yet as soon as you step out you find yourself in the desert. The special natural scenery of the region makes for an excellent backdrop in which many films and TV series have been shot. Being here makes you feel like you're in one of them.

中国观鸟首选之地
Birdwatching

“水绕沙丘天下绝，万鸟栖息苇中藏”。沙湖之美，美在沙水相融；沙湖之奇，奇在水绕沙丘……一座座松软的沙丘，被偌大的清澈湖水怀抱，凭借独特的自然风光和美丽的湿地，沙湖成为鸟的天堂。这里栖息着近200种、100多万只鸟，占宁夏鸟类总数的三成多，是“中国观鸟首选之地”和中国最美的40个景点之一。

Water encircles the sand dunes as thousands of birds rest hidden amongst the reeds. The beauty of Sand Lake combines sand and water. Really wonderful! When one walks into the area, past countless hills of sand, one is embraced by the water of the lake. The special natural scenery and beauty of the wetlands form a paradise for more than one million birds of almost two hundred species, more than 30% of the total in Ningxia. It's been lauded as the best site for birdwatching in China, and one of the 40 most beautiful places in China.

供图：宁夏画报社

摄影：钟培源

黄土高原的绿岛
Green Island

六盘山山清水秀，风光旖旎，人称此地“春去秋来无盛夏”。踏访六盘山，满眼都是沙棘、白桦、落叶松……还有郁郁葱葱的杂草。独特的地势造成六盘山峡谷中溪流交错，水流每到陡落处便会飞泻成瀑，而后落地成潭，于是形成潭、瀑、泉、涧、溪等多种水体景观。得天独厚的自然环境，赏心悦目的自然美景，为六盘山赢得了“黄土高原的绿岛”美誉。

Liupan Mountains are green, and the waters are clear, with the scenes charming and graceful. They transition from spring to autumn without a summer. When one sets foot in this area, one sees the common sea buckthorns, white birch, and larch as well as various grasses. The special topography of the season makes Liupan Mountains a place where streams inter-cross within mountain valleys, forming roaring waterfalls when they encounter sheer edges, and deep pools after. Pools, waterfalls, springs, creeks and streams are all about here. The distinctive natural environment earn Liupan Mountains the name “Oasis upon the Loess Plateau”.

神奇的纬度
Mystical Latitude

通常而言，北纬 38 度所在区域是较为适宜人类居住和生活的。北纬 38 度线刚好穿过宁夏，决定了宁夏的气候，年均温度介于12℃—14℃之间，气候条件较为舒适。宁夏是一个有温度的地方，西有贺兰山，东有黄河，依山带水，它的温度正如我们的体温，不高不低，不十分热，也不十分冷。

Generally speaking, 38 degrees north is a relatively suitable latitude for humans to live at. This line passes right through Ningxia and determines its climate, with a yearly average between 12 and 14 degrees. The climatic conditions are quite favourable. Ningxia has its share of heat, with Helan Mountains in the West, and the waters of the Yellow River in the east. Mountains and waters make for a climate that’s suitable for us, neither hot nor cold.

一园游遍宁夏
All of Ningxia

中国花博会每四年举办一届，被誉为我国花卉界的“奥林匹克”。从宁夏到海南、从河南到江苏，看四季海棠的红艳、赏狐尾椰的俊俏、观羽毛枫的秀雅……宁夏作为第九届花博会东道主，以“微缩宁夏”展示宁夏五个地级市各具特色的历史文化和地域特色，用集约有限的空间展现出美丽宁夏的精华。“一步迈进花海，一园游遍宁夏”。

The China Flower Expo happens once every four years, and is honoured as the “Olympics” of the flower world in China. From Ningxia to Hainan, Henan to Jiangsu, people can appreciate the charm and beauty of the Begonia semperflorens, the foxtail-leafed palms, and the feathered maples... Ningxia was the site of the 9th China Flower Expo, where plants from cities and counties all over Ningxia were brought together in one place to showcase the beauty of the province. Here you can see all of Ningxia.

挂在半山腰的绿丝带
Green Strips on the Mountain

驱车行驶在固原彭阳的田野上，忍不住停下来眺望远方的梯田，瞬间也改变了在中国看梯田不是云南就是贵州的印象。固原彭阳梯田没有水，多彩线条就像挂在半山腰的丝带，被誉为“中国美丽田园”“中国最美旱作梯田”。梯田本是防止坡耕地水土流失而形成的特殊农田形态，却也在无意中成了一道靓丽的风景。

Driving over the fields of Pengyang in Guyuan City, one can’t help but look out over the far-off terraced fields, and feel as if one is in Yunnan or Guizhou. The terraced fields of Pengyang are like strips of colour halfway up the mountains, and have been praised as some of the most beautiful in China. These fields serve a practical purpose, but are also excellent scenery to look upon.

供图：宁夏画报社

摄影：张永祥

沙与河的风情
Sand and River

浩瀚的沙漠，雄浑的黄河，沙水一体，古老原始的羊皮筏渡，遐思悠悠的沙漠驼铃……这就是沙坡头。刚刚还在感叹“大漠孤烟直，长河落日圆”的塞上奇观，转身却又遇见“春水碧于天，画船听雨眠”的江南美景。黄沙、绿草、碧水、蓝天在这里巧妙融合，交织出一幅色彩斑斓的五彩画卷。

The bold Yellow River flows through the vast desert. The old sheepskin rafts drift upon the water, and the sound of a camel bell rings from far out over the desert. This is Shapotou. Scenes from certain poems come to mind–“a single plume of smoke rises from the great desert, and the round sun sets over the long river” or “the waters of spring are as clear as the sky, and from the boat one listens to the rain”. Yellow sand, green grass, blue water, blue skies all come together here forming a wonderful painting.

堆积出来的浪漫
Romance

银川人的婚纱照里，览山公园恢宏壮丽的仿古罗马斗兽场风格的露天剧场建筑是少不了的浪漫外景地。镜头下阅海余晖中的新婚恋人彼此牵手依偎，眺望着远方的摩天轮，就这样手牵手一起白了头。10 年前这里还曾是一片荒地，城市环保治理工程用 310 万方建筑垃圾堆积成浪漫的览山，化作了城市绿肺，浸润呵护着碧水蓝天的运动休闲之都。

In Yinchuan, many wedding photos are taken at the open-air theatre built in the style of the Roman Coliseum, full of romantic atmosphere. Couples lean on each other and hold hands, looking out at the Ferris wheel in the distance. Just 10 years ago this was a barren land; the civil engineers turned a 3.1 million square-metre landfill into this site of romance, adding green to the landscape and providing a place of blue waters and skies to exercise and relax.

沙河共色相辉映
Hue of Sand

中卫，不同于人们印象中的西北。沙是中卫的名片，水是中卫的血脉。这座城市树绿、水清、空气湿润。“九曲黄河万里沙，浪淘风簸自天涯”，黄河呈“几”字形，千回百转，流经宁夏中卫，滋润着这片充满生机的热土；腾格里沙漠纵横，与黄河之水交相辉映，沙与河自然而然融合在一起，形成了“沙河共色”的景观。

Zhongwei is different from the North-western China in people's imaginations. Sand is the icon of the city, and water its lifeblood. This city has green trees, clear water, and clean air. The Yellow River left miles and miles of sand as it makes its multiple turns. Despite the rapid torrents and harsh winds, it never adjourns, forming the shape of the Chinese character 几. It irrigates the ground, crossing the Tengger Desert. In a place where water and sand come together, the nature of the desert and the river share the hue.

黄河漂流是一种享受
Floating on the Yellow River

被誉为国内独木舟海洋探险第一人的李华灿，从青海巴颜喀拉山的黄河源头，历经三个多月漂流至宁夏境内。李华灿说：“从黄河入宁开始，我发现黄河宁夏段植被非常茂盛，尤其是从吴忠至银川这段河岸，一马平川的稻田、清新的空气、凉爽的气温，让我的漂流之旅成为一种享受。”

Lauded as the first canoe explorer in China, Li Huacan started out at the source of the Yellow River in the Bayan Har Mountains, and over the course of three months drifted to Ningxia. Li said, "When I entered Ningxia on the Yellow River, I discovered that the vegetative coverage on the banks was very thick, especially from Wuzhong to Yinchuan. There were boundless stretches of fields, clear and fresh air, and nice temperatures, which led to me really enjoying my floating journey."

摄影：徐向红

宁静夏天最避暑
Cool Summer

宁夏的夏天很有诗意，白天温暖但不暴晒，傍晚就开始凉爽。宁夏基本没有酷暑，从5月到10月，天朗气清，蓝天白云，绿树成荫，久居南国的人如果想晒干被梅雨浇得有些发霉的心情，到宁夏晒晒太阳是最好的选择。穿行在沙湖之间，漂流在黄河之上，行走在沙漠深处，休闲避暑在森林绿洲，享受灿烂而宁静的夏日。

The summer in Ningxia is full of poetic feel. The days are warm, but the sun isn't overly intense, and things start to cool off as night falls. Ningxia doesn't really have a period of intensely hot summer. From May to October, the sky is clear and the air fresh, white clouds float by, and the ground is covered in green. If the people from Southern China want to dry off from the plum rains, then Ningxia is a good place to come. Passing through Sand Lake, floating on the Yellow River, walking through the depths of the desert, resting at a forest oasis, enjoying the warmth and quiet of the summer days…

秋色如童话
Fairytale Autumn

宁夏的秋天，更像一位迟暮的美人，美得心碎、美得彻骨。进入9月，"一场秋雨一场寒"。随着时令的渐行，天气越来越凉，尤其是早晨和晚上，那种蕴含温暖的凉意能给人神清气爽的感觉。而天高云淡的宁夏会变得浪漫悠远，整个塞上江南犹如一幅多彩的童话世界，瓜果飘香，稻田如画，景致绝美。

Autumn in Ningxia is like a senior beauty, thrilling and breathtaking. When September comes around, there is a series of rains before winter quickly sets in. As time progresses, it becomes cooler and cooler, especially in the early morning and late night. These warm feelings of coolness are refreshing in a way. Thin clouds float in the high sky with a romantic feeling, and the whole landscape blooms with the colours of a fairytale. Fragrances of fruits drift in the air, and the rice fields are picturesque.

摄影：钟培源

供图：宁夏文化和旅游厅

一百零八塔
108 Towers

宁夏青铜峡水库西岸崖壁下坐落着一个巨大的古塔群，塔群坐西面东，依山临水，依山势凿石分阶而建，自上而下按奇数 1、3、3、5、5、7、9……19 排列，构成一个共 108 座塔的等边三角形塔群。有人说这 108 座塔能化解 108 种人生烦恼，数一个塔就可消除一种烦恼，若能一口气数清所有的塔，烦恼便烟消云散。

There is a group of huge old towers on the western bank of the reservoir at Qingtong Gorge in Ningxia. The group of towers faces east, flanked by mountains and waters. They're made out of stone, and arranged in odd numbers: 1, 3, 3, 5, 5, 7, 9, all the way to 19. They form an equilateral triangle of 108 towers in total. It is said that the 108 towers can solve 108 human worries, with one disappearing as one counts each tower. If one can count all the towers in one breath, one's worries will float away like the scattering clouds.

欣赏蓝天也是一件幸福的事
Blue Sky

我在微信朋友圈发的图片里，宁夏的蓝天占有很大比重，有朋友甚至怀疑："加工过的吧？"我说，绝对没有。宁夏大学一位老师去外省读了几年书，有机会走出宁夏，但她依然回到宁夏，就因为这一片蓝天让人留恋。深圳的一位朋友来过宁夏后，感慨万千："宁夏蓝天真美！"其实，经常欣赏蓝天也是一件幸福的事。

I was posting on social media about the blue sky of Ningxia, and a friend asked me if I'd post-processed the picture. I replied I definitely had not. A professor from Ningxia went to another province to study for a number of years. She was happy to have the opportunity to explore outside of Ningxia for a while, but said, "It's hard to tear myself away from this blue sky here." When one of my friends from Shenzhen visited Ningxia, she remarked on how beautiful she found the sky. Actually, frequently looking at the sky and appreciating its colour is a fortuitous event.

被鸟儿唤醒的清晨
Awakened by Birds

作家肖彭写道:“在银川的第一个早晨,我是被鸟儿的歌声唤醒的。‘在清晨的鸟鸣声中醒来’，是这些年只有在诗情画意中，或者说只有在梦中出现的情景……对于在大都市生活的人们来说，的的确确多年未曾遇见过。”每天清晨在鸟鸣中醒来，你说银川人是多么幸福?

Author Xiao Peng wrote, “In the first morning in Ningxia, I was awakened by the chirpings of birds. ‘One awakes to the sound of birds in the clear morning’ is something that exists these years only in paintings and poems, or in dreams…’ For urban residents, these are memories years in the past.”

惟石能言
Speaking Stones

在贺兰山脚下，坐落着世界上规模最大的岩画专题博物馆——银川世界岩画馆，在这里可以倾听来自远古的呼唤。被誉为“民间文化抢救人”的作家冯骥才在看到雄浑壮阔、原始古朴的贺兰山岩画后，感慨良多，挥笔留下了“岁月失语，惟石能言”。冯先生的题词如今镌刻在这座目前中国唯一的岩画专题博物馆内，引得观者驻足深思。

At the foot of the Helan Mountains, there is the largest rock-painting museum in the world – the Yinchuan World Rock Art Museum. One can hear the calls of ages long past here. Author Feng Jicai, lauded as a saviour of folk culture was moved when he saw the primitive rock paintings upon the Helan Mountains, and penned a couplet, “Times remains speechless whilst the stones speak.” Feng’s words are now inscribed at the entrance to what is China’s only rock art museum, prompting viewers to think as they step in.

供图：宁夏画报社

摄影：王晓龙

黄河楼上看黄河
The Yellow River Tower

中华黄河楼是宁夏黄河金岸上的标志性建筑，有“黄河金岸第一高楼”之称，宁夏特有的黄河文化、西夏文化和大漠文化在此得到淋漓尽致的彰显。黄河楼总高 108 米，拾级而上，逐层登顶，青铜峡的黄河风光尽收眼底，大河奔流，波澜壮阔，你对“天下黄河富宁夏”会有更为切身的感受。

The Yellow River Tower is one of the representative landmarks of the Yellow River Gold Coast in Ningxia. Ningxia has the culture of the Yellow River, the culture of the Tangut civilisation and the culture of the desert, all of which are exhibited here. The tower is 108 metres in height. Ascending the stairs one is rewarded with a beautiful view of the Qingtong Gorge. The river flows wide and rapidly, with bold waves. It brings to life all those phrases that one hears about the wealth of the Yellow River in Ningxia.

宁静的夏天，惬意的冬天
Quiet Summer, Cozy Winter

一山一世界，一水一天涯。宁夏的夏天不冷不热，空气清新，阳光明媚，是个避暑的好去处。“宁静的夏天，天空中繁星点点……”，数着星星，度过一个宁静的夏天。萧瑟的冬季，阳光却是如此灿烂，一踏足会迷失在“千里冰封、万里雪飘”的北国风光里。溜冰、滑雪、逛灯会、涮羊肉、泡温泉，一壶暖茶、一杯葡萄酒，把时光温热在宁夏的冬天里。

A mountain is a world and a waterway is a universe. The summer of Ningxia is neither hot nor cold, and the air is clean and fresh. With pleasant sunshine, it is a summer resort to its true sense! Stars make for a nice sight in the summer sky. The sunlight is still bright during the bleak winter, and “the northern kingdom” fills with snow. Ice skating, skiing, lantern festivals, mutton hot pot, hot springs, warm tea, and wine all come together in the winter of Ningxia.

供图：宁夏画报社

贺兰晴雪
Helan Snow

由于气候原因，贺兰山一年四季清隽如铁，唯有落雪时节分外妩媚动人。一场凛冽的大风后，晴空万里，天湛蓝湛蓝的，山敦敦实实地立着，天与山的交汇处潋滟着雪白一线，形成一种晴天中白雪皑皑的奇美景观，这就是“贺兰晴雪”胜景。“满眼但知银世界，举头都是玉江山”。观贺兰晴雪能感觉心里装满纯洁，尘世少了许多羁绊。

For the climate reasons, the skies of Helan Mountains are clear year-round. It can be quite moving when it's snowing. Especially after a harsh cold wind, with boundless clear sky all around, the sky is deep blue. The mountain stands mighty, and the land and sky are connected by a rippling line of white snow, forming a beautiful scene. This is the "sunny snow of Helan", praised by the poet Chen Dewu of the Ming dynasty for its beauty. Looking upon the scene, one has a feeling of great purity, unrestrained by the fetters of the common world.

神秘的西夏王陵
Imperial Mausoleum of Western Xia

1938 年，德国出版的《中国飞行》一书中，收录了德国人卡斯泰尔在中国荒凉的大西北航拍到的一张照片，照片上是用黄土夯起的大土包。这大土包就是富有传奇色彩的西夏王朝的帝陵。有关西夏的文字记载很少，留给后人的是跨越时空的无限神秘、传奇的遐想。人们从那些废弃的建筑、出土的文物和残缺的经卷中，寻找着这个古老王朝的踪迹。

The book *China Flight*, published in Germany in 1938, contains an aerial picture taken over the barren north-western landscape in China. In the picture there are some large structures of rammed earth. These are the famed imperial Mausoleum of Western Xia. There are very little written record of the empire. It takes a great imagination to peer back through time. From the ruins here, a number of rare writings and scrolls were unearthed, providing us with traces to follow the paths of the ancient dynasty.

沙湖日出 Sand Lake Sunrise

“沙湖的日出既不亚于黄山日出的瑰丽奇迷，也不亚于泰山日出的壮观雄伟。沙湖的日出有北国大漠的气势，有沙海茫茫的奇谲，甚至还带着北国人那无遮无拦的狂放与炽诚。”于秀兰《大美沙湖》道尽了沙湖日出的别样美。在沙湖观日出，有一种毫无阻隔、一览无遗的壮观与通畅。

“The sunrise at Sand Lake isn’t second to the beauty of Mount Huangshan’s sunrise, nor the magnificence of sunrise at Mount Taishan. It has the power of the northern desert, the splendour of the sea of sand, and the unbridled wildness and passion of the northern people.” Yu Xiulan thus described this scene in *Grand and Beautiful Sand Lake*. Viewing the sunrise here one has a feeling of a grand and unobstructed view.

供图：宁夏画报社

最美盘山公路 Mountain Road

在宁夏，有一条风景如画的盘山公路——泾隆公路。公路位于固原市隆德县和泾源县之间，全长 28 公里。从隆德进入泾隆公路，两侧映入眼帘的都是金色的华北落叶松，到达山顶进入泾源县境内时，道路崎岖蜿蜒，有时几个急转弯连着，还有 360 度的转弯，让人胆战心惊，大有川藏线上的“怒江七十二拐”之气势。

The Jing-Long Mountain Road in Ningxia is truly a scenic thoroughfare. This road connects Jingyuan and Longde counties, and has a total length of 28 kilometres. Embarking upon the route from Longde, one will find both sides are flanked by the Prince Rupprecht’s larch. As one makes their way to Jingyuan county, on switchback after switchback, there are points where one is afforded a 360-degree vista. This is truly a path of breath-taking views.

摄影：陶克图

藏在黄河肚子里的博物馆
Hidden Museum

“妈妈，我看到黄河水里的鱼了！”孩子兴奋得手舞足蹈。这是发生在中卫黄河宫黄河博物馆内的一幕。黄河宫外形为水滴状，创意源自李白“黄河之水天上来”的诗词寓意。主题建筑半隐于地下，展示黄河在整个流域的多样气候、地质地貌、丰富资源物种等。在这里，人们能近距离感受黄河文化，透明的景观通道让你体验滔滔的黄河水，还可以欣赏到黄河里的鱼类及其他动植物。

“Mummy, I see fish in the Yellow River!” A child excitedly jumped about upon making this observation. This is a scene that unfolded at the Zhongwei Yellow River Museum. The outside of the building is in the shape of a drop of water, inspired by the words of Li Bai’s poem, “The water of the Yellow River comes from the sky”. Half of the construction is hidden underground, with the transparent construction allowing you to look into the waters of the river itself. One can appreciate the fish and other animals of the river from within.

供图：宁夏画报社

爱上一个人，恋上一座城
Love for the City

“曾经有一份真诚的爱情放在我面前，我没有珍惜，等我失去的时候我才后悔莫及。人世间最痛苦的事莫过于此。如果上天能够给我一个再来一次的机会，我会对那个女孩子说三个字：我爱你。如果非要在这份爱上加个期限，我希望是……一万年！”对于看过《大话西游》，甚至对此有一份情结的人来说，至尊宝的这段话是不会忘记的。因为《大话西游》你会迷上镇北堡华夏西部影视城。

“There was once a true love in front of me, but I didn’t value it. After I lost it I regretted deeply. This was the most painful experience. If I can have another chance, I would say to this girl three words: I love you. If I had to put a time limit on this love, I would say ten thousand years.” For those that have seen *A Chinese Odyssey*, or even someone who has a complex, these are valuable words to remember. Because of this film, you’ll become enamoured with the Zhenbeibu China West Film Studio.

一个因羊闻名的好地方
Famous for Sheep

几乎所有中国的美食家都认为，盐池滩羊肉质最佳。“去盐池吃羊肉”，成了一种食者的向往，就连二十国集团、金砖国家的领导人都曾品尝过它的美味。吃着大块羊肉、喝着羊奶粥，再品一品羊肝凉皮、荞麦饸饹、小吃汤、八宝菜等特色小点，推杯换盏后，登花马古城，观满天繁星，享清风拂面，细闻城头花儿小调……盐池是给心灵放假最好的去处。

Almost all Chinese gourmands believe that the mutton of Yanchi Tan sheep is of the best quality. “Have some mutton in Yanchi” is a well-known phrase among them. Even the national leaders of the G20 and BRICS were treated to the beautiful flavour of this delicacy. Here you can eat large chunks of the mutton, drink goat-milk porridge, try some mutton jerky cold noodles, buckwheat hele, snack soup and eight-treasure dishes, head out to the ancient Huama town, observe the stars in the sky, enjoy the cool breeze blowing over your face and listen to the folk songs. Yanchi is a wonderful place to give your soul a vacation.

沙漠里的自由
Freedom in the Desert

艺人蕾拉小姐来到宁夏，被中卫腾格里沙漠的美迷倒了，原来在极致的美景面前，一切试图记录的举动都是没有意义的，只需放下杂念，放飞心灵，融入此情此景。她想给三毛打个电话，问她怎么没来腾格里沙漠看看。一百种获得自由的方式，这里都有。

When artist Leila came to Ningxia, she was fascinated by the Tengger Desert in Zhongwei. It’s almost meaningless to record in words what one sees when confronted with such a scene of natural beauty. One can only let go of random thoughts, let the soul fly, and melt into the scenery. She wanted to give San Mao a call, and ask her why she hadn’t come to see the Tengger Desert. There are more than a hundred ways to gain freedom here.

摄影：牟将

摄影：娄星辰

月光下的水中束腰美人
Beauty Under the Moon

宁夏沙湖以水中有沙、沙中有水闻名世界，而沙湖水中的芦苇又被称为“水中束腰的美人”。湖面上的天是蓝的，云是白的，湖面周边地是绿的。每当月圆之夜，芦苇在微微的秋风中摇曳，此时，天上月光漏过微微颤动的芦苇洒在水面上，景致幽幽，月光点点，西部风情恍若那首唐诗：海上生明月，天涯共此时。

Sand Lake in Ningxia has sand in the water, and water in the sand. The reeds that grow in the water are the "corseted beauties" of the lake. The surface of the lake is blue, the clouds white, and green fringes the water. On the night of the full moon, the reeds sway in the autumn wind. At this time, the moonlight touches upon the gently rippling water as it peeks through the reeds. It's a calm scene flecked with moonlight. The landscape in the west frontier is best described by Tang dynasty poet Zhang Jiuling's, "The moon rises bright over the sea, as all who observe it enjoy it together."

百鸟叫来了春天
Birds in Spring

鸣翠湖是黄河古道向东移鄂尔多斯台地时留下的一片湖泊湿地，这里是百鸟的乐园。开春的时候，这里湖光戏柳，百鸟翔集。当地百姓说，银川的春天都是这里的百鸟叽叽喳喳叫来的。只要听见了鸣翠湖的鸟儿们脆脆的声音，就知道春天来了。地气热了，冻冰的湖面要化开了，冰下的鱼儿要出来透气了，树木要发芽了，桃树要开花了。

Mingcui Lake is a wetland upon the plateau as the Yellow River progressed east towards Ordos. Many birds flourish here. When spring begins, they flock about upon the lake and among the swaying willows. The locals say that spring in Yinchuan is filled with the sounds of birds all around. Their calls upon Mingcui Lake will definitely usher in spring. The ground heats up, the frozen surface of the lake melts, and one sees the fish underneath. The trees begin growing again, and the peach blossoms.

深呼吸小城
Breathing City

到了宁夏隆德县和泾源县，一定要放慢脚步，深深呼吸。这里山清水秀，满眼绿茵茵；这里是天然氧吧、洗肺天堂，呼吸的每一口空气全是负离子。在这里，睁眼、呼吸都是一种享受，两个字——舒坦。“深呼吸小城”是当地的绿色名片，是“绿水青山”转化为“金山银山”的纽带和桥梁。

When you come to Longde and Jingyuan counties, you must go for a slow walk around, and take in some fresh air. The mountains and rivers here are wonderful sights to witness. Natural oxygen cleans your lungs, and ions are always refreshing. Here, both your eyes and lungs will dwell in comfort. These places are spots of breathing, where the classic blue waters and green mountains are the most valuable treasure.

冬日暖情
Warmth in Winter

宁夏没有真正意义上的寒冷，而是冷暖相宜，四季皆游。在这里你不仅可以感受到北国的壮美，还可以深度分享文化探秘、冰雪运动、冬季垂钓、冰上龙舟、民俗展演、花灯灯会等变幻无穷的冬日快乐，吃一块手抓羊肉、喝一盅暖暖的八宝茶，收获一份悠闲自得、温暖如春的冬季之旅。

Ningxia doesn't have a cold winter in the true sense of the word, just one that mixes warm and cold; the four seasons are all suitable for sightseeing. One can not only feel the grand beauty of the northern country, but also deeply immerse in culture, play on the ice and snow, go winter fishing, see the ice dragon boats, folk performances and lantern festivals among other wonderful winter activities. Eating some mutton, drinking a cup of eight-treasure tea, you get a bit of relaxation and peace, and winter feels as warm as spring.

供图：宁夏画报社

摄影：左鸣远

中山公园
Yat-sen Park

中山公园，原本是西夏王李元昊建都兴庆府的第一大建筑“元昊宫”的遗址。1929 年为纪念孙中山，于此辟建公园，并正式命名“中山公园”。如今已成为银川最大的多功能综合性公园，更是市民休闲娱乐的好去处。“铁牛临池”“鸣钟问月”“文昌阁”，一步一景，一代代人在这里走过欢乐童年、放肆青春、甜蜜婚恋、携手暮年。生命轮回时代变迁，中山公园里一幕幕隽永深情永远没变。

This is the site of the remains of the “Yuanhao Palace” built by ruler Li Yuanhao of Western Xia. In 1929, in order to commerate Sun Yat-sen, a park was built here, and named “Yat-sen Park”. Today it is the largest multifunctional park in Yinchuan, and a place for the locals to entertain themselves. “Iron Cow Lake”, “Bell Ringing for the Moon”, “Wenchang Pavilion” are places you can visit as you slowly walk through the park. Many people spent childhood years here, grew up as youths, experienced first loves, and held hands through their later years. The cycle of life continues, and the deep feelings at the park persist year after year.

摄影：辛怡丽

民俗 · 轶闻
Culture and Anecdotes

定居在版画里的张贤亮
Zhang Xianliang

中国国家画院珍藏着一幅叫《怀念》的版画，这是版画家罗贵荣为纪念张贤亮专门创作的。作品以华夏西部影视城著名景点“月亮门”为主题，一只母鸡向着月亮门走着，距离这只母鸡不远的地方散落着一颗饱满的鸡蛋，天上一轮明月，地上一扇敞开的月亮门。版画怀念的是张贤亮把读书、生活、艺术坚持在一起，就会变成一只金蛋。

There is a woodblock print at the National Academy of Painting called *Yearning* by the artist Luo Guirong to memorialise Zhang Xianliang, a famous writer. The work features the “moon gateway” of the China West Film Studio, with a hen walking towards it, a big egg on the ground besides it, and a bright moon in the sky. The painting commemorates how Zhang Xianliang combined reading, life and art to produce golden works.

马兰花是个宝
Malan Irises

宁夏有两朵马兰花，一朵是民谣传唱“马兰花，马兰花，风吹雨打都不怕”中的盛开在宁夏大地的马兰花，独有一份坚忍不拔；另一朵马兰花，是口弦传人马兰花。老太太“一端口中衔，消愁解麻缠”，一生挚爱口弦，不识字却能够填词弹唱，她用悠悠曲调把口弦吹成了非物质文化遗产。

Ningxia has two Malan Irises. One is the folk song “Flowers of Malan”, which describes the Malan Irises blooming, firm and indomitable. The other “Malan Iris” isn’t a flower, but is the disciple of the traditional whistle Ma Lanhua. The veteran artist insists that playing the instrument can allay worries and annoyances. She’s loved the instrument all her life, and although she is illiterate she can compose lyrics and perform. She has made the instrument an intangible cultural heritage with her wonderful melodies.

供图：宁夏画报社

摄影：李靖

上门的财神
God of Wealth

老王每年农历冬至前后，和其他乡民们一起，身背褡裢，装着自印的《二十四节气表》外出送财神。“想财神，盼财神，财神主动送上门……”。财神们要是遇见社火，便成了乡民们的一场文化娱乐盛宴，热闹非凡。作家火仲舫在《花旦》里写道：“正月十五比花灯，十里长街昼夜明……”

Around each lunar new year, Mr. Wang and the people of his village put on traditional cloth jackets and head out with their self-printed copies of a publication on the traditional calendar to deliver the greetings of the God of Wealth. “Thinking of the God of Wealth, hoping for the God of Wealth, the God of Wealth comes to your door…” When these “Gods of Wealth” arrive at Shehuo parade, a kind of folk art performances, it makes for a very lively and entertaining scene. Author Huo Zhongfang wrote in *Young Actress*, “The lanterns shine brightly on the fifteenth day of the first lunar month, and all the streets of the city are bright…”

洁净的汤瓶
Clean Bottle

何奶奶随着儿子搬进了新楼房，有了专门而方便的沐浴器，可她沐浴还是要用那个看起来已经很旧很旧的绿色小汤瓶。她说，从汤瓶里出来的水慢溜溜，停顿的时候，就感觉自己在与清净的人生做对话。在他们看来，最洁净的水从这瓶口流出，可以抚平内心的喧嚣。

Mrs. He moved into a new house with her son. Although it has a modern bath, she still uses a small green bottle to bath; just looking at it you can see it’s very old. She says that the water flows slowly out of the bottle, and when it stops, you feel you’re having a dialogue with a clean life. For these people, the cleanest water flows out of a bottle like this; it has the ability to calm the clamour in one’s heart.

高台马社火
Horse Performance

隆德人喜欢马社火，而马社火在耍之前要扎高台。“扎高台呀耍社火，娃娃压成一摞摞，老汉笑成背锅锅，小伙儿闹成一窝窝，女子心野懒做活。”高台社火里高跷、花船、秧歌队、彩车等自然是少不了的，社火成为乡间群众性大型娱乐活动。倘若能赶巧看一场酣畅淋漓的高台社火，就如同享用了一桌美味佳肴。

There is a traditional horse performance quite popular with the people of Longde County. People young and old all come together to take part in the parade-like performance. Stilts, floats, yangge dancing and carts are all seen here; the entire affair takes place on quite a large scale. The chance to enjoy one of these performances involves many different sights and delights, like a great banquet.

摄影：李君杰

青苗水会
Pray for Rain

同心县张家塬乡每年农历四月十五日都要举行热闹非凡的青苗水会，以求风调雨顺，吉祥如意。每年水会七天前，参加仪式的老张和乡民们就开始斋戒，沐浴，禁食荤腥。到正日，二百多名男性青壮年齐聚莲花山下，祈雨、求福。这一融民俗、宗教于一体的活动于2014年列入国家级非物质文化遗产保护项目。

Zhangjiayuan Village in Tongxin County has a very lively Young Crop Festival every year on the 15th day of the fourth lunar month. It's held to pray for rains and good fortune. Seven days before the event, the local villagers will start to fast and bathe themselves. On the day of commencement, more than 200 male youths gather at the base of Mount Lotus, praying for rain and good fortune. This activity which combines folk customs and religion was listed as a national intangible cultural heritage in 2014.

踏脚舞
Step Dance

踏脚舞是一项健身防身的娱乐活动，相传已有上百年历史。参与者可分成两队进行群“踏”，或一对一、一对二、一对三，甚至村对村。你踏我躲，你攻我守，经过激烈决斗，最后选出“踏脚王”。“踏脚”已踏进了全国少数民族传统体育运动会的大家庭。专家评论：“该舞体现了西北青年粗犷、豪放的气质，给人以阳刚之美。”

Step dance is a kind of exercise and self-defence entertainment activity that has more than a century of history. Participants can go one on one, one on two, one on three, or even village on village. You step, I fade, you attack, I defend. In the end only one “king of stepping” will emerge. “Step dance” has been included in the National Ethnic Minority Games. An expert commented: this dance embodies the brashness of the youths of the Northwest, their bold character and the beauty of virility.

砚台中的书香气
Inkstone Fragrance

贺兰山以硬汉形象卓立于世，硬汉也有柔情的一面，用贺兰石制作的砚台，在文人墨客的案前散发着书香气。远看似“碧绿”嵌入“紫石”中，近看“碧绿”中山、水、云、月、龙、鹤、松隐隐约约。这种砚也称“碧子砚”。带盖的贺兰砚“存墨过三天”。贺兰砚承载着文人墨客的艺术梦。

Helan Mountains emerge from the ground tough and bold, but also have a soft side. The fragrance of the inkstones made from the rocks of the mountains is valued by the literati. Viewed from afar, it appears that verdure has been set within amethyst. Viewed up close, on it is carved with “verdure” mountains, waters, clouds, the moon, dragons, cranes, pines, and more. These inkstones are also known as “green stones”. They’re famous for their quality in the world of calligraphy in China, and have been immortalised in various phrases, and carry the dreams of those who deal with ink.

摄影：陶克图

砖雕
Brick Carving

砖雕在隆德普通人家的院子里很常见，最多的为一边是“耕读人家”，另一边是“书香门第”。“无雕不成屋，有刻斯为贵”，砖雕装扮着普通百姓的生活，也是村民对美好生活的一份向往，更是对文化的尊崇和热爱。

Brick carvings are frequently seen in the ordinary courtyards of Longde County. Most households have carvings like Farming While Reading or Cultured Family. These brick carvings are considered essential to a complete house, and decorate the lives of the ordinary people. They're an aspiration for better life and a sign of respect and love for culture.

摄影：陶克图

口弦
Traditional Kouxian

在清水河畔常会听到一种令人神往的“嘀嘀嘀、咚咚咚”的声音，那是弹奏口弦发出的。有一首花儿唱道：“三寸竹片片，两头扯线线。一端口中衔，消愁解麻缠。”口弦在清水河畔代代相传，无谱，全凭弹奏者手上的分寸、气流的强弱。弹奏者的心情通过口弦旋律传达，或忧伤或欢快，从心底深处流淌出来……

On the sides of the Qingshui River, or Clear Water River, you'll frequently hear the songs "dee dee dee, dong dong dong" ringing out. These are the sounds of *Kouxian*, a kind of lamellophone. A traditional Hua'er song talks about how playing the instrument can resolve one's worries. The instrument is quite popular in the area, and rather than playing off sheet music, enthusiasts just go with their own flow. It's a vehicle for the player to convey feelings, be they sad or happy, letting the feelings of the heart flow out…

回族武术
Hui *Kung fu*

宁夏回族人有尚武精神。长久以来流传的一句话“张家的枪，何家的棍，马家的软功，赵家的劲”。宁夏回族民间武术的流派繁盛。90 多岁高龄的回族民间武术家马振武仍在习武练功的场面，跌扑滚翻，样样精绝，潇洒利落，令人叹为观止，少数民族的智慧与创造力体现于此。

The Hui people of Ningxia have a warrior spirit. Listening to the lyrics of the traditional song: "The spears of the Zhang family, the batons of the He family, the soft *kung fu* of the Ma family, and the strength of the Zhao family", you can feel how martial arts are popular among the local people. Looking at Hui *kung fu* practitioner Ma Zhenwu, who is in his nineties, still practicing his moves, leaping and spinning about, you'll be amazed by the smoothness of his techniques. You can feel the wisdom and creativity of the Hui people in this way.

绞脸
Threading

在宁夏农村很多地方，姑娘出嫁之前都有绞脸的仪式，也叫“开脸”，出嫁的姑娘不能少这道程序。没绞脸是姑娘，绞脸后就是媳妇儿了。绞脸通常由女性长辈或自己母亲完成，红线一端咬在牙里，另一端挽个活扣用两手攥着，一开一合的力量在手指间游走，绞出的不仅是熠熠生辉的脸庞，还有姑娘脸上溢出的幸福和母亲心底最美好的祈福。

In many of the villages of Ningxia, before girls marry, they participate in a threading ceremony. This is considered an essential part of the process of marrying into a new family. One starts as a girl and emerges as a wife. The process is usually carried out by a female senior or one's own mother. One end of a red string is held with the teeth, and the other is held with the two hands. The string is run over the face, ripping out all small hairs, making for gleaming, smooth skin that exudes the joy of the bride and the best wishes of her mother.

摄影：陶克图

摄影：陶克图

剪纸三姐妹
Paper-cutting Sisters

在镇北堡华夏西部影视城，有个伏兆娥三姐妹剪纸很有特色。大姐剪的是农耕文化的缩影，二姐剪的是大自然与人的亲近，三姐剪的是现实生活的真实呈现。游人们喜欢看三姐妹剪纸，静静地伏在旁边，看她们用剪刀把自己平实的生活剪出了天地。

At the Zhenbeibu China West Film Studio, there are three sisters who make excellent paper-cut art. The eldest makes scenes of agricultural culture, the second those of interaction between humans and nature, and the third scenes of real life. Travellers enjoy viewing their paper cutting, observing how they use a simple pair of scissors to make these works come to life.

盐池麻雀能喝二两酒
Drinking Sparrows

到盐池吃饭，盐池人会唱一曲《下马酒》，请你喝一杯下马酒。饭吃得好不好要先看酒喝得好不好，还说，喝双不喝单，喝四不喝三，最后，醉眼蒙眬、东倒西趄时，盐池人会说你地道、真诚、可交。盐池挨着内蒙古，盐池人有着内蒙古游牧民族的豪放和热情，大碗喝酒，大块吃肉，如果不喝一点儿，他们会说你假故，会说盐池的麻雀都能喝二两呢。

When you eat in Yanchi, you'll hear people sing a song “Liquor off the Horse”, and they'll invite you to drink a few cups. Before you think about the food, you need to have a drink. It's also said you need to drink even numbers of cups – two but not one, four but not three. When you're tipsy and tilting, the people of Yanchi say that you'll be real, honest and easy to interact with. Yanchi is close to Inner Mongolia, and the people here have the bold and passionate character of the Mongolians. They drink liquor out of large bowls, and eat large piece of meat. If you don't drink, they'll say you are disingenuous. It's said that even the sparrows here can drink some liquor.

摄影：王洪喜

让农民画走向全国
Folk Paintings

隆德县是“现代民间绘画之乡”“书法之乡”。2017年，对于隆德县农民画代表李彦虎来说可谓双喜临门。4月，他的画在厦门大学校庆布展，部分作品被厦大和闽侯文化馆收藏；12月，他参加了启明星工程中国人民大学的课程。他希望通过大家的努力，能够让农民画走出隆德县，走向全国，走向世界。

Longde County has been described as “the village of modern folk paintings” and “the village of calligraphy”. In 2017, Li Yanhu, a representative of the crafts in Longde, said that this could be counted as a double blessing. In April, his paintings were exhibited at Xiamen University, with a few of the paintings collected by the university and the Minhou Cultural Centre. In December, he participated in the Venus project at Renmin University of China in Beijing. He hopes that through everyone’s efforts the paintings of Longde can travel all over China, and all over the world.

喊叫水的苦与喜
Crying for Water

中宁县有个村子叫“喊叫水”，村名直接道出了农民们心底最深处的渴望：给我一瓢水，天地间再无烦恼。喊叫水常年干旱，问起缺水的烦恼，他们却轻描淡写，好像上天从未慢待过他们，他们喊叫的不仅是水，更是对生存的一种呼喊。生命的厚度与韧度在现实与梦想的斑驳交错中，刻到了宁夏的黄土地里。

There is a village in Zhongning County called “Crying for Water”. The name of the village reveals the strongest desire of its residents: give me water and there will be no further worries in my world. The land of this place is dry year-round, and the lack of water is a constant worry, but they talk about it in calm terms, as if fortune smiles on them all the same. What they cry for isn’t just water, but survival. The thickness and toughness of life are interlaced with each other, and carved in the loess landscape of Ningxia.

泥巴人儿
Mud Men

看着手中捏的泥巴人儿，王永红仿佛又听到儿时村口渠边玩儿泥巴的嬉戏声，看到了那些面朝黄土背朝天、整天与泥土打交道的庄户人，觉得手中的泥土有了语言，有了动作，脑海中无数次构思的人物一下子鲜活起来。用不起眼的原色泥巴塑造淳朴的庄户人，承载了儿时无忧无虑的快乐和家乡纯朴的民俗民风。

Looking at the mud figurine in his hand, Wang Yonghong almost hears the sounds of children in his youth playing with the mud at the side of the canal, and sees the villagers backs to the sky, facing the loess. He feels the mud in his hands has language, has actions, and imagines all kinds of characters in it. He uses the material to build all kinds of things, all with the happiness and pure character of home that existed in the childhood of that time.

摄影：陶克图

汤瓶八诊
Bottle Health Check

汤瓶八诊是宁夏回族的保健医学疗法，主要是以内病外治的手法，舒经活络，对头、面、耳、手、脚、骨、脉、气八部位进行诊疗。回族人自古以来以汤瓶沐浴，蕴含着以崭新的面貌面对人生的意味，汤瓶八诊是丝绸之路上沉淀下来的文化底蕴，像一种静悄悄的仪式，净化着病人的心灵，给予人信念与力量。

The "bottle health check" is a method of maintaining the health among the Hui people of Ningxia. It mainly consists of methods for treatment of internal and external ailments of the head, face, ears, hands, feet, bones, veins, and "*qi*". The people have long washed themselves with a "water bottle", a kind of jug that resembles a large teapot. It makes them feel as if they become refreshed afterwards. The "bottle health check" is a remnant of the culture of the Silk Road. It cleans the spirit of the afflicted like a quiet ceremony, and gives one faith and strength.

赶集，从不褪色的一幅农民市井画
Bazaar

赶集，是农民的一种生活方式。人们从四面八方涌向小镇，只为在集市上，遇见人世盛极的风景。衣物农具、日用百货、瓜果蔬菜、鸡鸭牛羊，素日里常见不常见的东西，都开会般地聚集在一起。像马尔克斯在《百年孤独》中的那个在马孔多走着的吉卜赛人手里拿着的磁铁，人和物，全被吸到集镇上去了。赶集，就是四乡八邻的农人，为交易物产，为亲朋相聚与信息交流找的一个合理借口，这个借口，体面地存在了上千年。

The bazaar is a way of life for the farmers of Ningxia. People come to the town from all over; the flourishing exchange is quite an attraction. Clothes, farming tools, everyday items, fruits, vegetables, chickens, ducks, cattle, and items one doesn't see in everyday life are all here. Just like the magnets in the hand of the Gypsies in *One Hundred Years of Solitude*, the bazaar draws people and items here. At the bazaar, people from all about exchange goods and find an excuse to meet with friends. This tradition has existed for more than a millennium.

"五七干校"博物馆的三件镇馆之宝
Three Treasures in Museum

石嘴山"五七干校"博物馆有三件镇馆之宝。林汉达的《中国上下五千年》、汉语拼音之父周有光的打字机、倪海曙的长诗《贺兰山下》手稿。《中国上下五千年》是林汉达的女儿从火堆里抢救出来的。林汉达家乡办博物馆时，林汉达的女儿没有捐出，她认为，捐给"五七干校"博物馆更有意义，因为，这里有她父亲对人生和历史的记忆和思考。

In Shizuisan there is a May 7th Cadre School Museum which has three treasures: Lin Handa's *Five Thousand Years of China*, the typewriter of pinyin inventor Zhou Youguang, and the original handwritten manuscript of language planner and script reformer Ni Haishu's book *At the Base of the Helan Mountains*. *Five Thousand Years of China* was saved by Lin Handa's daughter from a fire. When Lin's home village constructed its museum, the daughter didn't hand it over, saying that she believed it was more meaningful to give it to the May 7th Cadre School Museum, because it was the place that held her father's memories and thoughts upon history and life.

摄影：岳昌鸿

回族婚俗“耍公婆”
Teasing the Parents

在宁夏回族聚集的乡村，婚礼过后第二天有隆重的“耍公婆”场面。亲戚朋友越多，说明主家人缘越好。乡亲们要给公公脸上抹鞋油，梳小辫，戴红头巾，穿婆婆衣服；又给婆婆画胡子，戴黑墨镜和草帽。一通折腾后，公婆互换角色，隆重出场，唱歌跳舞，逗笑玩乐。“结婚三天没大小”，这磨炼公婆脾性的仪式，能让人感受到回族人的热情与淳朴。

On the day after a wedding the villagers of the Hui people will gather to “tease the parents”. The more friends and relatives there are, the better a fate for the parties involved. Shoe polish is rubbed upon the father-in-law’s face, and plait is combed for him. He wears a red scarf and the women’s clothes. The mother-in-law has a beard drawn upon her, and wears sunglasses and a straw hat. After this process, they switch roles, and sing and dance for the amusement of all. This test of the parents’ disposition lets you feel the passion and simplicity of the Hui people.

上梁洗泥
On the Roof Beam

谁家要是盖新房子，会在上梁的时候，宴请工匠和亲朋好友前来“洗泥”，大家或提着各色干果，或牵一头羊，或拎一只鸡，前来贺喜。匠人和亲朋好友用绳子将正梁拉到屋顶，梁上绑个包裹，匠人坐在大梁上，解开包裹，抛撒糖果等，众人就齐齐地喊：“上梁洗泥喽！”正梁上贴上“上梁大吉”之类的标语，表达欢喜之情，祈求吉祥如意。

On the day when the roof beam is laid in place, the owner of the newly built house will invite friends and relatives for a “mud washing”. People bring dried fruits, or a sheep, or a chicken to celebrate. The carpenters, friends, and relatives use ropes to raise the beam to the required height, upon which a package is bound. A carpenter sits on the beam, opens the package, and throws candies and the like downwards, whilst the people below yell “The beam is done after the wash”. A banner commemorating the occasion is affixed to the beam, reflecting the high spirits and wishes for luck of everyone.

三块钱的心灵恪守
Three Yuan

有位乘客，从固原火车站搭了一辆出租车赶往十公里外的汽车站，到站后匆匆付了钱，进入候车室等车。大约过了半小时，年轻的出租车司机气喘吁吁地跑进候车室，好不容易找到这位乘客，将三块钱塞给他，说：“你多给了三块钱，是你的钱，你拿上。我拿上，心里有罪呢。”说完腼腆地笑了笑，轻轻地舒了一口气。

A passenger took a taxi from the Guyuan train station to the bus station more than 10 kilometres away. He hurriedly paid the fare upon arriving at the station, and went into the waiting lobby. After more than half an hour, the young driver of the taxi ran panting with exertion into the lobby, and through much effort found the passenger, handing him three yuan. He said “You paid three yuan extra, please take it. I’d feel awful if I’d kept it.” He smiled shyly, and let out a sigh of relief.

戴着小圆帽创作泥塑
Round Hat

杨栖鹤老先生创作泥塑的时候，总是要戴一顶民国年间的小圆帽，帽顶上缀核桃大小的一颗红玛瑙，这顶小圆帽让他忘却自己世俗的身份，沉浸在雕塑艺术里。他说，戴着小圆帽创作是对艺术生命的一种敬畏，每个泥塑都是有生命的，像自己的孩子一样，每创作一个，都要为之起名，好让这些泥塑人在泥塑的世界里也有一席安放之地。

When Mr. Yang Xihe creates his clay works, he always wears an old round hat, upon which is stitched a red agate the size of a walnut. This hat allows him to forget his simple identity and immerse himself in the activity of sculpting. He says that wearing the hat is a kind of gesture of respect for his art. Every sculpture has a life, just like one's own children. "Whenever I have a child, I give it a name, so that this clay figurine can have a place in the clay world."

摄影：陶克图

喜庆的古尔邦节
Gorban Festival

古尔邦节是喜庆的，回族人要会礼、宰杀牛羊、炸油香、互相拜贺……临近古尔邦节三天，主妇们要做大量油炸馓子和点心，以便招待来贺节的亲朋好友。男子们把献祭的牲畜宰好，大块连骨肉炖到锅里后，开始互相串门，拜贺节日；妇女们则换上新衣服，留在家里摆上食品、准备茶水，迎接客人。节日的喜庆，洋溢在每个人的脸上，敞亮美好。

Gorban Festival is a celebration where the Hui people conduct rites, slaughter cattle and sheep, fry cakes and give greetings to each other. In the three days leading up to the festival, the women prepare a large amount of fried dough twists and other snacks to receive friends and relatives. The men slaughter livestock, and cook big chunks of meat in large pots. They start to visit each other at their houses, delivering congratulations. Women put on new clothes and stay at home arranging food and tea to receive visitors. The good spirit of the holiday is on everyone's faces, clear and cheery.

宁夏麻编
Ningxia Linen

编艺传承人张璟带着宁夏麻编去毛里求斯做展览，外国友人直竖大拇指，夸赞她是“金手指”。她说：“细细编织，慢慢品味，很多老祖先传下来的道理会很自然地浮现。”麻编富含生活美学，的确有一股质朴的魅力，麻编富有光泽，韧性十足，来源于大自然又回归大自然，上天对它友好，它也绝不给自然徒增压力。

Zhang Jing continues the Ningxia tradition of weaving. When she took her linen goods to Mauritius for an exhibition, she received many thumbs up from foreign guests. She says, “When weaving these articles, you must appreciate them slowly, and you’ll see many principles of your ancestors naturally float to the surface.” Weaving flax fibres into articles is full of the aesthetics of life, and has a true and simple attraction. The fibres glow, tough yet pliant, coming from nature and having a natural feel. Heaven is favourable to them, and they exert no pressure on nature.

摄影：左鸣远

三两清油换不走一盏荞面灯
Buckwheat Lamp

诗人谢瑞在《一盏心灯伴明月》里写道，老家人过元宵节不叫过元宵节，叫过正月十五，不吃元宵，而吃荞面灯。这一天，家家户户不管光景好坏，哪怕用一碗白面换半碗荞麦面，也要做荞面灯，不仅全家每人一个，而且大门和各个屋门的门头、院坝、灶台、粮仓、牲畜圈里都要摆放一盏点燃的面灯。在六盘山地区，即便拿三两清油，也换不走祈祷吉祥安宁的一盏荞面灯。

Poet Xie Rui wrote in *A Lamp in the Moonlight* that the Lantern Festival for old people was called the "fifteenth of the first lunar month" instead; they didn't eat sweet dumplings as are traditional for others, but rather buckwheat lamp, a kind of paste in the shape of little candles. Rich or poor, each family will make a buckwheat lamp for each member of the family, as well as one for the main door, courtyard, kitchen, granary, and livestock pen, even if they have to trade a bowl of buckwheat flour with wheat flour. Around Liupan Mountains, an amount of oil can't replace these buckwheat lamps that bring the wishes for peace and prosperity.

万种风情轻薄如纸
Profound Emotions on Thin Paper

雷红霞夫妇织出的纸织画，无论山水还是花鸟，画面朦胧、迷离，有如覆盖着一层薄纱。细观画面，会看到上面有十字布绣一样分明的小方格，用手摸上去，立体感很强，有些许凹凸感。含蓄不外露，内秀不张扬，万种风情织于轻薄之纸上。

Lei Hongxia and her husband produce paper-weaving pictures. Whether they be of landscapes or birds and flowers, they have a dreamy, misty feeling, as if they're covered by a layer of chiffon. One sees clearly defined little squares as in cross-stich, and there's a strong feeling of texture when you run your hand over them, with countless peaks and valleys. They're restrained in character, and contain countless emotions in the paper.

说唱·声音
Songs and Voices

摄影：钟培源

凤凰于飞
Two Phoenixes

《凤凰于飞》这首源自《诗经》、富有感染力的比兴吟唱一直流传在这片土地，就像花儿，简单的曲调声音却带着一种不可言说的力量。张贤亮初次踏入银川，眼前一座寂寞、荒凉、破落的古城，耳边伴着《凤凰于飞》华丽甜美的歌声，这种强烈的反差让他终生难忘。骨子里那种永不放弃的、积极向上的精神，就像涅槃重生的凤凰。

The Two Phoenixes Fly Side by Side originated in *the Book of Songs*. Metaphorical and infective, the song enjoys a constant popularity over the years on this land. Just like the local Hua'er, the simple melody carries an unspeakable power. When Zhang Xianliang first set foot in Yinchuan, looking out over the lonely and desolate city, the sweet sound of this song in his ears made a contrast that became an unforgettable memory. The spirit of perseverance and resilience is like that of the reborn phoenix.

供图：宁夏大庆办

Mia 气“滴”很
Mia~

Mia 是宁夏方言的一个音，字典里没有这个字，宁夏人就用拼音代替。因为只有 Mia 才能表达出那种“美得不要不要的感觉”，因为爱这 Mia，宁夏人独创了自己特有的一系列悠闲、随性、快乐、开心的 Mia 事。“Mia 气麻将”“Mia 气奶茶”“Mia 气微电影”……宁夏，Mia 气“滴”很！

"Mia" is a descriptive word in the Ningxia dialect, one that you won't find in dictionaries. Thus, people write it in pinyin. The word means "awesome" and is often used in phrases like "awesome mahjong" "awesome milk tea" "awesome microfilm"... Ningxia, of course, is awesome!

《清平乐 · 六盘山》

Mount Liupan

毛泽东是运筹帷幄之中、决胜千里之外的统帅，也是征途吟诗、马背成章的诗人。1935 年 10 月 7 日，毛泽东率部队翻越六盘山时，以无产阶级革命家的伟大胸怀，观赏六盘风光，展望革命前景，挥毫写下了《长城谣》，后改写成《清平乐 · 六盘山》。这也是毛泽东在长征途中写的最后一首诗词。

As Mao Zedong was mapping out his strategies, winning decisive victories, he was also penning poems on horseback along his journey. On October 7, 1935, he led his troops over Liupan Mountains. When this proletarian revolutionary looked out over Liupan Mountains and the prospects of the revolution, he boldly penned *Great Wall Melody*, which he later changed to *Liupan Mountains to the Tune of Qingping*. This was the last poem he wrote on the Long March.

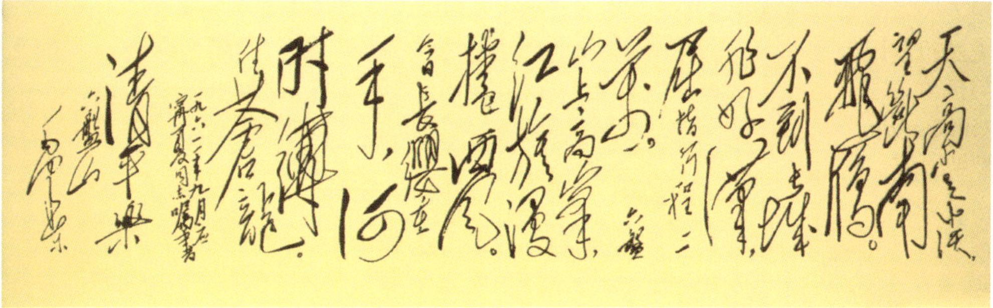

摄影：彭文润

摄影：钟培源

《西行漫记》与抗战之声
The Song of War

《西行漫记》是美国著名记者埃德加·斯诺的不朽名著。一部文笔优美的纪实性很强的报道性作品，向全世界报道了中国工农红军及其长征、西征的真实情况。书中用很大的篇幅描述了红军在宁夏境内的活动，记录了群众与红军战士的鱼水深情。扉页上英姿飒爽的红军号手照片——“抗战之声”——传遍了全世界。

Red Star over China is a famous book by American Journalist Edgar Snow. It documents the revolution from the perspective of a reporter, telling the world about the Chinese Red Army, the Long March, and the Westward Expedition. A large part of the book tells about the activities of the Red Army in Ningxia, especially the bond between the soldiers and the local Hui people. On the title page, there is a picture of a Red Army trumpeter, and the words “The Song of War”. This picture went on to become famous all over the world.

悲欢浅唱一人生
Joy and Sorrow

柳萍天生是唱秦腔的“好坯子”，舞台是她生命中很重要的部分。在舞台上，她演活了苏三、芸香、刘妃、穆桂英、潘金莲、林娘子……成为银川市秦腔剧团的“台柱子”。她在《武松杀嫂》《月下来迟》等折子戏中的高难度、高水准表演打动了中国剧协主席李默然和梅花奖评委，柳萍把花旦守在心中，悲欢浅唱，浓妆一场一人生。

Liu Ping has a voice naturally suited for Qin Opera. The stage is a large part of her life. On the stage she has brought Su San, Yunxiang, Liu Fei, Mu Guiying, Pan Jinlian, Lady Lin and others to life... She’s become the pillar of the Yinchuan Qin Opera Troupe. In *Wu Song Kills His Sister-in-law*, *Late Under the Moon* and others, her excellent performance amazed Li Moran, head of the China Theatre Association, as well as other judges and won her the Plum Blossom Award. Liu keeps her roles in her heart and feels real empathy for their joy and sorrow.

铁骨柔情女侠梦
Kind-Hearted Heroine

小时候因为对穆桂英、梁红玉等女性英雄的崇拜，执着的她选择了在舞台上演绎这些人物。武旦很适合她大大咧咧的性格，在武旦角色里也寄托了她对女侠的一种情怀。她就是宁夏京剧院优秀青年演员袁红玉。她说，舞台表演是一种享受，台上三分钟，台下十年功，每一次都做好出征的准备，独当一面是戏曲教会她的。

As a child she admired heroines like Mu Guiying and Liang Hongyu, so she persisted in playing their roles on stage. These martial roles are suited to her casual character, and allow her to express her feelings for their heroic deeds. This is the story of the outstanding young actress at the Ningxia Peking Opera Theatre, Yuan Hongyu. She says that performance on the stage is a kind of enjoyment. Three minutes on the stage involves ten years of preparation backstage. She always makes meticulous preparation for each performance. Through theatre, she knows how to find her feet.

中国电影从这里走向世界
To the World

作家张贤亮创建的镇北堡华夏西部影视城在影视圈赫赫有名。在这里，朱时茂和丛珊脱颖而出，姜文穿着大裆裤摘走“百花奖”的桂冠，巩俐坐着“我奶奶”的轿子颠进了世界的电影高峰……在此拍摄的影片之多，升起的明星之多，获得国际、国内大奖之多，皆为中国各地影视城之冠，故被誉为“中国一绝”，享有“中国电影从这里走向世界”的美称。

Zhenbeibu China West Film Studio, founded by writer Zhang Xianliang, is very famous in the film circle. Here, Zhu Shimao and Cong Shan showed their outstanding talents. Jiang Wen picked up his Hundred Flowers Award, and Gong Li became world-famous with the release of *Red Sorghum*. Many films have been made here and many stars have risen to fame through them, winning domestic and international awards. This is the starting point for Chinese movies to go out into the world.

供图：宁夏画报社

中国第五代导演与《红高粱》
Red Sorghum

提到中国电影，张艺谋及以其为代表的第五代导演是怎么也绕不过去的。张艺谋之所以能变成一个符号，就因为他在中国电影发展史上具有一种与众不同的特质和地位。他以自觉或不自觉的行为方式改变着中国电影。回顾张艺谋的创作之路，入行近30年，打响头炮的，就是在宁夏镇北堡华夏西部影视城拍摄的电影《红高粱》。

电影海报

When one brings up Chinese films, there will of course be mention of Zhang Yimou, the representative of the fifth generation of Chinese directors. He is an iconic figure, because his films secure a position in the history of Chinese cinema with their distinctive features. Consciously or unconsciously, he has changed the landscape of Chinese films. Looking back over his three-decade career, we'll find that his first blockbuster *Red Sorghum* was produced at Ningxia's Zhenbeibu China West Film Studio.

《画皮》，宁夏电影的骄傲
Painted Skin

《画皮》是宁夏电影集团出品的一部东方魔幻爱情电影，影片讲述了人妖殊途、你心换我颜的故事，影射了当今社会中爱情与价值的选择。国家电影局电影频道在第21届上海国际电影节上主办了“2018电影频道之夜”，推出改革开放“40年40部”年度影片，《画皮》荣获2008年度影片，成为宁夏电影史上的标杆。

电影海报

Painted Skin is an oriental fantasy love story film produced by the Ningxia Film Group. It reflects choices about value and love in society at the time of its production. The State Film Bureau's film channel organised the “2018 Film Channel Night” at the 21st Shanghai International Film Festival, and showcased “40 Films over 40 Years” since the Opening Up and Reform. *Painted Skin* was the film of the year for 2008, and is one of the pillars of Ningxia films.

两种死亡的生命意义
Two Kinds of Death

获鲁迅文学奖的作家石舒清的短篇小说《清水里的刀子》，被改编为同名电影。2016年，影片获得第21届釜山电影节新浪潮大奖。影片用纪实又古典的方式，讲述了马子善的老伴儿和一头老牛关于生命和死亡的故事，体现出生与死的干净与体面。通过这种看待生与死的态度，进而演绎出作品的生命之意义。

Knife in the Clear Water, by Lu Xun Prize recipient Shi Shuqing was adapted into a movie of the same name. In 2016, it won the New Tide Award at the 21st Busan International Film Festival. In a documentary and classic manner, the film tells the story of Ma Zishan's spouse and an old cow living and dying together, showing the purity and dignity of life and death. Through this perspective, it showcases the meaning of life in the original work.

宁夏川
Ningxia Valley

对于西北腔，可能很多人都依旧停留在"一群羊""一个旱烟袋""一条白手巾"和"一个苍凉的眼神"上。苏阳的《宁夏川》这首歌用民歌语言唱出对这片土地的认识，寥寥几句，对宁夏的地理概况和这片土地的富饶作出精炼的概括："宁夏川，两头尖，东靠黄河，西靠贺兰山，年种年收水浇田，金山银川米粮川。"

Traditional impression of the Northwest is nothing but "a flock of sheep", "a tobacco pipe", "a white towel" or "a bleak gaze". *Ningxia Field,* a song by Su Yang, however, provides a vivid picture of this land with concise lyrics: "Pointed at both ends, the Ningxia Field borders the Yellow River to the east and Helan Mountains to the west. Well-irrigated, the fields produce a bumper harvest. The granaries in Yinchuan and Jinshan are therefore the greatest."

摄影：王鹏

供图：宁夏大庆办

《灵与肉》与贺兰山
Novel and Mountain

张贤亮的小说《灵与肉》被改编为电视剧，剧中呈现了塞上江南——宁夏独有的风情，电视剧一开始，老郭赶着马车，以雄浑粗犷的声音，唱道："贺兰山啊贺兰山，一条大路望不到头河边呦……"以宁夏花儿的形式，唱出了宁夏的地貌。《灵与肉》是宁夏影视剧的一大亮点和高峰。

Zhang Xianliang's novel *Soul and Body* was made into a television series, which offers a glimpse of the southern-style landscape in North China, a rare sight found only in Ningxia. The series begins with Mr. Guo driving a horse-drawn carriage, singing in his bold and coarse voice, "At the foot of Helan Mountains is a road leading to the river beyond." In the style of Hua'er, a music tradition in North-western China, this song is a description of the land hereof. This series is blockbuster produled in Ningxia.

羊圈里写出的《王贵与李香香》
Written in a Sheep Pen

"山丹丹开花羞红了脸，哥哥你让我咋跟你言？"王贵与李香香这一对在革命斗争中成长起来的青年农民，革命斗争与爱情两不误，在革命中产生阶级兄妹般的爱情。时任陕甘宁"三边"报纸记者李季，以陕北民歌"信天游"的形式，在盐池的羊圈里写出了长篇叙事诗《王贵与李香香》，也因此打开了我国新诗运动的新局面。

"The mountain flowers are red, like my face. How can I talk about it with you, my brother?" Wang Gui and Li Xiangxiang are a pair of youths that grew up during the revolutionary war. Love blossomed while they fought shoulder-by-shoulder against the enemy. Hence the emerging of a proletarian story of conjugal love. As a newspaper reporter at the time, Li Ji wrote this long poem in the style of a local Shaanxi melody in a sheep pen in Yanchi, thereby opening up a fresh dimension in the new poetry movement in China.

宁夏坐唱
Sit-and-sing

宁夏坐唱是土生土长的曲艺形式，两人坐唱。“石榴子开花吗叶叶子黄呀，姨娘吗教子女贤良……”苏阳乐队翻唱的《贤良》就是在宁夏坐唱的基础上的再创作。电影《美丽的大脚》里王树的扮演者孙海英学唱过，陈凯歌导演的电影《边走边唱》引用过……宁夏坐唱唱的是一种坚守和地方曲艺传承的情怀。

Siting and Singing is a local artistic form in Ningxia: two people sing while seated. “The pomegranate blooms when the leaves are yellow, and auntie teaches virtues to the children...” Su Yang’s song *Virtues* derives from the sit-and-sing tradition. In the film *Pretty Big Feet,* Sun Haiying, who played Wang Shu, learns the tradition. It also appears in Chen Kaige’s *Life on a String*. Sit-and-sing is a way of continuing the traditions here.

像辣辣缨一样活着
Live an Ordinary Life

“你是世上的奇男子呀，我就是那地上的辣辣缨。”苏阳的音乐把宁夏的民间花儿和西北传统曲艺秦腔等与当代音乐嫁接、解构，创造出了一种全新的音乐语言。也只有像辣辣缨一样，实实在在生长在这片黄土地上，感受过人们的劳动、生活、爱情，那些涌动在胸腔的炽热与高亢、戏谑与调侃才会迸发出来。

“You’re an exceptional man in this world, and I am the spicy grass in this place.” Su Yang’s music combines elements of Hua’er with those of Qin Opera. He deconstructs them and reconstructs components for a new kind of musical language. Just like the spicy grasses here, it grows solidly out of the loess. Without a taste of the daily life here, one can hardly understand the passion and banter of the local people.

摄影：张鹏

供图：宁夏画报社

我的宁夏川
My Ningxia Field

很久没有听到这样的一首歌，闭上眼似是身在黄土高原；一回头远处山坳里传来一声嘹亮高亢的西北调调。马希尔《我的宁夏川》给了我们这样的惊喜，传达给我们苍茫辽阔、气度恢宏、一派高原尽收眼底的意境。马希尔高亢悠远的声音将灵魂赋予这首歌的每个音符，敲打着心灵深处的渴望。

I haven't heard a song like this for a long time. With my eyes closed, I feel like I'm on the loess plateau. Ma Xi'er gave us such a surprise with *My Ningxia Field* we seemed to command a marvellous view of a landscape vast and magnificent. His voice, distant but resounding, imbues each note of the song with soul, and touches on the desires deep in our hearts.

"以泪示爱"的花儿
Tears of Love

花儿主要传唱于六盘山区及同心、海原一带。六盘山自古以来就是征战的场地，萧关古道亦是六盘山儿女出外闯荡的必经之途。在萧关古道上洒满了情人的热泪，他们用自己的眼泪诉说着心中的爱。"花儿是眼泪谱写的歌"，"只要任意从花儿的海洋中舀出一勺来品尝，那毫无疑问是苦咸的精灵"。

Hua'er, or "flower" is a style of traditional song from the areas around Liupan Mountains, Tongxin and Haiyuan. Liupan Mountains has long been the site of battles, and the Xiaoguan Pass is one that you must take to exit the region. The road is soaked with lovers' tears, which betrayed their true feelings. "Hua'er is the song of tears." "If one ladles a portion of water out of the sea of Hua'er, they will definitely discover a bitter and salty spirit in the taste."

呶（nāo）头子
One *Nao*

有人向张大爷问路，张大爷抬起手指，指着方向说：“呶头子”。“呶头子”是个模糊的说法，三五十米的距离是一个呶头子，三五十里的距离也是一个呶头子。路的远近，根据“呶”的声音长短区别。呶头子是一个概略的地理位置，也是宁夏人一种热情而率性的自然生活的体现。

If asked of directions, an old man will point to a certain direction and say “One *Nao*”. A *nao* is a vague descriptor. The specified distance depends on how long the speaker draws the syllable out. It reflects the candid passion of the local people.

互联网电影节与金杞奖
Online Film Festival

马孝礼是从宁夏海原县搬迁出来的移民，16 岁就独自出去闯，如今事业好转，总想能给家乡做点事。2017 年，在他的努力下，银川举办了首届互联网电影节，奖项是金杞奖。马孝礼说，他要让银川成为互联网电影中心，让宁夏的枸杞升值，成为金杞，让以后每一个业内人士以领到金杞奖为荣。通过他的努力，可以让更多的人知道宁夏，了解银川。

Ma Xiaoli is an emigrant originally from Haiyuan County in Ningxia. He left home at sixteen, and he has been thinking about contributing to his hometown since he made it in his career. In 2017, his efforts resulted in the first Online Film Festival, with the prize of the Golden Goji Berry Award. He says that he wants to make Ningxia the centre for online films, and help the local goji berries increase in value and fame. The Golden Goji Berry Prize is expected to be a widely coveted award and ultimately help Ningxia be better understood.

摄影：钟培源

黄河今流
Course of the River

两千多年的黄河文化与民间文化，如何能通过音乐、绘画、影像等多样式的新媒介，激活“现代人”骨子里深藏的民间文化基因，使民间艺术在今天再次发芽，重新焕发出新的生命力和价值。当来自银川的摇滚音乐人苏阳站在纽约的舞台上，让音乐的民族性和世界性话题碰撞摩擦，“黄河今流”计划应运而生。一如苏阳所言，黄河沿边的土地，一直在变迁，我们的脚步也一直没停下……

The Yellow River culture has a history of more than two millennia. Through new media like music, paintings, and video can it activate the hidden genes of folk culture in modern people and give new life to folk art? When Su Yang, a rock-and-roll musician from Yinchuan stood on the stage in New York, combining the ethnic character and international character, the "Course of the Yellow River" plan came to life. As Su said, the land along the Yellow River is continuously changing, and our steps never cease…

摄影：刘泉龙

就让它绿绿地长
Let Them Grow

“院子里长着绿韭菜，不要割呀，就让它绿绿地长着。”《绿韭菜》是宁夏花儿的经典，唱的是青年男女对生活的热爱和对美好爱情的向往。来自宁夏的“花儿精灵”黄亚在山西卫视《歌从黄河来》节目中以一曲《绿韭菜》亮相，让观众对花儿充满了好奇，对宁夏充满了期待。她真正的梦想是继续做一名花儿歌手，把传统文化唱起来，让花儿“活起来”“火起来”。

"Green leeks are growing in the courtyard; don't cut them down, let them grow tall and green." *Green Leeks* is a Hua'er classic about the love between young men and women. Popular Hua'er singer Huang Ya performed *Green Leeks* on the Shaanxi satellite TV program *Songs from the Yellow River*, which sparked interest in Hua'er as well as Ningxia itself. Her true dream is to continue singing Hua'er songs and popularise the art form.

走咧走咧去宁夏
Let's Go to Ningxia

"走咧走咧去宁夏；我的心啊恋宁夏，我的爱啊在宁夏。"唱红《走咧走咧去宁夏》的歌手徐千雅说："我演唱过很多地方的歌曲，而这首歌是非常有特色的音乐作品，歌词和旋律都很讨喜，极具宁夏的独特韵味，相信这首歌会带动更多的人去美丽的宁夏。"有人评价，这是继《眼泪花儿把心淹了》后，宁夏地区现代音乐作品的跨时代标杆之作。

"Let's go, let's go to Ningxia; my heart longs for Ningxia, my love is in Ningxia." Singer of *Let's Go to Ningxia*, Xu Qianya, said, "I've sung the songs of many places, and this one is a very special musical work. The lyrics and melody are both enjoyable, and it's full of the special tones of Ningxia. I think this song will encourage more people to visit the beautiful place." Some believe this is one of the most important songs after *Tears Inundate My Heart* in the contemporary music realm of Ningxia.

西海固符号
Sign of "Xihaigu"

一提起西海固，总会和贫穷联系起来，"贫瘠甲天下"。用山、沟、赤、谷、梁、崖这些符号组成的西海固是孤独的，是岑寂的。然而只要你唱起花儿就不再是贫穷的，就不会再感到孤寂。"花儿本是心上的话，不唱时由不得自家……"花儿是西海固粮食之外的粮食、爱情之外的爱情、生命之外的生命。

A mere mention of "Xihaigu" will remind us of poverty, "world-class impoverishment" indeed. Features such as mountains, gullies, barrenness, valleys, ridges and cliffs make up this desolate area, quiet and still. Nevertheless, a single song of Hua'er will disguise poverty and disperse loneliness. "Hua'er is the language of the heart, which you can hardly part." Hua'er itself is food, love and life to the people of "Xihaigu".

供图：宁夏画报社

《灵与肉》
Soul and Body

《灵与肉》是作家张贤亮的代表作。他曾用《苦难的历程》里的三句话来描述自己的人生经历：在清水里泡三次，在血水里浴三次，在碱水里煮三次。这部作品反映的是他在宁夏贺兰山农场劳动时的经历。体现的是劳动创造人、在与劳动人民结合的实践中形成知识分子优秀品格和真正灵魂的哲理。《灵与肉》发展了伤痕文学，启发了新时期人格意识的追寻，开启了改革文学及先锋文学。

Soul and Body is Zhang Xianliang's masterpiece. He once used three sentences from Aleksey Nikolayevich Tolstoy's *The Road to Calvary* to describe his own life experience: soak three times in clear water, bathe three times in blood, boil three times in alkaline liquid. This work is an account of his work on a farm in Helan Mountains. It demonstrates such philosophical ideas: how labour shapes people and how his immersion among the people forges the noble soul of the intellectuals. *Soul and Body,* an evolution of the Scar Literature, inspired a search for personal identity in a new age and sparked off avantgarde literature in China.

一个城市的卓别林
Chaplin of the City

“一二三四五六七，说一个的哥叫哈喜喜，七六五四三二一，他的婆姨叫夏莉莉，酸甜苦辣一台戏，听听别家咋显眼。”坐上银川出租车的人都能听到这档本土广播娱乐节目。“哈喜喜”讲的是老百姓自己的故事，本土本色。“哈喜喜”成了这座城市的卓别林，有了“哈喜喜”，整个城市欢喜风趣起来了。

A taxi rider in Yinchuan will have a chance to enjoy "Jolly Joy", a local radio program that features the blissful daily life of a guy and his wife. Passionate and entertaining, Jolly Joy is a local version of Charlie Chaplin.

为诗歌而来
Come for the Songs

“如果你来看我，越过丘陵，穿过沟壑，会有成万吨阳光迎接你……”“我喜爱这小城里的烟火气……”同心诗人周瑞霞用带着泥土气息的美丽诗句抒写贫困，为精准脱贫创造精神财富。2017年，中国诗歌学会授予同心“中国诗歌之乡”称号。中国诗歌学会是为诗歌而来，也是为脱贫而来，为良心而来。

"If you come and see me, crossing the hills and traversing the gullies, tons of sunshine will welcome you." "I like the earthly pleasures in this small city." Zhou Ruixia, a poet of Tongxin describes poverty with her earthy lines, trying to contribute her spiritual wealth to its alleviation. In 2017, the Poetry Institute of China (PIC) bestowed the title of "Home of Poetry" upon Tongxin. The PIC came for poetry, poverty alleviation as well as conscience.

不与朴素争美的花儿 Beautiful Flower

“花儿本是心上的话，不唱是由不得自家；刀刀子拿来头割下，不死还是这个唱法。”天高地远随心所欲地吼上几句花儿，是宁夏人与大自然水乳交融的对话。宁夏的花儿有30多种曲调，高亢嘹亮、激越动听，散发着醇厚的泥土清香。对于百姓来说，花儿就像一束灿烂的火源，把生命从忧愁和苦难中解脱出来。庄子说“天下莫与朴素争美”，宁夏花儿就是这样。

“Hua’er is the language of the heart, which you can hardly part. I would rather die than give up the art…” Singing out a few lines of these songs at their own will on a vast landscape is actually a dialogue between the locals and nature, an amicable pairing. There are more than 30 types of melody in Hua’er, clear and resonant, bold and exciting, and full of the fragrance of the soil. For the people here, these songs are like a blazing fire that burns away the worries and difficulties of life. Zhuangzi said “Do not compete for beauty with that which is plain”. And plainness is precisely the essence of Hua’er.

王洛宾和五朵梅的邂逅 Wang Luobin

王洛宾的大半生都是在西北边陲度过的，高原、戈壁、牧场、毡房……有一次，王洛宾和作家萧军等人来到宁夏六盘山，住了三天，临走时，店里来帮工的五朵梅唱起了“走哩走哩（者），哟……远（哈）了。眼泪的花儿漂满了……”。一首“花儿”让王洛宾很动情，因为五朵梅他留在了中国西部创作民歌。

Wang Luobin spent more than half his life on the north-western frontier, on the plateaus, the Gobi desert, the pastures, and in the yurts. Wang and author Xiao Jun once spent three days in Liupan Mountains. When they were about to leave, a waitress called Wuduomei, literally “five plums”, in the restaurant sang a Hua’er song, “Oh, you’re to go far away. A flower is shedding tears at the gateway…” This Hua’er song caught the imagination of Wang Luobin, so thanks to Wuduomei, Wang was motivated to stay in the west of China and write folk songs.

摄影：徐立刚

摄影：王占生

盐池是个好地方
Yanchi is a Nice Place

“盐池是个好地方，三边四地好风光，原野阔，五谷香，遍地甘草和滩羊，唱花儿，吼秦腔。”盐池是草原牧歌、秦腔秦韵、红色歌谣和宁夏花儿的汇聚地。出生于盐池县的兰州军区战斗歌舞团青年歌唱演员孙学翔唱了许多歌曲，但他说，歌唱家乡是他的荣幸，感恩家乡是他的福分。一曲《盐池是个好地方》唱出了孙学翔对家乡情有独钟的情怀。

“Yanchi is a nice place with stunning scenery: wide fields, bumper crops, and the sheep on the lush greenery. The Hua’er songs is pleasant and Qin Opera resonant.” Yanchi is heaven to herding songs, Qin Opera, red songs, and Hua’er songs. Sun Xuexiang, a singer of the Lanzhou Military Troup, was born in Yanchi and has sung many songs. He says singing about his hometown is the greatest honour, and it’s his good fortune to be able to pay thanks to Yanchi. His special feelings for his hometown finds expression in the song *Yanchi Is a Nice Place*.

宁大话
University Dialect

宁夏是一个移民地区，二十世纪五六十年代，一批批怀揣理想的青年，响应国家建设西部的号召，从四面八方来到宁夏。为了便于和各地人交流，不知从何时起，从宁夏大学的校园里开始，一种宁夏当地方言融入了普通话的特殊“方言”很快就流行起来，当地老百姓戏称这种半土不洋的话为“宁大话”，吃的是宁夏的草料，开的是南腔北调的花。

There are a lot of migrants in Ningxia. In the 1950s and 1960s, a number of youth flooded into Ningxia from all directions to fulfil their dreams in response to the nation’s call to build up the west. In order to facilitate communication, on the campus of Ningxia University a “dialect” began to emerge that combined the local language with Putonghua. It quickly became popular, and the locals came to playfully call this semi-local language “university dialect”.

方言的语言艺术
Language Art

在宁夏方言中，一些看似毫不搭边的文字声调，经过组合变换，就成了有声的生活艺术。中卫话自带喜剧效果："来（làn）就来（lan）吆，还包包蛋蛋提的是点心！"抑扬顿挫地呈现出一幅生动的情景剧；纯正与幽默兼具的吴忠话仿佛自带放大滤镜，那种夸张让人忍俊不禁："姐姐唷，锅里的面条子要潽了，麻溜儿搁马勺溜些子水啥"；中宁话对叠字情有独钟、对"子"字格外偏爱，"尝了我（wò）们的枣枣子，吐了一地的胡胡子，又不买我（wò）们的枣枣子。"

In the dialect of Ningxia one will hear sounds and tones that don't normally go together. Collocated in a local way, they end up a vocal art. While the dialect of Zhongwei has a dramatic effect itself, with each sentence presenting a vivid picture of daily life; the dialect of Wuzhong has an exaggerating and exhilarating ring to it. The dialect of Zhongning is characterized by juxtaposition of certain characters frequently followed by *–zi*, a common suffix.

摄影：连伯宴

时尚·生活
Times and Fashion

通透的宁夏
Transparent

宁夏的天是通透的蓝，可以是一丝云彩也没有，一直看到山边；宁夏的山是通透的，一览无余，可以看到天边，没有遮挡；宁夏的太阳是通透的，从升起到日落，全景照射；宁夏的空气是通透的，可以一口气吸到底；宁夏的人是通透的，热情好客不拐弯。通透的宁夏，敞开胸怀，迎接南来北往的客。

The blue sky of Ningxia is intense, sometimes without a cloud in sight. At times like this, you can see all the way to the mountains. The mountains are intense, too, stretching vast and wide; from them you can see the sky without obstruction. The sun is intense, too, illuminating the entire landscape from rise to set. The air is intensely clean, and taking in a deep breath of it is wonderful. The people are also intensely hospitable and transparent. Intensely transparent, Ningxia warmly welcomes visitors from all directions.

疏朗的银川
Elegantly Sparse

宁夏自古享有“塞上江南”的美名，而银川则首得其中之利。这座城市始终与周边环境相契合，日渐增高的城市建筑的海拔，永远不会高于贺兰山的天际线。无论站在哪一个方位眺望，都可以看到远方莽莽苍苍的贺兰山脉。文化学者余秋雨说：“到了宁夏以后，我感到天高地阔，图像疏朗，色彩单纯。”

Ningxia has long been famous for its southern-style landscapes although it's in the north of China – the city of Yinchuan is a prime example of this. This city has always existed in harmony with its surrounding environment. As time progresses, it's built up further and further, but the view of Helan Mountains in the distance will never be blocked out. No matter where you are in the city, when you look out you can see the magnificent view of the mountain range in the distance. Cultural scholar Yu Qiuyu said, “After I came to Ningxia, I found the sky high and the earth wide; it was sparse in image and simple in colour.”

摄影：王鹏

摄影：连伯亭

夜游让你邂逅另一种美
Beauty at Night

每当夜幕降临，银川人一面坐上古画舫游船，畅游阅海湾的小西湖，饱览阅海湾灯火斑斓，一面可以看一场独一无二的水幕秀——民乐、交响乐、现代音乐、古典音乐等多主题创意水秀，提供了美轮美奂的视觉体验。银川在时间和空间上都能给市民和游客提供惬意的服务。斑斓的彩灯照亮了银川的夜，也照亮了银川的“夜经济”。

Each night, the people of Yinchuan board traditional leisure boats, and travel around the Small West Lake at Yuehaiwan, taking in the beautiful sight of the sparkling lanterns, as they listen to all kinds of music: folk, orchestral, modern, and classical. It's a wonderful combination of sight and sound. Through time and space, Yinchuan gives its residents and travellers comfortable services. These flecks of light and lilting notes illuminate and enliven the night time of the city of Yinchuan. Local economy also benefits from the picturesque landscape.

文化上了榜
Culture on the List

易中天教授来到宁夏，看到街道两边广告牌上，高高悬挂着宁夏七位版画家的照片。他说，真没想到，宁夏对文化是如此地尊崇，版画家在宁夏有着如此之高的地位，这是宁夏版画在全国占有举足轻重地位的原因。历史的沧桑扑面而来，可宁夏没有染得半点世俗的沧桑，反而让沧桑变成了文化与时尚。

When professor Yi Zhongtian came to Ningxia, he saw billboards on either side of the road with the pictures of seven woodblock print artists from Ningxia. He remarked that he hadn't expected Ningxia to have such respect for traditional culture. With woodblock print artists having such a high status in Ningxia, the province is one of the main areas for the art form in all of China. As the various changes of history have come, Ningxia has still not given up the tradition, and has rather turned it into a symbol of fashion and culture.

农民女作家的手机写作

Novels on the Phone

"为什么每次只写 100 多字，还没看就完了。"喜欢写作的红寺堡农民女作家马慧娟说。她喜欢手机写作，摁坏了 7 部手机，写出了几十万字的作品。她一手种地一手写作，她在自己的一片黄土地里种出了属于自己的文化庄稼。不仅通过北京卫视和鲁豫对话，还当选为全国人大代表，向全国人民讲述 23 万宁夏移民乡愁的新归宿。

"Why do you only write 100 characters at a time? I'm not done with the story." Ma Huijuan of Hongsibu, or Red Temple Fort thus speaks. She likes to write on her mobile phone; she's worn out the keyboard of seven units doing so, writing hundreds of thousands of characters. She works the ground with one hand and writes on the phone with the other; on her plot of loess she's not just grown plants but also a crop of culture. She's had a dialogue on Beijing Satellite TV with famous host Chen Luyu, and served as a deputy to the National People's Congress, introducing the new home of 230,000 migrants in Ningxia.

绿色写意方格

Green Grid

腾格里沙漠身上的网眼迷彩，网住狂野的流沙，拽住沙生植物的根。在铁路和黄沙之间，隔着的一带绿色，润泽了眼睛。治沙的人们在方格子里创作，写上诗句，有胡杨、沙棘、花棒……沙漠的格子里不断地有人在创新、构图。写意治沙方格，凝结着劳动人民的智慧与创造。

Upon the face of the Tengger Desert are connected grass grids which hold the wild sands in check, and anchor the roots of the plants that grow in the sand. Between sand and the railway, there are pleasant strip of green. The people who work at controlling the sand grow poplars, commen sea buckthorns, and bluestem within. There are always people constructing upon these grids, innovating and building things. This interesting way of managing the sand is a testament to the wisdom and creativity of the people here.

摄影：徐胜凯

摄影：钟培源

跑的是风景不是比赛
Running for Fun

银川连续举办了两次马拉松赛，分半程和全程，参与者积极性很高。顾大我说，马拉松是一项痛并快乐着的运动，奔跑过程中达到身体极限的痛苦，完赛后苦尽甘来的酣畅淋漓，是享受健康体魄的一种权利。马拉松赛是一个城市素质的体现，也如人生，重要的不是到达目的地，而是沿途的风景。

Yinchuan has two marathons, half- and full-length. A number of people participate with great enthusiasm. According to Gu Dawo, the marathon is a sport that combines pleasure and pain – it’s a huge struggle when you’re running the race, but after you finish you’re full of joy, enjoying your healthy physique. The marathon is the realisation of the character of a city, and just like life, isn’t about the destination, but rather the scenery on the way.

微博银川
Weibo in Yinchuan

搜索新浪微博银川用户，排名第一的不是明星、学者、专家，而是政务微博“微博银川”。微博银川的“粉丝”已近 300 万，发布微博 13660 余条，被 @ 的微博超过 50000 条。500 多个政务微博组成的微博集群，连着整个银川市民的心。网民们评价说，回答问题萌萌哒，直面问题很犀利，解决问题很给力。

When you search the users of the Sina microblogging site Weibo in Yinchuan, you’ll find the first-ranked isn’t a celebrity, scholar, or expert: it’s the Yinchuan government’s “Weibo Yinchuan” account. It has more than three million fans, 13,660 posts, and has been mentioned more than fifty thousand times. More than five hundred government microblogs have come together to make this account, connecting the hearts of all the people of Yinchuan. Online users say that it responds to questions in a nice manner, asks trenchant questions, and solves problems effectively.

黄河大桥的今昔
Big Bridge

小时候，王文金的家住在黄河边的河滩村，渡黄河的工具是小木船和羊皮筏子。看着新修的黄河大桥，王文金感慨地说："现在你看看黄河东岸，学校、小区、医院、工厂，啥都有。原来的荒滩变成产业新区，世界级的能源化工基地，马路宽阔，交通便利，我们农闲时，想去内蒙古的上海庙玩儿，一步就能跨过黄河。"

In his childhood, Wang Wenjin lived at Hetan Village on the banks of the Yellow River. At that time, people crossed the river in small wooden boats or sheepskin rafts. Looking at the new big bridge, Wang remarks with emotion, "Look at the east bank of the river, with schools, residential communities, hospitals, factories – it's got everything. It's great to see barren land turn into a new productive district, with world-class energy and chemical industry bases, wide roads, and convenient transport. I think that when I have time I'll go to Inner Mongolia to see the Shanghai Temple; crossing the river is so easy now."

供图：宁夏画报社

满城找寻耳蜗
Looking for the Cochlea

2013 年，先天失聪的 4 岁女孩在银川步行街丢失了人工耳蜗。在小女孩耳蜗失踪的 114 小时里，银川全城的人用焦灼的眼、热腾的心，终于找出了耳蜗。这一年，步行街中轴线上矗立起一座名为"爱心之城"的雕塑。雕塑是全国网友馈赠给银川城的一座爱的丰碑。有耳朵的城市，全城的风景都可以依着它而定位。

In 2013, a girl who was born deaf lost her artificial cochlea at the Yinchuan Walking Street. In the following 114 hours, the people of the city looked everywhere with their sharp eyes and warm hearts, finally finding the object. This year, a sculpture titled "A City of Loving Hearts" was erected at the Yinchuan Walking Street – it's a gift from Internet users around the country to the city, a monument to commemorate the love of the city. It's a landmark that helps people find their way to all the scenic spots in Yinchuan.

环保志愿骑行团
Environmental Volunteer Ride

“青春助力生态立区，碧水蓝天志愿行。”一批身穿绿马甲、骑着小黄车的青年志愿者节假日出现在银川街头，引得众多路人关注。志愿者们还纷纷邀请路上的行人一同参与到骑行活动中。一位市民说，以骑行的方式宣传环保更加深入人心，每个人都可以参与其中，为环保尽一份力。

“More young volunteers, more ecological awareness.” A group of young volunteers wearing green vests and riding yellow bikes make their way around Yinchuan on holidays, attracting the attention of those on the streets. The volunteers continually invite others to ride around with them. A city resident says that this method of riding bikes to promote environmental protection really touches the heart, and that with everybody able to participate, it’s a great contribution to awareness for the cause.

真爱 CP 稻田蟹
Paddy Crabs

稻田养蟹以蟹养稻、以稻促蟹。2016 年央视《远方的家》专访宁夏稻田蟹，节目一经播出，稻田蟹和稻田米受到众多“吃货”的青睐和追捧，成了宁夏知名的“真爱 CP”。秧苗，稻子和螃蟹一起成长。一旦各种病虫害开始侵扰，螃蟹们便使出浑身“蟹”术捉虫，为水稻减少了病虫害、除了杂草、施上农家肥。宁夏的“真爱 CP”是时尚，更是健康。

Crabs in rice paddies help with the cultivation of the rice, and the paddies sustain them. In 2016’s TV programme *The Faraway Home*, this ecosystem of Ningxia was documented. The crabs and rice of the paddies are both appreciated by gourmands, and have been known as the “true love couple” of Ningxia. The sprouts, plants and crabs grow up together. If bugs invade the paddies, the crabs head out and eat them, reducing the number of insects and other pests that would harm the crop. Their waste also provides fertiliser to the crop. These “true love couples” of Ningxia are both fashionable and healthy.

摄影：王鹏

摄影：左鸣远

不止一次限高
Height Limitations

每一个城市都在逐步变高。银川的发展史上却因自己的特殊原因，而一再在一些特殊地方“限高”。出于对明代的玉皇阁、清代的钟鼓楼的保护，周围的建筑规定不能超过这两座建筑，这种保护到现在依然有效。而银川新区阅海湾中央商务区，随着现代建筑技术的提高，“银川高度”不断被刷新。100米以上的超高建筑已经有20座。

All cities gradually grow taller. However, for some historical reasons, there have been quite a few height limitations in Yinchuan. Because of protection for the Ming dynasty Jade Emperor Pavilion and the Qing dynasty Drum and Bell Towers, the surrounding architecture can't exceed them in height; these protections are still in place. In the Yuehaiwan Central Business District, as construction technology improves, the "height of the city" is continually increased – there are already 20 buildings there with a height of more than 100 metres.

幸运鸟窝
Birds' Nests

唐徕小区是20世纪80年代的老旧小区，2013年要拆旧建新。小区里老树很多，工人们准备挖掉移走时，发现树上很多鸟巢里有刚孵出的小鸟。于是建议以后凡是拆迁时，发现鸟巢里有小鸟，就一律停工，小鸟什么时候长大飞走了，什么时候再动工。这一建议得到了政府和百姓的称赞，也得到了小鸟们叽叽喳喳的奖励。

The Tanglai Residential Compound is an old one, built in the 1980s. In 2013 it was to be demolished and rebuilt. There were many old trees in the compound, and when the workers prepared to remove them, they discovered that many of them had nests with small birds. For this reason, they recommended that whenever birds' nests were discovered, work be halted, and only resumed when the birds had grown and flown away. This suggestion gained praises and approval from the people and government, as well as the chirping appreciation of the little birds.

闽宁协作脱贫
Poverty Relief

20 世纪 90 年代，福建与宁夏响应国家号召跨越千里而牵手，开启了对口协作发展之旅。从此，宁夏中南部山区，迎来了一批又一批福建援宁挂职干部，帮助大山深处的群众摆脱贫困。“你从八闽大地走来，带着海风，带着温暖；儿回回梦里回到六盘山，闽宁情谊割不断……”这曲流传在宁夏的新花儿，道出了当地老乡对福建援宁各界人士的朴实感激之情。

In the 1990s, Fujian and Ningxia jointly responded to the call of the central government to link up and cooperate. A number of temporarily assigned officials came to the mountainous area of south-central Ningxia. These officials helped with poverty relief of the people deep in the mountains, helping them write a new chapter in their lives. “You come all the way from Fujian, bringing sea breeze and warmth; in dreams one returns to Liupan Mountains; the friendship between Ningxia and Fujian do not fade.” This popular new Hua’er expresses the gratitude of local people.

摄影：陶克图

雕像有尊严
Statues

银川海宝公园矗立着 30 多座青铜制成的雕像，雕像高 2 米多，他们有古代宁夏籍的状元，也有古代历史上为宁夏做出过重大贡献的外地人。银川风沙大，鸟儿多，但雕像落成 10 多年来，走入公园散步的人们，任何时候看到的雕像都是簇新光亮的。海宝公园的工作人员说，把它们擦得干干净净的是对文化的尊重。

There are more than 30 bronze statues in the Haibao Park of Yinchuan City, more than two metres in height. They represent famous figures in the history of Ningxia, as well as people from other places that made great contributions to Ningxia. Yinchuan has lots of wind and sand, and many birds, but even 10 years after they were erected, one will find these statues brilliantly clean whenever walking into the park. The staff at the park say maintaining these statues in a pristine state is part of their respect for culture.

供图：宁夏画报社

绣娘绣出非遗花
Embroidery

穿针，引线，一双巧手带着五彩丝线在洁白的布架间翻飞，渐渐地，洁白的布匹上绽开了一朵朵艳丽富贵的牡丹，飞来了婉转啼叫的黄鹂，奔来了洁白乖巧的小羊……绣工解志霞说："说起这绣花剪纸，咱海原的女子没有不会的，这些手艺成了咱女人的金饭碗，刺绣、家务、农活三不误。""非遗"不仅仅是"守艺"，更是让传承者受益。

Threading the needle, stitching; deft hands carry coloured threads over the pure white cloth in the embroidery frame. Slowly, a beautiful peony come into existence on the white background. Orioles cry and sheep roam. Embroidery fan Xie Zhixia says, "When it comes to paper-cut art and embroidery, none of the girls here don't know how to do it. These are our treasures: embroidery, housework and farming are the pillars of our lives." These "intangible heritages" aren't just a matter of "protecting traditions", but also something that yield benefit to those who practice them.

骑着骆驼去上班
Camel Commute

有好多外地朋友曾经打趣问，你们宁夏人是不是都骑着骆驼上班？确实，处在毛乌素、腾格里、乌兰布和沙漠自东、南、西三面呈"倒U形"包围中的宁夏，没有骆驼是说不过去的，城市里还真没有。不过，自银川实施机动车限行交通管理措施后，有两位姑娘为保护蓝天行动，还真骑着骆驼上了一次班，成了网红。

I've been asked by a number of people if we ride camels to work in Ningxia. In fact, in the Mu Us, Tengger and Ulan Buh deserts in the west, south and west, camels are everywhere, but they're absent from cities. However, after Yinchuan implemented restrictions on the number of cars in cities, two girls as part of their environmental protection efforts rode camels to work one day, and became instantly famous online.

情人节新宠
New Favourite

在情人节这样一个特别的日子，没有什么比一部温情脉脉的电影和一杯温和慵懒的桃红酒更能带给你温暖和美好，1995 年上映的经典爱情电影《云中漫步》就是最好的证明。也许穷极一生也找不到那个云中小镇，但一杯地道的宁夏酒庄桃红酒却能让味蕾体验甘醇，让灵魂在云端徜徉，让这个日子更具温情与浪漫。

On a special day like Valentine's Day, nothing will make you feel better and warmer than a romantic movie and a glass of rosé. The 1995 film *A Walk in the Clouds* is the best proof of this. Even if you can't find that village in the clouds, a glass of Ningxia rosé can awaken your senses, letting your spirit wander among the clouds, filling the day with warmth and romance.

摄影：陶克图

摄影：王鹏

生态农场托管出生态产业链
Ecological Chain

贺兰县的黎伟以新阿里共享生态农场项目走上了他的梦想之路。他说，45 岁的肖华把 70 亩地全部交给农场托管，流转费已高于肖华自己种植的收益，还把他从土地中解放出来通过打工挣取了第二份收入。城里人也爱上了这里的优质水稻、生态水产、生态禽蛋、优质葡萄等，还有备受期待的生态牛羊基地、金山特产基地、生态餐厅、乡村住宿等。

Li Wei of Helan County accomplished his dream with the New Ali Shared Ecological Agricultural Park. He said 45-year-old Xiao Hua entrusted all 50,000 square metres of his farm to him; the fee he got for doing so was more than he made farming the land anyway. This also freed him up to go out and work for a second source of income. The people of the city like the rice of good quality, the ecological production of aquatic products, eggs, grapes, and other foodstuffs from here. They also enjoy the ecological animal husbandry area, full of cows and goats, the Jinshan Local Products Base, the ecological restaurant, the village inn and other attractions.

两个老头儿和一个小丫头的世界举动
Two Men and a Little Lady

“贺兰晴雪”本是宁夏的一处自然景观，然而他们却用以命名一个酒庄。因为酒庄酿造的“加贝兰”酒，打开了世界业内人士认识和了解宁夏的窗口，让宁夏的葡萄酒走出中国，走向世界。做出这一举动、打开这扇窗的正是容健、王奉玉两个老头儿和一个名叫张静的小丫头。

The “Sunny Snowscapes of Helan” is one of the natural views of Ningxia, and their name has also been used as that of a winery in Ningxia. This winery produced the “Jiabeilan” wine, and has opened a window for the industry professionals of the world to know and understand Ningxia, taking the wine of Ningxia outside of the gate of China and into the rest of the world. The people behind this movement are two old men Rong Jian and Wang Fengyu, and a young woman named Zhang Jing.

供图：贺兰晴雪酒庄

供图：宁夏画报社

清凉广场清凉一夏
Cooling off in the Plaza

老李是一位在银川打工的外来务工者，劳作一天后老李最享受的是，坐在清凉广场看一场电影或一台文艺节目。天天如此，再多的乡愁都被这一晚上的文化节目稀释在夜色中，回去后倒头就睡，第二天迎着太阳，继续一天的劳作。清凉广场的清凉文化是外来务工者消解乡愁和心锁的钥匙，是银川这座城市的温度计。

Lao Li came from elsewhere to work in Ningxia. He enjoys cooling off and watching a film or a TV show in the plaza after a day's hard work. Each day is like this; no matter how much he misses his hometown, these feelings of melancholy will be washed away in the colours of the night. Back at home, he falls asleep as soon as his head hits the pillow. The next morning, he wakes up to the bright sun and heads out to work again. This culture of Qingliang Plaza, or "Cooling Plaza" is a key to resolving the longing for home for these migrant workers, and a thermometer for the warmth of the city of Ningxia.

以素食谋善缘
Vegetarian Food

陈涛是一位80后，也是一名主厨，他说他做的是中国第九大菜系。原来，第九大菜系就是，心怀对所有生灵的善意，所有原料及调料都不采用动物制品及添加品的植物善菜。吃着素手撕牛排、糖醋里脊，心怀善意，舌尖上咀嚼的是健康。

Chen Tao is a chef born in the 1980's. He says that his cooking is of the "ninth Chinese cuisine system", in reference to the traditional eight. He says that his food is full of the good intentions of the spirit, with all ingredients and spices not using any animal products or additives, being purely plant-based. You'll be delighted by his vegetarian steak, and sweet and sour pork filet – not only are they delicious, they're healthy too.

彦妮的文学梦 Literary Dream

彦妮是他给自己起的笔名，从 14 岁起，他就有个文学梦。后来，一家人在银川开了一家报刊亭维持生活。他坚持写作，试图通过写作改变生活，实现文学梦。然而，随着电脑、手机、网络的兴起，报刊亭关闭了。生活成了最大的问题，再说起文学梦时，他说，杰克·凯鲁亚克在小说《在路上》说了，永远年轻，永远热泪盈眶。

Yan Ni is the pen name that he gave himself. From the time he was fourteen, he had a literary dream. Later, he came with his family to Ningxia where they started a magazine stand. He persisted in his writing, trying to use composition to change his life, and realise his literary dream. As computers, mobile phones and the Internet became popular, the magazine stand closed. Surviving became his central problem, taking precedence over literature. He said, just like in Jack Kerouac's *On The Road*, one must be forever young, eyes full of tears.

夜生活从环湖夜跑开始 Nightlife Starts at the Lake

“今天跑得累吗？”李姐问孙子。每天晚上李姐带着孙子环湖夜跑。不知从啥时候开始，环湖夜跑成为银川人夜生活的一部分，由最初的三五人、十来人，到成千上万人。随着夜跑人数的增加，沿途树起了里程碑，单单北塔湖就设了 17 个，记载着夜跑人的运动、时尚、健康、文明。

“Are you tired from the night's running?” Mrs. Li asks her grandson. Every night she takes him for a run around the lake. People don't recall exactly when it started, but running around the lake has become a part of night life for the people of Yinchuan. It started with a handful of people, then became a few dozen, and now thousands partake. As the number of participants has increased, milestones have been placed along the route; North Tower Lake alone has seventeen of them. They serve as recorders of the fitness, fashion, health and culture of the city.

摄影：陶克图

怀远夜市
Huaiyuan Night Market

银川怀远夜市原本是下岗职工和大学生的生活天地。自从央视财经频道《消费主张》栏目“中国夜市全攻略”报道之后，每晚都是人满为患。丁铁民的烤蛋，附近的大学生几乎没有没吃过的，宫廷酥牛肉饼几乎成了怀远市场的代名词，阿里木羊肉串儿肉块大、味道好，还有辣糊糊、羊蹄、辣条……地道特色小吃应有尽有。约三五个好友，就着啤酒撸串儿，惬意而美好。夜市让市民们慢下来，仔细品味城市的滋味。

Yinchuan's Huaiyuan Night Market is a place where people visit after work and university students mingle. After the CCTV Finance Show *Consumption Proposals* released a report on "the night markets in China you must hit up", the market was jammed with people every night. Almost every students nearby has eaten Ding Tiemin's Baked Eggs; The Imperial Court Crispy Beef Pancake has become almost an icon of the market. Alim's Mutton Skewers are huge and delicious, and there's also spicy noodles, lamb hooves, spicy strips, and more… All kinds of authentic flavours come together here.

新华街的女人
Women of Xinhua Street

新华街算是银川最古老最繁华的商业街，商业街里女人们自然是主角，新华街的女人只问时尚，不论季节。一半火焰一半海水，风情万种，往往上半身是白雪皑皑，裘毛大衣，下半身则是烈日炎炎，大冬天露着大腿不怕冷。新华街的女人们，就是银川时尚的风向标。

Xinhua Street is one of the oldest and busiest commercial streets in Yinchuan; the women who browse and shop here are the main actors. They're fashionable, no matter what the season is. They show off all kinds of styles, with snow-top-like fur caps and coats, and hot skirts and dresses that reveal their legs even in the middle of winter. These women are the weathervanes of fashion in Yinchuan.

爸爸去了沙坡头
Going to Shapotou

“爸爸，你看，好大片沙漠！哇，居然沙漠那头还有绿洲！”湖南卫视《爸爸去哪儿》剧组将爸爸和孩子们带到了沙坡头，全国观众也聚焦到沙坡头。孩子们尽情地在沙子中撒欢儿，爸爸们开心地陪伴着孩子们。爸爸带着孩子来到沙坡头，让心灵放了假，也给孩子留存了一个温暖如沙的童年。

"Dad, look, what a large desert! And there's even an oasis within it!" Hunan Satellite TV's show *Where Are We Going* brought the fathers and sons to Shapotou, bringing it into the focus of the eyes of people around the country. The children had fun playing in the sand, and the fathers happily accompanied them. Taking your children to Shapotou is like a vacation for the soul, and a journey that will form warm memories for the young ones.

摄影：李君杰

立体化稻鱼共生
Coexistence

贺兰县的稻田里养鸭、养蟹，环田还养鱼，构建了稻、蟹、鸭、鱼共生互促系统。稻田里产出的大米，为城市餐桌上添加了健康有机成分，成为时尚。

The rice paddies of Helan County support ducks, crabs and fish, making for an ecosystem where harvesting of rice and crabs, hunting for ducks and fishing are all possible. These fields produce excellent rice, providing wonderful grain for the tables of the city.

又趁东风
Go Fly a Kite

银川的广场多，人民广场、光明广场、大团结广场……休闲玩耍的人多，放风筝的更是争先恐后。蓬头的稚子、鹤发的老人、偶得闲暇的中年人……个个撸起袖子，在湛蓝湛蓝的天空摇曳绮丽多彩的梦。高手自在悠然，新手屡败屡战却急坏了随行的“军师”，最甜蜜的是那个放得又高又远的帅小伙，女朋友的赞叹在他心里绽开了花。

There are many plazas and squares in Yinchuan: People’s Square, Guangming Plaza, Datuanjie Plaza. There are many people who come here to relax and play; flying kites is a popular hobby. Youths with unkempt hair, old people with white hair, relaxed and chill middle-aged individuals… everyone rolls up their sleeves and flings these beautiful vessels of dreams into the deep blue sky. Veterans calmly fly their kites high, and beginners battle with the winds, sometimes succeeding, sometimes failing. The sweetest of all is the handsome young man who flies his kite far and high, the exclamations of admiration from his sweetheart blooming like flowers in his heart.

供图：宁夏画报社

农家书屋就是精神家园
Book Room

秀花的孩子放学后就到农家书屋去读书，她不用再给孩子买书看。秀花说：“我不识字，也不知道给娃娃买啥书，而且娃娃放学回来还给我念了如何种瓜，我照着书本上的方法，种出的瓜又甜又大。”顺口溜说：如今农民跟时代，钢笔本子随身带；农闲时节不摸牌，有空就到书屋来；读书看报取真经，富了脑袋富口袋。

Xiuhua's child goes to the Village Book Room after school, so Xiuhua doesn't have to worry about buying her books anymore. She says, "I'm illiterate, so I don't know what books to buy for her. When my daughter got out of school one day, she brought me this book on how to grow melons. She read it to me, and I followed the instructions. The melons grew big and sweet!" With this resource, pen and notebook become important tools. Rather than playing cards during the agricultural slack season, people can go to the Book Room to read, gaining knowledge through reading books and newspapers that they can later convert into wealth.

爱上这座城市的记忆
City Memories

富宁街的羊杂、怀远夜市的烤串儿，苏阳、布衣、赵牧阳的音乐，这些都是开始爱上这座城市的原因。“我开始流浪，才找回了故乡”，离开故乡，才知道酸甜苦辣的成长都留在了这座城市。北京路长长的2路公交，周末轧马路的时光……仍然是爱上这座城市的记忆。

The goat tripe at Funing Street, the skewers at the Huaiyuan Night Market, the music of Su Yang, Bu Yi, and Zhao Muyang – these are all reasons that I started to fall in love with the city. "I did not find my home village until I started to wander around." Only after I left my hometown did I discover all the vicissitudes of life and decide to remain in this city. The Number Two Bus on Beijing Road, weekend strolls… These are all memories of how I fell in love with this city.

从沙窝芦草洼到良田
From Reed Creek to Fertile Fields

“干了大半年，挖了十里，转头让沙子埋了八里……”移民老马说，等这一大片荒地长出绿油油的庄稼，好日子就来了。30 多年过去了，沙窝芦草洼变成了良田美景，良田镇成为宁夏美丽生态乡镇。从贫瘠荒芜到美丽富裕，一砖一瓦都是人与自然抗争、融合的见证。老马说，永远也不会忘记那些垦荒奋斗的日子，永远不会停止对生活的感激。

“I worked for half a year, digging for five kilometres, but in the blink of an eye the sand had filled four kilometres back in…” Mr. Ma, a migrant to Ningxia, says that as soon as the green farm appeared in this wasteland, life got better. Thirty years have passed, and “Reed Creek” has turned into beautiful cropland, and is now classed as a beautiful ecological village of Ningxia. Each brick and tile is a testament to the battle between man and nature, as well as evidence of their merging. Mr. Ma says that he'll never forget those days that he spent developing the area, and will be thankful for life for good.

供图：宁夏画报社

包容不排外
Inclusive

一位在宁夏挂职的福建干部说：“挂职一年多，感觉自己成了真正的宁夏人，很快就习惯了宁夏的习惯，舒服、自在，少了客套。宁夏人包容、不排外，生活在这里没有异乡人的焦虑。”在宁夏居住一段时间，心便会很快安定下来，也就会踏踏实实地待下去。

An official from Fujian dispatched to Ningxia says, “After I was here for a year, I felt I was really a part of Ningxia. I quickly got used to the customs and comforts of this place, managed to relax and dispense with formalities. People here are inclusive, and accepting of outsiders. There's no kind of worries being an outsider here.” If you live in Ningxia for a while, your heart will quickly be calmed, and you'll settle down physically and mentally.

摄影：王猛

心中有爱天地阔
Sky and Earth in the Heart

在西吉白崖乡待过的支教老师说，只要回忆起白崖乡，似乎脚丫子一下子就能够触碰到清冽的河水，手一下子就能够触及高高又蓝蓝的天，心里也已品味到那淳朴的乡间气息。有时在漆黑的夜晚躺在白崖乡的黄土高坡上，看星星和城市里看不到的空灵的星空。在那时就只觉得，心中有爱，天地好广阔。

A teacher who spent time in Baiya Town, Xiji says, whenever he thinks about the place, he feels like he has instantly stepped into the clear and cool water of the river, that he can feel the high and clear blue sky just by sticking his hands out, feeling the simple and clean atmosphere of the place in his heart. On pitch-black nights lying upon the loess slopes of the township, one looks out at the sky and sees all kinds of stars not visible from the city. At that time, you just feel that your heart is full of love, and that the sky and earth are vast and wide.

时尚是一种穿越
Fashion is a Passage

尽管外面依然是寒风嗖嗖，然而，银川的美女们已经穿上了超短裙、露脐装穿梭于步行街、万达广场……把南方的时尚温度穿在了身上，置寒冷于不顾。脑海中突然闪出石窟西夏壁画中的西夏少女，她们的穿着也是，露脐装、短袖衫、超短裙和织有精美图案的透明丝袜。原来，时尚是一种穿越，与年代无关。

Even among cold weather and harsh winds, the women of Yinchuan still wear very short skirts and tops that bare the midriff at the Walking Street and Wanda Plaza. Wearing these fashions of the south here, they don't feel the cold. This makes one think of the women depicted in the rock paintings in the grottoes of the Tangut civilisation. They also wear tops that bare the midriff, short-sleeved shirts, very short skirts and beautiful silk stockings. Fashion after all is something that passes through time without obstruction.

高老头儿的天堂
Mr. Gao's Heaven

高老头儿是 1958 年从北京到宁夏的，刚来时采购图书是用毛驴车和搬夫。书放在车上，人走着回来。几十年过去了，图书馆有了微信公众平台及文化数字化服务平台，地方宽畅了，读书的人更多了。看着曾经翻阅过的书、坐过的椅子，回望那些在图书馆流连忘返、沉迷读书的日子。高老头儿说，这就是他心中天堂的模样。

Mr. Gao came from Beijing to Ningxia in 1958; when he first got here he used a donkey cart and porters to purchase books. He'd put the books in the cart and walk back. Decades have passed, and now the library has a WeChat platform and a digitised service platform. The space has been enlarged, and many more people come here to read. Looking at the books read in the past, the chair sat in, thinking about the comings and goings and changes within the library, days spent immersed in books… Mr. Gao says that for him, this is a heaven in his heart.

幸福像花儿一样
As Happy as Flowers

王林从 20 岁开始当灵武塔桥村的村支书。见证了塔桥村近 30 年的三轮脱胎换骨般的蜕变，从"吃粮靠回销、花钱靠救济、种田靠贷款"的"三靠村"到全国有名的"蔬菜村""花卉村"。如今，以花卉装点幸福日子。看着满地的花卉，村民李梅说，花卉使我们富裕，我们的幸福像花儿一样。

Wang Lin has acted as the village party secretary of Taqiao Village, Lingwu City since he was 20 years old. He has seen the massive changes in the village over the course of three decades; a place where originally grain was bought back from the government, spending money came from assistance, and loans were taken out to plant rice paddies, transforming into a village known nationwide for flowers and vegetables. Today, the flowers add happiness to the village. Looking at them growing all over the village, villager Li Mei says that they are the prosperity of the village, and that our happiness radiates like the fragrance from flowers.

供图：宁夏画报社

微约车队
Smartphone Reservations

开了16年出租车零事故的马建雄，组建了宁夏第一支可用微博、微信预约的出租车“微约车队”，尝试把“网络”和“的士生活”连接起来。“微约车队”除了开通和安装了微博、微信、支付宝等软件外，还在队员的车上安装了充电宝、配备了各种型号的充电数据线，为有需要的乘客提供方便。“微约车队”是银川出租车的豪华车队。

Ma Jianxiong had driven a taxi for sixteen years before he formed the first team of taxis in Ningxia that accepted reservations via Weibo and WeChat, in the hope of connecting the Internet with taxi life. His “Micro-reservation Car Team” also started providing portable power packs and various charging cables in addition to Weibo, WeChat, Alipay and other software services in order to make journeys more convenient for passengers.

红运果嚼出健康好运
Lucky Fruits

煮茶、煲汤、泡酒，曾是人们服用枸杞最常见的方法。森淼红运果换了一种方式，将鲜枸杞清洗干净后直接低温冷冻制干，口感酥脆，直接嚼着吃。邻居大妈连续吃了大半年森淼红运果，吃出了健康，晚上睡觉明显踏实了，干眼、泪眼、老花眼等症状有了改善，精力好了，感冒也少了。

Boiling tea, making soup, and soaking them in liquor – these are frequent ways that people consume goji berries. Green Ocean has come up with a new method, in which the berries are quick-frozen at low temperature after being cleaned and dried. They’re crispy and sweet, and can be eaten directly. When my neighbour ate them for six months, she became healthier, sleeping better at night. They can treat xerophthalmia, watery eyes, and presbyopia, among other conditions, improve one’s state, and help with cold resistance.

摄影：李君杰

全城寻找老兵纪念章
Searching for a Badge

抗战老兵高永福，把佩戴的一枚“中国人民抗日战争胜利70周年”纪念章弄丢了。街坊邻居们主动自费印制寻物启事，当地媒体立即行动起来，仅银川交通音乐广播微信平台关注量就达到6902次。捡到纪念章的仇冬萍无意间看到了微信，把离开老人30多个小时的纪念章，送到高永福家里。老人两脚一并，精神抖擞地给她敬了个军礼。

When old soldier Gao Yongfu lost his commemorative badge for the Second World War, all his neighbours came together to put up funds for lost and found notices; the local media became involved and even the Yinchuan traffic radio station's WeChat post about the incident received 6,902 likes. Qiu Dongping just happened to see the post, and after 30 hours of worry brought the badge back to him at his house. She was greeted with a true salute.

寻找马银川
Looking for Ma Yinchuan

获得第二届“最美银川”微电影金鹊奖的《寻找马银川》，讲述了一个北京摄影师来到银川，寻找帮他相机失而复得的恩人马银川。一路上他遇到了热心帮忙的的哥德新、诚信担当的老板娘、爱心传递的陈总……最后马银川虽然没有出现，但他却了解了银川的风土人情，他恍然醒悟，原来在银川，人人都是马银川。

Winner of the second Golden Magpie Award for short films, *Looking for Ma Yinchuan* tells the story of a photographer from Beijing who comes to Yinchuan, looking for Ma Yinchuan, who returned his lost camera to him. On his way he meets a number of characters – the warm-hearted taxi driver, the honest shopkeeper, the loving businessman. In the end, although he doesn't find Ma Yinchuan, he comes to understand the local customs, and awakens to the fact that everyone in the city is a Ma Yinchuan.

越户外越青春
Youthful Outdoors

西夏磨房是宁夏近千人户外“驴友”爱好者自发组织的群体。有位“资深驴友”说，迈出脚就是一场说走就走的旅行。连续十几个小时的户外行走，疲惫的双肩、起泡的脚掌……都被夜晚的星空或山巅的一缕清风瞬间治愈。户外活动的收获是挑战自我、收获友谊、感受自然的过程。越户外越青春，户外让生命精彩不断。

The "Xixia Mill" is a community of almost a thousand outdoor travelling enthusiasts in Ningxia. One of its members describes it as a group of people who just head out when they want to. After you've walked for more than a dozen hours, you're tired and your shoulders are heavy, your feet blistered… but you forget all of this in an instant when you look at the starry sky or the mountain peaks. Through these outdoor activities you improve yourself, meet friends, and get closer to nature. The more time you spend outdoors, the younger you feel; outdoor activities make for endless excitement in your life.

候鸟迁徙路上的“快乐驿站”

Happy Station

如果雅克贝汉到过宁夏平原，也许他会将《迁徙的鸟》的拍摄机位架设在滨河的青铜峡鸟岛、银川鸣翠湖湿地或沙湖。每到春天，数以万计的各类鸟儿开始了大迁徙，“塞上湖城”银川就是鸟儿迁徙路上的必须留宿的“快乐驿站”。鸟儿“错把银川当天堂”，人与鸟儿互动的和谐画面，引来了全国各地摄影师的镜头。

If Jacques Perrin had come to Ningxia's plains, he may have taken pictures of the birds at the Bird Island of Qingtong Gorge, the wetland of Mingcui Lake, or the Sand Lake, like in his work *Le Peuple Migrateur*. Every year in spring, thousands of birds of all kinds begin to migrate from here; beautiful Yinchuan is a “happy station” at which they must stop over to rest on their long path, one which may even make them mistake Yinchuan for heaven. People and birds interact in a harmonious scene, making for sights that attract photographers from all over the country.

摄影：王大勇

摄影：张慧

宁大，六秩辉煌
Ningxia University

2018年2月1日，央视《远方的家》对罗马尼亚东辉运动器械有限公司（DHS）总裁杨茜做了专访，DHS工厂是欧洲最大的自行车生产基地。2018年1月，85后的郑元世参与的“网络化动态系统的分析与控制”项目获国家自然科学二等奖。他俩有一个共同的身份——宁夏大学校友。2018年，宁夏大学迎来六十周年校庆。60年来，宁夏大学为社会培养了几十万人才。

On February 1st, 2018, the CCTV Show *The Faraway Home* featured an interview with Yang Qian, president of Donghui Sports Equipment in Romania, which operates the largest bicycle production base in Europe. In January 2018, Zheng Yuanshi, born in the latter half of the 1980s, was awarded the second national prize in natural sciences for his “Analysis and Control of Networked Dynamic Systems” project. These two people have something in common – they’re both from Ningxia University. In 2018, the university had its sixtieth anniversary. Over the course of these six decades, it has turned out hundreds of thousands of talented individuals.

摄影：陶克图

世相 · 面孔
Ways and Faces

黄土旱塬上的文学庄稼
Literature Nourishes on the Loess Plateau

作家铁凝来西吉时曾说，文学是西吉最茁壮的庄稼，西吉文学是中国宝贵的粮仓。因为一本书改变一生命运走上文学之路的康鹏飞，用文字爬出家暴恐惧成长为新时代女性文学代表的单小花，背着"门板诗作"赶集的残疾文学爱好者马建国……他们就像长在山里的"文学庄稼"，在最贫瘠的土地上不屈不挠，收获着文学的果实。

Once when author Tie Ning came to Xiji County, she put it this way, "Literature is Xiji's most flourishing crop. Xiji literature is China's most bounteous granary." Kang Pengfei's life was changed by a book, and so he started on his own literary journey; Shan Xiaohua defeated domestic violence with the power of her writing, and became a leading figure in modern Chinese women's literature; poet Ma Jianguo once wrote his poems on door panels, carried them on his back and took them to the market… These writers are like literary crops in mountains, growing strong and steady on this barren land, and with the fruits of their literary labour there is a bountiful harvest for the nation's literature.

梁衡寻柳
Liang Heng Seeking the Old Willow

作家梁衡在《百年震柳》文中写道："我从北京飞到银川，又坐汽车颠簸了四个多小时，终于在一个深山沟里找到了它。"梁衡找的就是被震惊世界的 1920 年海原大地震撕裂的、海原县西安镇哨马营的一棵柳树，是地震的活见证，人称"震柳"。

Author Liang Heng wrote in his *Willow in the Earthquake*, "I flew from Beijing to Yinchuan, then piled onto a bus bumping for more than 4 hours, and finally found the old willow tree in a deep ravine." The willow tree Liang Heng was looking for is in Xi'an Town, Haiyuan County, in a village called Shaomaying. It survived the world-shocking Haiyuan earthquake in 1920, though it was torn almost completely in two. It remains a living witness to this earthquake and so is called the Earthquake Willow.

最美银川人面条儿哥
The Kindest Man in Yinchuan, Mr. Noodle

河南人郭良山带着妻儿来到银川，在石油城开了一家手工面条儿店。面条儿店对前来买面条儿的残疾人和 80 岁以上的老人，一律免费赠送。郭良山还资助了 40 多个城市贫困孩子。而他和家人却挤在一间 10 平方米的加工车间里，儿子想要一件羽绒服都舍不得买。他用一碗最普通的面条儿，感动了银川200万人，成为"最美银川人"。

Guo Liangshan came from Henan to Yinchuan, bringing along his wife and kids, and started to run a handmade noodle stall. For the disabled and people over 80 years old, he gives away his noodles for free. In addition, Guo Liangshan also sponsors more than 40 poor kids throughout the city. Actually, he and his family live in a processing workshop that's no more than 10 square metres in size. He is so thrifty that he would hesitate to buy his son a down coat. His simple bowls of noodles have touched the hearts and stomachs of 2 million Yinchuan citizens – truly, he is the kindest man in Yinchuan.

陕甘宁边区盐池与毛泽民
Yanchi on the Shaanxi-Gansu-Ningxia Border and Mao Zemin

盐池县是红军西征在宁夏解放的第一县，也是陕甘宁边区的重要组成部分。1936 年，毛泽民来到盐池，指导盐业生产和贸易工作，组织了盐池第一个城区消费合作社，成立了盐池县税务局，保障边区用盐供给。抗战时期和解放战争时期，盐池县作为陕甘宁经济的大后方，为抗战胜利和保卫陕甘宁边区做出了不可磨灭的历史贡献。

Yanchi County was the first county the Red Army liberated in Ningxia during the West Expedition, and soon became one of the most important areas of the Shaanxi-Gansu-Ningxia Border. In the year 1936, Mao Zemin, who was in charge of salt production and trade affairs, founded the first urban consumer cooperatives in Yanchi, as well as the region's revenue department to manage and safeguard the salt supply throughout the border region. During the War of Resistance Against Japanese Aggression and War of Liberation, Yanchi County made indelible contributions to the ultimate victory of the Red Army over the Japanese Aggressors and to the protection of Shaan-Gan-Ning Border Region.

本土诗人的心灵栖所
The Spiritual Homeland of Native Poets

“在我心中，西海固永远是一个诗歌的、文化的西海固，我诗意地栖居在这块苍凉的大地上，我的思想延伸的方向，是在有限的生命中寻找永恒的家园。”诗人杨建虎和他的诗歌兄弟们，常常在永不熄灭的传奇中眺望西海固的壮美，希望找到灵魂的出口。

"'Xihaigu' has always been a land for poetry and culture for me. I live poetically on this desolate land. My thoughts extend far and wide, seeking an eternal homeland for my brief time in this world." Poet Yang Jianhu and his fellow poets often stare out at the grand beauty of "Xihaigu" passionately, hoping that their souls find the answers they seek.

供图：宁夏文化和旅游厅

供图：《新消息报》

登顶珠穆朗玛峰的汉子
A Man Among Men, atop Mount Qomolangma

宁夏汉子马兴江终于让“塞上江南，神奇宁夏”的旗帜首次飘扬在珠穆朗玛峰。他曾三年穿越四个无人区，多次挑战人类极限。逐梦路上，这宁夏汉子身上带有一股子不畏艰险的激情，他始终在用耐力和智慧与生命交谈。马兴江说，要把儿时心灵深处种下的梦想在余生撒到世界各地去，让世界了解宁夏。

Ma Xingjiang, who hails from Ningxia, finally planted his flag that reads “Wonderous Ningxia, southern-style landscape beyond the Great Wall ” atop Mount Qomolangma. Among his many tests of human limitations, he once travelled through four no-man areas in just three years. On his journey to pursue his dream, he carries with him a fearless passion. Ma Xingjiang described his goal as being the following, “Through my whole life, I want to spread my childhood dream that I hold deep at the bottom of my heart to the whole world, and let the world know about Ningxia. ”

一个过日子的过程
An Ordinary Life's Journey

王征被誉为“西海固影像代言人”，他以一种虔诚的心态拍摄自己的家乡长达七年，让人们真实地认识这块“干涸得纯净、荒芜得神圣”的土地。编辑李媚说：“对于西海固的人，王征不是一个外来者，也不是一个见证者。他离开过西海固，再回来。这是一个回来的过程，是叩问心灵和追索心灵史的过程，更是一个过日子的过程。”

Wang Zheng is dubbed the representative photographer of “Xihaigu”. He has been shooting his homeland with quiet devotion for 7 years, helping people see for themselves the land’s dry purity, and its barren sanctity. Editor Li Mei said, “To the people of ‘Xihaigu’, Wang Zheng is not an outlander, nor a mere witness. He once left ‘Xihaigu’ and then came back again. This for him has been a journey home, a journey of asking and seeking within his own heart, and more importantly, a journey of leading an ordinary life.”

任重，“少年张大千”
Ren Zhong, a Young Chang Dai-chien

银川青年画家任重 3 岁起即临池学书，少年时即屡获国内外大奖，人称“大千早年”。他在花鸟、山水、人物、草虫、走兽、舟楫等各科各法皆有突出表现，笔墨体势，典丽精髓，画风渊雅静穆、高古清逸。任重也从不想掩饰他的野心，超越唐人，超越宋人。他说，成功是有捷径的，而执着就是成功的捷径。

Ren Zhong, a young painter from Yinchuan, started learning calligraphy from when he was 3 years old and has won numerous domestic and international prizes in his teenage years, winning the title “the teenage Chang Dai-chien”. He specializes in painting birds and flowers, landscapes, portraits, grass and insects, wild animals, boats, etc. His style is elegant and precise, from which audiences can feel a sense of serenity and the spirit of the medieval era. Ren Zhong, never one to conceal his ambitions, has said that he wants to surpass the artists of the Tang and Song dynasties. He believes there’s a shortcut to success, and that shortcut is persistence.

笨拙又深情的西海固人
Clumsy but Affectionate “Xihaigu” Residents

作家石舒清说，西海固人给他的感觉是又笨拙又深情的。清淡的生活状态下，西海固人很真，看向客人的眼神是童稚的、纯净的。你有所求的时候，他们会热情又浓烈地帮助你，好像你不是客人，而是值得他们付出一生的挚友。那种笨拙又深情的感觉，深深地感染到每一个过客。

Writer Shi Shuqing said, “My impression of the people living in ‘Xihaigu’ is that they are clumsy but warm-hearted. They have a simple and peaceful life style and an honest heart. When they greet tourists or guests, you can always tell there’s purity and innocence in their eyes. When you need help, they’ll pitch in with all their heart. It feels like you are their lifelong friend rather than a stranger. This clumsiness and warm-heartedness infect everyone who ever visited the region.”

小巷总理
Minister in the Alley

银川孙仙梅从事社区工作 30 多年，每天早晨不到 7 时就出门，有时晚上 12 时都回不了家。社区的面貌一天比一天好，居民都亲切地称她“小巷总理”。在孙仙梅的感召下，儿媳妇、大女儿先后走上社区工作的岗位。谈起家规，孙仙梅搬出经常对子女唠叨的一句话：“干一行爱一行，珍惜岗位，不自私，要有爱心。”

Sun Xianmei has been working in Yinchuan to help the community for more than 30 years. Every morning she leaves home before 7 AM, and sometimes won’t get home before 12 PM. Thanks in part to her great efforts, the community is improving day by day and the residents here call her the “Minister in the Alley”. Inspired by Sun Xianmei, her eldest daughter and daughter-in-law both decided to work for the community as well. When it comes to the principles of her family, the most often-quoted one is “Fall in love with what you do, cherish the position you have and don’t be selfish. Always be warm-hearted and ready to help.”

福建挂职干部
Temporary Officials from Fujian

宁夏与福建对口扶贫协作20多年。福建挂职干部陈星说，是固原贫困群众不服穷的精神一直在鼓舞着他。“闽宁友好使者”林月婵先后40多次往返闽宁两地开展工作，落实帮扶项目20个；林承祥资助140名贫困学生……一大批干部挂职宁夏，既是福建人才、资金、技术等植入宁夏发展的过程，也是宁夏人思想观念解放的过程。

Ningxia and Fujian have been cooperating on poverty alleviation for more than 20 years. Chen Xing, a temporary official from Fujian, said that it was the spirit shown by the poor people of Guyuan to shake off poverty that has inspired him from the start. As the Goodwill Messenger between Ningxia and Fujian, Lin Yuechan has travelled between the two provinces more than 40 times, during which time she had completed 20 poverty alleviation projects. The temporary official Lin Chengxiang has sponsored 140 poor students to continue their studies… Thanks to a large number of Fujian officials serving temporary positions in Ningxia, not only have talent, funds, and technology been shared, it's also proved to be a process of liberating Ningxia people's minds and thoughts.

摄影：陶克图

张贤亮的宁夏心情
Zhang Xianliang's Love of Ningxia

张贤亮18岁来到宁夏，一待就是一辈子。在这里受伤，也在这里痊愈，宁夏大地上自然浓郁的风土人情温暖了他的心，留下了他的情，也塑造了承载他一生情怀的镇北堡华夏西部影视城。他说：“宁夏的自然和人情，对一向生活在大城市的我，完完全全弥补了失落感。宁夏的空旷、粗狂、奔放及原始的裸露美，竟使我不知不觉喜欢上了它。”

Zhang Xianliang came to Ningxia when he was 18, and has been living here ever since. He was both hurt and then healed again here. The rustic customs nourished by this land so close to nature warmed his heart. He gradually fell in love with this barren region, and built a film studio in Zhenbeibu, the China West Film Studio. He said, “Previously, I had always admired big city life, but the natural landscape and customs of Ningxia filled a hole in me I didn't know I had. Ningxia is wide, empty, rugged, wild and primitive. I couldn't help falling in love with it.”

宁夏妈妈“暖洋洋”
A Warm-hearted Ningxia Mama

“喂？你在干啥着呢？”点开暖洋洋的微信头像，视频语音串联起两边的笑容和声音。暖洋洋是妈妈的微信名，她属羊。因为不识字，出门不方便，所以不愿意出门。今年春节，快80岁的妈妈学会了微信，每天给儿女打一个视频电话、听听姐妹给她发的语音，看看孙子的图片，很是开心。暖洋洋微信里没朋友，只有她心头最惦念的人。

“Hey, what are you up to?” The minute I answered my mom's video call on WeChat, we both started laughing and giggling. Nuanyangyang is her WeChat name, meaning warm, to represent the warmth of her heart. In Chinese, “yang” also sounds like the word for sheep, and my mom was born in the Year of the Sheep. Because she can't read, she barely goes out and is not keen to, either. So during the last Spring Festival, my nearly 80-year-old mom learned how to use WeChat. From then on, every day she would give her kids a video call, listen to her sisters' voice messages and look at her grandchildren's pictures. Now she has a much happier life. She doesn't have too many contacts in her WeChat, only those she cares about the most.

马背梦
A Dream of Roaming on Horseback

宁夏西吉小伙子史泰龙从小有一个江湖武侠梦，他曾和自己的马“平安”信步由缰，走走停停一个月，完成了骑马旅行的梦想。这一次，他要在马背上重走丝绸之路，从西安到罗马，骑行三年。史泰龙的想法很简单，去看看丝绸之路沿途的风景和不同地方的人生活的模样，也想去陌生的地方挑战自己。

Shi Tailong, a young man from Xiji County in Ningxia, always dreamed of becoming a wandering hero like those in the martial arts tales he loved as a child. He used to ride on his horse, Ping'an (meaning safe and sound) and wander around for a month, thus fulfilling his travel dream on horseback. This time, he will set off again with his horse, and retrace the old Silk Road: from Xi'an to Rome, which will take him a total of 3 years. What drives Shi Tailong is quite simple: to see the landscape along the Silk Road, as well as meet the people of many different places with their different life styles, and to challenge himself in strange new places.

文化苦旅的终结点
The Last Stop on Yu Qiuyu's Chinese Culture Quest

走遍全国各地的余秋雨，将文化苦旅的最后一站选择在宁夏。他说：“我把宁夏放在全国的最后一站，这绝对不是轻视，往往最后的才是最重要的。宁夏这一站是我心目中最重要的一站。”真正踏上宁夏后，城市的视觉图像带给他莫大的惊喜，单纯、干净、开阔、明朗，这是这位文化学者眼中的宁夏。

The famous Chinese writer Yu Qiuyu travelled around the whole country, and chose Ningxia as his journey's end. He said, “I chose Ningxia as my last stop, not to suggest that I look down on this place. On the contrary, I was saving the most important for last, and Ningxia is the most important part to travel to for me.” When stepping into Ningxia, the vivid images of cities shocked him. Simple, pure, open and lively; this is Ningxia through Yu Qiuyu's eyes.

搬出一片新天地

Moving Forward into a Whole New World

从很早的时候，西海固的王志珍就想“搬出去”。移民搬迁的想法一直压抑了好多年，真的搬家的日子来了，太阳还没露脸，王志珍一家五口人，连脸都没洗，就带着几瓶水、几个大饼走出父母家的大门。到了新家，一进屋，王志珍就掏出一大摞政府发的宣传资料，招呼女儿给他读。“这里有很多机会，比在老家强多了。就是自己打工，赚钱机会也多的是。”王志珍的一个朋友对他说。搬出苦地方，走出轮回。

Wang Zhizhen came from “Xihaigu”, and wanted to move out of this land for many years. This thought had hidden at the bottom of his heart for much of his life, and when the day finally came, he and his family didn’t even take the time to wash their faces, just grabbing a few bottles of water and some pancakes and leaving his parents’ house. It was break of dawn, the sun had barely begun to peek over the horizon. The minute he moved into his new place, he took out a big pile of government pamphlets and asked his daughter to read them for him. “There are a lot of opportunities here, much better than your hometown. As long as you work hard, even if not a boss yourself but an employee, you can earn good money.” One of his friends put it this way. He had moved out of his poor town as well as his poor fate.

摄影：刘泉龙

从乔治·海德姆到马海德
From George Hatem to Ma Haide

宁夏回族中的马姓最多，当年，伟大的国际主义战士、美国医生乔治·海德姆到达同心豫旺堡后，得知回民中姓马的人很多，于是改了个中国姓，自 28 岁以后的大半生叫马海德。他来到红军西征前线，为军民治病。1950 年入中国籍，是新中国成立后第一个加入中国籍的外国人。

Ma is the biggest surname among Hui people in Ningxia. When the great internationalist and early pioneer of modern medicine in China, American doctor George Hatem, arrived at Yuwangbu in Tongxin County in Ningxia, he learned that most Hui people have the surname Ma and picked it as his own Chinese surname. Ever since he made that choice as a 28-year-old youth, he has been known by the name Ma Haide to the end of his life. He followed the Red Army to western China, and gave medical aid to soldiers and citizens. In 1950, he changed his nationality to Chinese and became the first foreigner granted citizenship in the People's Republic of China.

创造世界奇迹的农民
The Farmer Who Worked a Miracle

有一位农民与黄沙打了一辈子交道，有一天偶然把麦草秆与一把铁锹同时插在沙丘里，第二天返回原地，发现麦草秆还在，而铁锹却让活动的沙子不知带到哪儿去了。后经专家几十年的实验，形成了现在的麦草方格。即在流沙表面用麦草、稻草扎成 1 米 ×1 米的方格，以此达到固沙的目的。这样简单，这样平凡，然而它创造出了“世界奇迹”。

There's a farmer whose life is surrounded by sand. One day, he happened to stick a wheat stalk along with a shovel into a sand dune. The next day when he came back, he found that the wheat stalk was still there but the shovel had been carried away by the flowing sand. Experts then performed numerous experiments, and finally managed to build a sand-net made from wheat stalks. They made 1m×1m grids of straw on the surface of shifting sands, so that it can hold the sand in place. Although the theory and method are so simple, this discovery has worked miracles around the world.

心里要亮堂
A Clear Conscience

在宁夏，提到做人，老人们常常挂在嘴边的话是，做人“心里要亮堂”，不能偷、不能抢、不能拐、不能骗，不能把做人的本分忘记。一盏心灵的灯，照亮了他们行走的脚步。在他们看来，无论何时何地，做人要诚实、本分、善良，只有这样，人心里才能更亮堂。

In Ningxia, when speaking of how to be a good person, old people would always quote "you must have a clear conscience." Don't steal, don't rob, don't abduct, don't deceive, always remember who you are. This moral code is like a torch burning in their hearts, brightening their way through life. These old people believe that, no matter when or where, one should be honest, responsible, and kind. Only with these traits can one have a clearer conscience.

小任果业市场大

Ren's Prosperous Fruit Business

任爱民最初在银川东环水果批发市场做进口水果、精品水果的批发生意，几经周折，他对水果、干货等 80 多个品种进行超市联营。短短几年时间里，他就在银川 20 家大型连锁超市联营销售，在全国各地均有固定采购批发点，每天几十辆标有“小任果业”字样的配送车穿梭于银川大街小巷，“小任果业”慢慢成了一个响当当的品牌。小任说，品牌是干出来的。

Ren Aimin first had a fruit stall at Donghuan Fruits Wholesale Market in Yinchuan, mainly wholesaling imported and other high-quality fruits. Gradually, he began to sell fruit and dry goods to supermarkets and within only a few years he had managed to cooperate with more than 20 big supermarket chains in Yinchuan and had fixed purchasing channels from all over the country. Every day, scores of trucks with the “Ren's Fruits” logo pass back and forth on the streets of Yinchuan. Ren's Fruits has also become a famous local brand. Just as Ren put it, a brand is built up through hard work.

“东财西发”的陈玉明

Chen Yuming, the Man Who Brought a Fortune from East to West

30 多岁的陈玉明，作为闽宁结对优秀企业家代表之一，来宁投资 12 年，为西吉带来了一个大项目——总投资 10 亿元打造宁夏（西吉）闽宁产业园，打破了西吉零工业现状，为西吉人民摆脱生活与就业困境创造了条件。西吉对于陈玉明已渐渐成为一种责任、一种使命、一份情怀。

Chen Yuming is a man in his 30s, a representative of distinguished entrepreneurs of Ningxia and Fujian Cooperation project. He has been investing in Ningxia for 12 years, during which time he brought an investment of 1 billion to build the Ningxia and Fujian (Xiji) Industrial Park. It transformed the lack of industry in Xiji, and created employment opportunities for Xiji people to rid themselves of poverty. For Chen Yuming, Xiji is already not just his responsibility, but his mission and passion.

片儿警侯今知

Officer Hou Jinzhi

32 岁的警察侯今知负责的片区有 6 个小区 30000 多居民、6 家单位及 300 个商业网点。几乎人人都认识片儿警小侯。“小侯，假期能给学生搞个专场的家庭安全和外出安全的讲座吗？”……除了例行工作，小侯每天利用两部手机回复处理 17 个微信群和 11 个 QQ 群里辖区居民的各种问题。一名片儿警就是一片社区的百事通。

Section-policeman Hou Jinzhi is 32 years old, and is in charge of 6 neighborhoods, covering some 30 thousand residents, 6 institutions and more than 300 commercial outlets. Almost everyone knows Hou the section-policeman.“Hou, can you give a speech about safety tips for staying at home and going out during student vacations? ” … In addition to his day job, he has two mobile phones, and every day he checks 17 WeChat groups and 11 QQ groups, replying to all sorts of questions asked by residents. He is like an encyclopedia for this community.

摄影：陶克图

下马关，一家人的长城

Xiamaguan, One Family's Life Beside the Great Wall

下马关古城最初叫长城关，是明长城固原镇重要关隘。红十五军团的军团长徐海东曾在这里办公，徐海东在这座城楼上与斯诺长谈过一整天。村民杨国兴父亲临终前嘱咐杨国兴，一定要保护好，任何人都不能再动城墙一块砖。杨国兴遵守着父亲的诺言，领着两个女儿和母亲共同守护在这长城的脚下。守护长城也守护着清贫和寂寞。

The Xiamaguan section of the Great Wall was originally called Changchengguan (the Pass on the Great Wall), and served as a vital pass on the Guyuan section of the Great Wall during the Ming dynasty. The commander of the Fifteenth Red Army Xu Haidong used to work here and it was here, on this particular fortification, that he talked with famed journalist Edgar Snow for a whole day. Villager Yang Guoxing's family live beside Xiamaguan. His dying dad made him promise that he would protect the Great Wall so well that no one could take even one brick away. Yang Guoxing pledged his word, and so protected the Wall along with his two daughters and his mother. To this day they guard the wall day and night, living humble, lonely lives in service of this great monument.

模特儿女孩邂逅银川

A Model Visitor to Yinchuan

模特儿玛蒂耶第一次来到银川走秀后，就爱上了这座城市，凉爽的气候、可口的美食以及热情的人是她热爱这片土地的缘由。在银川行走之后，她的感受是："西临贺兰山，东边黄河环绕，这真的是一块被赐福的地方，我的心在这里感到前所未有的宁静。"

Brazilian model Maite took part in a runway show in Yinchuan and it was then that she fell in love with this city. The pleasant weather, tasty food and hospitable people are the reasons she fell so hard for the place. After she travelled a bit in Yinchuan, she said, "West of Yinchuan is Helan Mountains, east of it is the Yellow River... this is a promised land and my heart found serenity here."

宁夏的江南才子们
Southern Talents in Ningxia

宁夏文化艺术界名人以江南人居多，比如文学大家张贤亮，书画名人曾杏绯、吴善璋、周一新、罗贵荣……这些江南才子们，因为种种原因来到了宁夏，几十年过去了，不管他们原来的根在哪里，艺术之花却开在了宁夏。现在的他们，无论从性格性情还是生活习惯都已成了地道的宁夏人。周一新说，他虽生在南方，长期在北方生活，已经把自己当成了当地人，一生都把他乡作故乡了。

Intellectual celebrities in Ningxia mainly come from Jiangnan (the areas south of the lower reaches of the Yangtze River). For instance, well-known writer Zhang Xianliang, brush painting Zeng Xingfei, Wu Shanzhang, Zhou Yixin, and Luo Guirong...These Jiangnan talents came to Ningxia for all sorts of reasons. After a few decades, no matter where their roots were originally, their art works bloomed in Ningxia. They have all become Ningxia natives now, life style-wise and personality-wise. Just as Zhou Yixin said, "Although I was born in the south, I've lived in the north for a long long time, now I think myself a native and Ningxia my hometown."

回归精神的故乡
Coming Back to the Spiritual Homeland

作家雷达曾在《走宁夏》中说过："切莫用施舍者的眼光看西部，西部不是可怜巴巴的施舍对象。"是的，虽然宁夏长期以来被认为是荒凉、落后的西部省区，但是其在历史的长河中醒目而光辉，为人类珍藏了深厚的精神财富。正如雷达所言，不管人类文明发达到了何等程度，我们永远需要不断回归精神的故乡。

Writer Lei Da once said in his *Travels in Ningxia*, "Don't look at Western China hoping to provide help, here is not a place which begs for your charity." Indeed, Ningxia has long been considered a barren and underdeveloped region in China, but it is unique and distinguished in historical terms, and contains a considerable spiritual fortune. Just as Lei Da put it, no matter how civilized human beings are, we will always need to go back to our spiritual homeland.

供图：宁夏大庆办

长在土里的“山花儿”
Down-to-earth Folk Song Performer

马生林老人是穿着布鞋去北京大学唱花儿的人，每当他唱起“尕妹你是牡丹花园长，二阿哥是空中的凤凰”时，他的眼睛湿润了……旁边的小鸟叽叽喳喳，院子里的阳光干净利落，农具就那么安静地摆放着。那一刻，花儿让马生林感到，生活中的每一个细节都如此美好感动。

Ma Shenglin is an old man who is a performer of Ningxia Hua'er folk songs. He once went to the top university in China, Peking University, to put on his performance wearing a pair of cheap cloth shoes. Every time when he sings "My girl, you are the peony queen, and I'm a phoenix in the sky", tears well in his eyes. This is his ordinary life: birds singing in the trees, sunlight falling onto his clean and tidy courtyard, farming tools placed orderly around. At that moment, Hua'er makes Ma Shenglin feel life's beauty and deeply move him.

繁华跌落的荒凉
From Comfort to Tribulation

20 世纪 50 年代初，因写《大风歌》的张贤亮从中国最繁华的都市上海，到了中国最荒凉的宁夏，在宁夏劳改农场待了 20 多年。从繁华跌落到荒凉，他开始坐牢、写作、经商。他说，他坐牢的时间比作家时间长，他像一个心灵深处孤独的旅行者。文学评论家许子东说，张贤亮是一座城，是文学思想解放的旗手。

In the 1950s, writer Zhang Xianliang published a poem titled *Song of the Great Wind* and thus was sent to Ningxia from Shanghai. He was forced to leave metropolitan Shanghai and was imprisoned in desolate Ningxia for more than 20 years. From a prosperous city to a barren land, a luxuriant life to a bitter one. He began to write, and later started his own business. His prison life ended up being longer than his life as a writer. Critic Xu Zidong once put it, Zhang Xianliang is as deep as a city, and also a flag-bearer of the idea of liberty in literature.

雨中外卖小哥
Delivery Man in the Rain

一外卖小哥在大雨中骑行，看见一位妈妈正推着婴儿车等待过马路，雨落在了母子身上，也落在了外卖小哥的心里。他停下送餐的脚步，脱下身上的雨衣盖在了婴儿车上，并将这对母子送到了家门口。外卖小哥是穿梭在城市里的飞人，时间就是生计，但遇到他人的难处，这两者自不必权衡，心灵的善意自然而然地迸发出爱的相送。

A food delivery man is riding through the pouring rain. He saw a mom pushing a baby stroller and preparing to cross the road. The rain came down on the mom and her child, and also soaked into the delivery man's heart. He stopped his deliveries for a moment, took off his raincoat and covered the stroller. Then he escorted them home. Couriers are like racers zooming through their cities, their time strictly bound to their payment. But when other people needed help, they didn't hesitate for a moment. The delivery man showed his cares and helped them with a heart of gold.

浙江知青又来了
The Educated Youths from Zhejiang's Return

当年的浙江支宁青年小李，如今已是李大爷。他第三次来到宁夏时，感叹地说，每来一次都不一样，宁夏变化好大啊！小陆的父母插队落户时年龄小，体质弱，当地农民把他们当成自己孩子一样关爱照顾。几十年过去了，浙江知青们念念不忘永宁老乡，看着老乡花白的头发，李大爷说，岁月苍老，知青不老，宁夏成了他们一生的牵绊。

Once an educated youth from Zhejiang Province to Ningxia, Mr. Li is now already an aged man. During his third time going to Ningxia, he sighed that every time it's a brand new place so different to previous times. In another such case, when Lu's parents were sent to Yongning in Ningxia as educated youths, they were small and fragile, and local farmers took care of them as if they were their own children. Time flies, and now several decades have passed, but these educated youths from Zhejiang can never forget the kindness of these fellow-villagers in Yongning. Seeing these villagers all have grey hair now, Mr. Li said, " Though everyone will grow old eventually, but the memory will not. Ningxia will be a part of us forever. "

摄影：陶克图

人和画就是中药厚朴
Personality and Paintings Just like Traditional Chinese Medicine

国内美术界一位大咖说，宁夏画家周一新的画和人，怎么看都像中药厚朴。他笔下的人物关公像是巡视人间忠义的英雄，仿佛随时从画上走下来主持正义；喜乐弥勒快乐得像是随时和大家一起开心一笑；笔墨中的荷花像是要透过宣纸开在心里一样。周一新把中国画那种陶然的逸气完美地表达了出来。他的画风与人品有一种骨血相融的密切。

A famous Chinese artist once said, Ningxia painter Zhou Yixin's personality and paintings are like the features of a kind of traditional Chinese medicine: Houpu "strong and plain". Portraits painted by him are famously vivid and lifelike, for instance, it seems the hero in his paintings of Guan Yu will burst out; His Maitreya, the Future Buddha, is so joyful that it seems he will laugh along with whichever ordinary people are there viewing the painting. He shows the reclusive nature of Chinese paintings perfectly. There's a deep connection between his art style and his own character.

宁夏引黄古灌区护渠人
Protector of Ningxia Irrigation Waterway

护渠人最重要的工作就是巡堤。“每天两到三次巡堤，用水高峰期或者降雨期增加一到两次，主要看有没有人私开斗口放水，有没有人乱挖树毁渠，甚至需要细致地观察堤坝上有没有蚁穴。”护渠人杜永新说。几十年来，巡堤的路从坑坑洼洼的泥泞路变成了混凝土路，下雨天也可以骑摩托车或开车去巡护了。工作方式变了，但不变的是工作的琐碎和枯燥，还有护渠人的坚守和严谨。

The main job of a waterway protector is to patrol along the riverbank. "Every day I need to patrol the area around 2 or 3 times. During peak usage times or when it rains, I'll patrol again another 1 or 2 times, in order to see whether people have been secretly making openings on the bank, digging out trees and destroying the waterway, or whether there's any ants-nests along the riverbank." said waterway protector Du Yongxin. After a few decades, the patrol route has transformed from a mud path to a concrete road, on which protectors can ride a motorcycle or drive a car on rainy days. The way they work may have changed, but the protectors' perseverance and rigorousness remain.

傻子与沙子
The Fool and the Sand

20年前踏进荒漠治沙的刘宝川，再也不愿意离开青铜峡这片土地，他散尽家财，苦苦守着这片荒滩。周围人不解，都叫他"刘傻子"，"傻子"和"沙子"从此结了缘。刘宝川说："虽然坚持造林治沙会导致经济返贫，但我内心是富足的。"黄沙吹尽人间惆怅，却吹不走治沙"刘傻子"的一片赤诚和执着。

Liu Baochuan came to Qingtongxia City 20 years ago, and once there he decided not to leave and instead focus on sand control. To pursue this aim, he spent all his savings and remained living on these desolate sands. Other people can't understand him and call him "Liu the Fool". For him, "fool"and "sand" (which sound alike in Chinese) are therefore tightly bound together. Liu Baochuan said, "Although sand control caused me temporary financial problems, in my heart I am fulfilled." With time, sand blows away both his problems and sadness, but it couldn't blow away Liu the Fool's passion and persistence.

一手菊花一手烈酒
Flowers in One Hand, Alcohol in the Other

唐荣尧是一位一手拿着菊花一手端着烈酒写作的作家。因为热爱历史，痴迷文字，他像一位苦行僧，行走在寂寞、苍凉的戈壁荒原。他的性情像宁夏的山水，柔软的内心戴着一副坚硬的盔甲，在纸上穿越历史。《宁夏之书》《贺兰山——一部站着的史诗》《神秘的西夏》……他用笔墨复活英雄，行走在历史和现实中。

Tang Rongyao is a writer who would hold a chrysanthemum in one hand and liquor in the other while writing. He's always been fond of history and writing, and pursues them as his dream, therefore choosing to live like a stoic. He walks in the lonely and desolated Gobi desert. His personality is just like the mountains and rivers in Ningxia – soft and tender on the inside, with unbreakable armor outside– and travels through history with his pen. *Book of Ningxia*, *Helan Mountains—A Standing Epic*, *The Mysterious Western Xia*… He has brought these heroes of history to life and lives his own between the real world and history.

牛红旗，坚守着失守的城堡
Niu Hongqi, Safeguarding the Last Forts

作家牛红旗原本是个摩托车专卖店的老板，五年来，他自掏200多万元走遍了西海固，开坏了两辆越野车，坚守着那些快要失守的大大小小的城堡。他发现，那些城堡散落在村镇、山坡、沟壑，湮没在颓废的老街旧巷，隐身于黄昏枯树身后，每一个都有故事。这些城堡不仅是一个个历史、地域符号，还是一种文化、精神的象征。

Writer Niu Hongqi once owned a motorcycle shop. He has travelled around the "Xihaigu" region over 5 years, costing him more than two million yuan. Along the way, two of his off-road vehicles broke. His goal is to safeguard those deserted forts. He noticed that forts are scattered throughout villages, on mountain slopes, in gullies, and in deserted alleyways. Hidden behind withered trees, and basked in the setting sun, each of them has its own story. As Niu Hongqi put it, "These forts are not only a symbol of the history of a region, they're also a symbol of culture and spirit."

牧羊诗人
Shepherd Poet

"我 17 岁的时候，嗜书如命。那时刚学会读书，知识的诱惑让我疯狂不已，家乡是真正的穷乡僻壤，我是个阅读饥渴严重的放羊娃。而书，在这个黄土深埋的世界里却是真正的奢侈品。"红寺堡区农民诗人王学军说。他只读到小学三年级，辍学后，便成了放羊娃，闲暇时读书，如痴如醉……而今，他是新月文学奖得主，一位朴实的牧羊诗人。

"When I was 17 years old, I loved reading with all my heart. I had just learned how to read back then, and the allure of all that knowledge drove me mad. My hometown is in a rural area, and I'm a shepherd who was keen to read. Books are a real luxury in this sand-buried land." says shepherd poet Wang Xuejun from Hongsibu District. He dropped out of school at grade 3 and became a shepherd boy. When he had some leisure time he would always read, and indeed read like a man possessed... Now, he has already won the New Moon Prose Award, a simple shepherd poet.

贺兰山下三鞠躬
Bowing Three Times Under Helan Mountains

画家韩美林登上贺兰山，看到贺兰山岩画时，面对宁夏贺兰山深深地鞠了三躬，说："贺兰山数千乃至上万年前苍茫朴拙的岩画，是我艺术和生命生生不息的精神家园。远古先人留下的痕迹，让人惊叹，让人崇拜，让人敬畏，让人热血沸腾又让人回味无穷。"韩美林的三鞠躬是对艺术的敬畏。

The artist Han Meilin once climbed Helan Mountains. When he saw the rock paintings there, he bowed to them three times and said, "These paintings can be dated back thousands of years or even to ten thousand years ago. The art style is rough and simple, and it's an endless source of artistic inspiration for me as well as a symbol of my spiritual homeland. This cultural wealth our ancestors left us is astounding. We worship it, respect it. It is breathtaking and leads us to meaningful musings." Han's bows showed his awe and respect for the art.

摄影：陶克图

当代《呼兰河传》

A Modern Tales of Hulan River

1982 年出生于西吉县的马金莲，原来是位民办教师，因为酷爱文学，2000 年开始文学创作，现为宁夏作家协会副主席，备受文坛注目。她的中篇小说《长河》被誉为“当代《呼兰河传》”。她的短篇小说《1987 年的浆水和酸菜》获第七届鲁迅文学奖。有读者说：“太美了，真的太美了，这篇小说让我重新燃起了对文学的激情。”

Ma Jinlian was born in Xiji County, Ningxia, in 1982. A former rural schoolteacher, she is passionate about literature and began writing in 2000. Ma now serves as vice-president of the Ningxia Writers Association, having received a lot national attention for her works. Her novella *A Long River* was compared to the renowned 1940 novel *Tales of the Hulan River*. Her short story *Sour Solution and Vegetables in 1987* won the 7th Lu Xun Prize. As one reader put it, “Too beautiful…really! This story ignites my passion for literature.”

供图：《新消息报》

误把马燕当莫言
Mistaking Ma Yan for Mo Yan

莫言获得诺贝尔文学奖后，一位西方读者想买一本莫言的书看，因为不太清楚具体书名，误把马燕当成莫言，于是买回了宁夏姑娘的自传《马燕的日记》。读完全书后，他十分高兴，认为自己犯了一个“幸运的错误”。“妈妈，如果我上不了学，我的眼泪一辈子都流不干。”因为“这个幸运的错误”，农村失学姑娘马燕圆了自己上学的梦。

After Mo Yan was awarded Nobel Prize in Literature, a western reader wanted to buy his works and confused his name with Ma Yan. So he ended up bring home *The Diary of Ma Yan*, an autobiography of a schoolgirl in Ningxia. He thought he was very lucky to have made this mistake and was deeply touched after reading the book. In the book she wrote, “Mom, if I can’t go to school, I will never live a day without tears. ” Because Ma Yan’s story is well-known by the public, a fund was set up to send Ma Yan and children like her to school.

郭文斌的安详时光
Guo Wenbin’s Peaceful Life

作家郭文斌因创作《寻找安详》而开启了新时期的安详文学潮流，让人们在这个浮躁喧嚣的现代社会里，寻找内心安详的力量。他说：“我非常感激上苍没有把我降生在城里，包括豪门显贵之家，却投放到宁夏西吉县将台堡一个名叫粮食湾的小山村，它让我能够从童年开始就享受大年所带来的那种刻骨铭心的快乐，销魂的快乐，无缘无故的快乐。”

Writer Guo Wenbin’s work *Seeking Peace* kicked off a new literature trend. Its style makes readers feel calm and at peace in this flighty and rash modern world. He said, “I’m grateful that I wasn’t born in a big city and an upper-class family and was instead born in the small village of Liangshiwan (literally ‘grain harbour’), in Xiji County’s Jiangtaibu region. It gave me the chance to fully experience the excitement of enjoying Chinese New Year as a child. It’s unforgettable and enchanting, and as a kid, sometimes you don’t even need a real reason to get excited.”

雷抒雁的第二故乡
Lei Shuyan’s Second Hometown

作家雷抒雁大学刚毕业时，在青铜峡包家滩插队种田三年。参军入伍后经常向《宁夏日报》投稿，和战友在中卫沙坡头植过树。每当再次路过沙坡头时，雷抒雁都很感慨，看见那些树，他就想起自己在宁夏度过的时光。“我把生命的一部分留在了这里，这里是我的第二故乡。”

When writer Lei Shuyan first graduated from college, he was sent to Baojiatan in Qingtongxia City to live with the farmers and farm the land as part of the Down to the Countryside Movement. Later he joined the army and during this time, he often contributed to *Ningxia Daily*. During his service, like many of his comrades, he was assigned to plant trees in Shapotou District, Zhongwei. Passing by Shapotou now always reminds him of those years he spent in Ningxia, “I left part of my life here, and this is my second hometown.”

皮实的山里娃
Tough Kids in the Mountains

一张苹果般红的小脸蛋儿、一双纯净澄澈的大眼睛、一身不太合体的单薄衣裳、一副憨态可掬的萌萌表情……在宁夏中南部山区，随处可见走在路上的山里娃。人们常说，乡下孩子皮实得很，天天风里来雨里去，习惯了，倒也不觉得苦累。有的孩子家离学校太远，甚至有好几里的山路，就早起一会儿，掰个窝头饼子一路走一路啃。

Little rosy cheeks, a pair of pure black eyes, with loose but thin clothes, charmingly naive… In the mountain areas of south-central Ningxia, one can see this kind of cute kid everywhere. People always say that children living in the mountains are rugged and strong; they work and go to school regardless of the bad weather, and so they learn to bear hardships early on and don't let such things bother them. Many kids live far away from school, some of them needing to walk a few kilometres through the mountains every day. They would just get up early, grab some corn bread and set out on their way.

供图：宁夏画报社

一棵树一个人一辈子
A Tree, a Person, a Life

当时毛乌素沙漠边缘有个地方叫“一棵树”。白春兰28岁来到这里，那时除了遍地沙子，根本就没有树，周围十里八里连个人影都看不到。从那时起，白春兰一棵树一棵树地栽，被沙漠埋了，再栽。30多年过去了，70000多亩的沙漠绿树成荫。因为嫁到了一棵树这个地方，一个人与沙漠做着较量，栽了一辈子树，人称她“沙漠王”。

There's a place called Yikeshu (a single tree) on the edge of Mu Us Desert. When Bai Chunlan first came here aged 28, there were no trees and barely any inhabitants, just endless sand. From then on, Bai Chunlan has been planting trees one by one. If a tree got buried by the sand, she just planted another one. After 30 years, more than 46.7 square kilometres of desert has become oasis. She moved to Yikeshu because this is her husband's hometown, and fought with the sand alone, planting trees for her whole life. People now call her the queen of desert.

在出租车上传递本土文化

Spreading Local Culture in a Cab

保剑君的作家身份比出租车司机身份更有知名度。银川交通音乐广播请他做了一档15分钟的节目《保师傅带您逛银川》，讲述老银川的民俗、传说、典故、历史。讲着讲着，他开始尝试写作，出版了30多万字的《银川文化地图》,这书成了银川的哥的姐的"掌中宝"。《人民日报》称保剑君为"流动的宣传栏，文化的活地图，文明的展示点，道德的传播者"。

Bao Jianjun is well-known as a writer rather than a cab driver. Yinchuan Traffic Music Radio asked him to put together a regular 15-minute program called *Mr. Bao Shows You Around Yinchuan*, telling about customs, legends, anecdotes and history about Yinchuan. After doing the show for a while, he tried his hand at writing. His writings were eventually collected into a book named *The Cultural Map of Yinchuan*, which is over 300,000 Chinese characters. It has become an encyclopedia for taxi drivers in Yinchuan. *People's Daily* crowned Bao Jianjun as "A moving column, a living map, a display of culture, and a spreader of morals."

抄写《毛泽东选集》的农民

The Farmer Who Copied out *The Selected Works of Mao Zedong*

农民李忠勤，用两年半时间以毛笔抄写整部《毛泽东选集》，共计4册106万字，全卷铺开长达3500米。李忠勤还想教娃娃们练书法，把传统文化传承下去。真正的文化，除了在博物馆里流芳千年，更是那些来源于生活、根植于心底的觉醒。李忠勤书写的是经典，留下的是那股被文化滋养过的精气神儿。

Li Zhongqin is a farmer who spent two years hand-copying the entirety of *The Selected Works of Mao Zedong*, which is some 4 volumes and 1.06 million Chinese characters in total – the paper he wrote it on is 3500 metres long end-to-end. Li Zhongqin strongly wishes to teach children calligraphy, so that they can help pass down this essential part of traditional Chinese culture. Real civilization not only exists in museums, but is also awakened in the lives and hearts of the living. Through the copying of a classic, Li Zhongqin showed us his spirit and cultural pursuit.

奇特的感受

A Strange Feeling

来自江南水乡的"驴友"说，在宁夏同心走一趟会有一种很奇怪的感觉。当你适应了这里的气候和环境，竟然会觉得身处青山绿水的优越感慢慢消退，有时候看到那依附在地皮上的羸弱的小草，都会爱意涌动。再慢慢欣赏经过身旁的普通人，心中顿觉天地辽阔，生命坚韧。活着就要拥有这样一种简单朴素的姿态。

Hikers from the south are often heard to say that walking through Tongxin County gives them a strange feeling. Once you get used to the climate and environment here, the pride of coming from a big city starts to wane and everything here seems lovely to you. Even the tiny blades of grass on the barren soil work their way into your affections. Gradually, you learn to appreciate the ordinary people passing by, and you start to feel the broadness of this world, the toughness of this life. Life is best lived with this simple attitude.

宁夏文学三棵树
The Three Big Trees of Ningxia Literature

作家们在宁夏这片土地上孜孜不倦地写作，于是宁夏文学不再是“寂寞深村里”。20 世纪 90 年代，陈继明、石舒清、金瓯以令人瞩目的文学成绩被文坛称为“三棵树”，卓然西部；20 世纪初，又有季栋梁、漠月、张学东“新三棵树”。“三棵树”逐渐蔓延成林，荫护宁夏或贫瘠或坚实的土地，是宁夏文学的诗和远方，成为中国西部文学不可低估的力量。

More and more authors are writing diligently in Ningxia, and so the literary community in Ningxia is no longer like a small and lonely village. In the 1990s, Chen Jiming, Shi Shuqing and Jin Ou were dubbed the “Three Big Trees” in Ningxia literature and were famous in western China because of their prominent achievements. In the early 2000s, Ji Dongliang, Mo Yue and Zhang Xuedong were named the “New Three Trees”. These writer trees gradually grew into a forest and the shade of this literary forest now covers the barren or solid lands of Ningxia. They are the hope of Ningxia literature. These “trees” are a mainstay of western china literature.

写给世界的绿色答卷
A Shining Example of Environmental Protection

有专家在 1991 年就曾预言，以当时中国土地沙化的速度，10 年可以吞没一个宁夏。然而，宁夏创造了沙坡头、白芨滩等世界治沙奇迹；给全球沙漠治理交出了一份绿色答卷，被联合国粮农组织誉为“中国治沙奇迹”。作家周涛赞叹说，与风沙抗争的人就如同填海的精卫。

Experts once predicted in 1991 that, with the speed of land desertification in China, Ningxia could be completely devoured within 10 years. But against all odds, Ningxia has worked sand-control miracles in such areas as Shapotou and Baijitan. Theirs is a shining example of environmental protection to the world, and they have been hailed as working miracles in Chinese desertification control by the Food and Agriculture Organization of the United Nations. Writer Zhou Tao praised the people battling the sands and sandstorms by comparing them to Chinese mythological tale of bird Jingwei trying to fill up the sea.

8 年还债 20 万
A Debt Repaid over 8 Years

丁芳是灵武市郝家桥镇关渠村十组的一名普通家庭妇女。2007 年的一天，她的老伴儿带着两位老乡外出时遭遇车祸，老伴儿当场身亡，而两位老乡身负重伤。两位老乡的 20 万医疗费由她来承担。当时近 50 岁的她，披星戴月，勤俭节约，用了 8 年时间，替亡夫还清了欠债。

Ding Fang is an ordinary housewife in Group 10, Guanqu village, Haojiaqiao Town, Lingwu City. In 2007, her husband had a car accident after going out of town with two fellow villagers. Her husband passed away on the spot and the two fellow villagers were seriously injured. She was responsible for paying for their medical bills, a sum of more than 200,000 yuan. She was almost 50 back then, but still worked day and night and lived an extremely frugal life in order to make the money back. Finally she paid off the debt after 8 years.

宁夏文化的一张名片
A Representative of Ningxia Culture

张贤亮是一棵从江苏移居来宁夏的文学大树，也是宁夏文化的一张名片。20 世纪 80 年代，张贤亮几乎一个人站在宁夏的黄河岸边和茫茫草原上独吟。他的《灵与肉》《邢老汉和狗的故事》《肖尔布拉克》《初吻》《河的子孙》《龙种》《土牢情话》《绿化树》《青春期》《男人的一半是女人》《一亿六》等作品，成为一个时代的绝唱。

Zhang Xianliang is a great writer from Jiangsu. Now he has become a representative of Ningxia culture. In 1980s, he was almost alone in Chinese literature as a Ningxia-based writer, standing by himself along the banks of the Yellow River and wailing in the endless grasslands. His works, like *Soul and Body*, *The Story of Old Xing and His Dog*, *Xiorbrag*, *First Kiss*, *Descendants of the River*, *Dragon Seed*, *Love Words in Prison*, *Green Tree*, *Puberty*, *Half of Man is Woman*, and *One Hundred and Sixty Million*, all stand at the forefront of Chinese literature.

舒婷来宁夏追忆童年
Shu Ting Recollected Her Childhood in Ningxia

诗人舒婷来宁夏，首选到中卫喝牛杂汤吃凉拌野生沙葱，夜宿沙坡头，枕着黄河涛声入睡，陪着星星看沙漠里的萤火虫。记得有天晚上，窗外一只小鸟在叫，它的叫声轻柔妩媚，像江南娇羞的少女，它羞涩地叫一声，躲起来再叫一声，缠绵得让人不敢呼吸。舒婷说，她一次次来宁夏的缘由，就是这里能圆她一个完美纯粹的童年记忆。

When poet Shu Ting visited Ningxia, she first went to Zhongwei City and had beef innards soup with a wild onion appetizer. She stayed the night in the Shapotou District, stared at the fireflies under the stars, and fell asleep to the sound of the flowing Yellow River. One night, a bird was singing outside her window. It sounded so gentle and charming, just like a timid girl from the south. It tweeted once and then hid away, waited a short while, and then twittered again. It was a song so tender that one dared not even breathe lest one might interrupt it. Shu Ting said, “Now I come to Ningxia over and over again, searching for my ideal childhood memory.”

供图：宁夏画报社

毛乌素沙漠边缘践行“美丽中国”
Building Beauty on the Edge of the Mu Us Desert

一个人在 20 多年的时间里可以做很多事情，而王有德只做了两件事——让沙漠绿起来，让职工富起来。王有德是以治沙成名的全国劳动模范、感动中国人物……荣誉很多，而他说他就是为治沙而生的。他三句话不离本业：谈他的治沙体会，谈他的治沙乐趣，谈得更多的是浸透在他骨子里面的生态忧患。

One can achieve many things in 20 years, but for Wang Youde, he just did two things. One is to bring green into the Mu Us Desert, and the other is to help the workers here get richer. Wang Youde focused on sand control, and thus became a National Model Worker, and was picked as a “People Who Moved China”, etc. Despite being given numerous honours, he considers himself just an ordinary person who focuses on sand control. He’s forever thinking about his job and the task at hand: his experience in sand control, how much he enjoys it, and his concerns regarding the wider environment as a whole.

梦随蝶舞
A Butterfly Dream

蝴蝶的生命是短暂的，但有着像蝴蝶一样美丽名字的宁夏作家陆梦蝶的生命却是顽强的。15 岁开始与疾病抗争，从重病瘫卧床上到能拄杖行走，她经历着自己的“人生长征”。读书、写作、剪纸，开办服务农民的“田野书舍”，出版了《梦随蝶舞》《偶是农民》等作品。她说：“我从不吝啬对生命饱含的深情和希冀，我像蝴蝶飞舞一样，实现着自己人生的梦想。”

Butterflies have a short life, but one girl called Mengdie (a beautiful name which means butterfly dream) is leading a strong and tough life against all the odds. She is Lu Mengdie, a writer of Ningxia. She has been fighting a painful disease since she was 15 years old. From being paralyzed to walking with a stick, she has struggled through her very own “long march”. Against such a fate, she has surpassed all expectations – reading, writing, doing Chinese paper cutting, organizing a reading room for farmers, and publishing her own works such as *A Butterfly Dream* and *I, A Farmer*. She said, “I never gave up and am always passionate and happy with my life. I will fly like a butterfly, and fulfill my dream.”

摄影：陆梦碟

羊杂西施

A Beauty Selling Lamb Innards Soup

作为一名吃货，旅游除了领略当地的风土人情，对于美食简直毫无抵抗力。来宁夏，必吃吴忠的杜优素羊杂碎，因为来吴忠不吃杜优素，就不算来过吴忠。比杜优素羊杂更具盛名的是漂亮的老板娘，人称"羊杂西施"。据说许多外地游客也为了看一眼"羊杂西施"，专程去吴忠吃碗羊杂。"羊杂西施"成就了杜优素，更成了一道风景，这正印证了那句：秀色可餐。

When the foodies are travelling, they will find out about the customs of a place, and in particular which local food is a must-have. Coming to Ningxia's Wuzhong City, one has to try Duyousu Lamb Innards Restaurant. If one doesn't visit Duyousu, it is as though they haven't visited the city at all. What is most famous about the restaurant is that the owner is a beauty, and people call her "Beauty Selling Lamb Innards Soup ". It is said that many tourists go try lamb innards dishes just to get a glimpse of her. Her beauty helped make Duyousu what it is today, as she herself became an attraction. One might almost say: a delectable beauty!

千金一诺

A Golden Promise

银川女孩张钰最好的朋友得了白血病，因为治疗剃光了头发。为了安慰好友，张钰说："等我头发长长了，就匀你一半。"没想到好友治疗失败，遗憾地离世了。张钰却把头发的事记在心中，她寻觅了很久，终于在公益平台"青丝行动"中将自己的头发捐赠出去。千金一诺，她把对好友的承诺像温暖的种子一样播撒到那些因化疗而失去头发的女人心中。

Zhang Yu is a girl from Yinchuan. Her best friend got Leukemia and had to shave her head. Zhang Yu comforted her by saying, "I'll give you half of my hair when it grows longer." What she didn't expect is the treatment would not be effective – her friend ended up passing away. But Zhang Yu took the promise of giving away her hair. She looked around and finally found the Qingsi Hair Donation Charity, and donated her hair to them. Hers was a golden promise, made out of care and affection for her friend but which became a seed that blossomed into her helping other Leukemia patients.

摄影：连伯亨

物产 · 馈赠
Local Specialty – Gifts

自然的馈赠
A Gift from Nature

宁夏地处北纬 38 度，阳光充足、气候适宜，广袤的无污染的优质土地，得以黄河水灌溉，加上两千多年的农耕历史和现代种植技术，宁夏，菜有菜香、果有果味、瓜有瓜甜。供港的蔬菜、优质大米、枸杞、长枣、硒砂瓜、羊肉、葡萄酒等物产，是大自然对宁夏最好的馈赠。

Ningxia is at 38° North, so it receives plenty of sunshine and has pleasant weather all year round. The Yellow River irrigates the fertile and unspoiled land each year, and with over two thousand years of farming history and techniques, crops here are all of excellent quality. Vegetables are succulent, fruits are juicy, and the melons are fragrant. Here, we have vegetables that handily beat the standards for export, as well as world-class rice, goji berries, jujubes, Xisha melons, lamb and wine, among many others. These are the sublime gifts mother nature has given us.

摄影：吴宏林

上帝也会微醺趔趄的地方
A Place Where God is Merrily Tipsy

如果上帝端个空酒杯来到人间，他希望往里倒的红酒，一定是产自北纬 38 度、黄金葡萄种植带的贺兰山东麓产区，如果让他在这些红酒中选一款，估计很难。百座酒庄，瓶瓶精品，如果让他来这里豪饮一次，贺兰山东麓产区一定会成为上帝在诗意与酒意中微醺趔趄的地方。

If God were to descend into the human world with an empty glass, the wine he would fill it with would surely be from the vineyards on the eastern slopes of Helan Mountains. Located at 38°N, this is a golden region for grape-planting. If he could pick only one kind of wine from this part of the world, the choice would be a tough one. The slopes are home to hundreds of vineyards, and each of their bottles is exquisite. If God could have a day to sample them all, then he would be sure to get intoxicated in this poetic land.

摄影：王鹏

金砖国宴会上的红宝石
The Ruby at the BRICS Banquet

绚丽如“红宝石”的宁夏百瑞源枸杞，出现在金砖国家领导人第九次会晤的餐桌上，成为宴会餐桌上的“明珠”，备受各国元首青睐。宁夏枸杞美誉在外，靠的是好品质和好口碑。百瑞源让宁夏枸杞以鲜明的地域文化特色，成为中国枸杞的代表性符号，荣登国际舞台。

The Bairuiyuan goji berry is as red as a ruby. This kind of goji berry was served at a banquet of the ninth BRICS Summit in 2017 and instantly caught the eyes of those assembled, becoming an immediate favourite among the leaders of the various countries. Ningxia's goji berries have earned an excellent reputation worldwide thanks to their fine quality. Bairuiyuan goji berries are an icon of the Chinese goji berry, lending Ningxia a strong regional flavour and finding favour worldwide.

传杞故事
The Legend of Golden Chinese Goji Berry Wine

张金山是宁夏最早做枸杞酒的老总。他说他要用宁夏枸杞酿造出中国味道的顶级干红。喝酒喝的是味道，一款“传杞”枸杞酒，让法国波尔多葡萄酒学院院长杜德先生高度评价，舌尖的味道是纯中国的，法国葡萄酒颜色多为玫瑰色，香气浓烈，这款酒的香气与中国人一样，含蓄内敛，金黄中充溢着贵族气息。

Zhang Jinshan was one of the earliest businessmen to invest in goji berry wine. He said, "I aim to make top-rank dry red wine with a unique Chinese style by adding goji berry." The essence of wine is its taste. This Golden Chinese Goji Berry Wine has been highly praised by Denis Dubourdieu, the director of the University of Bordeaux's Institute of Vine and Wine Sciences, with him complimenting its strong Chinese features. French red wine is mainly a burgundy colour, with a strong aroma. This Gogi Berry Wine is golden, and the taste is like the Chinese people, noble though restrained.

拍摄：杨宏峰

天然脑黄金
A Natural Brain Supply

“沙湖水暖鸟先知，正是花鲢肥嫩时。”在宁夏，游沙湖不吃沙湖大鱼头，不知塞上鱼美味。沙湖大鱼头是农产品地理标志产品。鱼肉细腻，味道鲜美，鱼头汤嫩、鲜、肥、白、滑，食过回味悠长。鱼头里含有丰富的胶原蛋白、维生素等，被称为天然的“脑黄金”，因此，也成了国宴佳品。

The humble duck is the first to know when Sand Lake becomes warm in spring, and so it is time once more to feast on the many species of carp that inhabit the lake. When visiting Sand Lake, one simply must try carp head, a renowned delicacy of this border region. The carp head has been selected as a China Geographical Indication Agro-product. It has a velvety texture and delicate flavour. The broth made from the carp is creamy white in colour with a smooth and savoury in taste that lingers in the mouth. There's all kinds of nutritious goodness in this kind of fish head, including collagens, vitamins, and so on – so much so that it has been crowned "gold for the brain" and often selected for national banquets.

李白也知滩羊皮
Even Li Bai Knew of Tan Sheepskin

据说，李白创作《将进酒》时，曾经看到过一位贵族小姐穿着羊毛皮披肩，那时正值深秋，一阵微风过后，只见身披的千金裘，毛色倾垂，犹如平湖生波，瑞雪飞舞，又恰似玉簪飞光，梨花纷纷醉落。李白受其启发，创作了“五花马，千金裘，呼儿将出换美酒，与尔同销万古愁”。这千金裘就是宁夏滩羊皮制作而成的。

An old story says that when the famed Tang poet Li Bai was writing *Bring in the Wine*, he saw a noblewoman wearing a scarf made from Tan sheepskin. It was late autumn, when a breeze blew over, the scarf rippled like wave or falling pear blossoms. Inspired by this poetic image, he wrote, “My treasured horse, my wool robe worth a thousand gold pieces! They are ready to be swapped for fine wine, and together with you I’ll wipe out the worries of ten thousand ages.” This thousand-gold-piece robe he mentions was made from Ningxia Tan sheepskin.

一条葡萄黄金种植带
A Golden Region for Grape-planting

葡萄是葡萄酒的原料，所以说好葡萄酒是种出来的。全球绝大多数葡萄园位于南北纬 30° 至 50° 之间，在这条著名的葡萄酒纬度线上，阳光适合酿酒葡萄的生长和成熟，山地、丘陵是葡萄树最喜欢落地生根的家园。法国波尔多、勃艮第，意大利托斯卡纳，美国加州纳帕山谷……宁夏贺兰山东麓也在这个纬度内，不同于新老世界，它被全球葡萄酒业界人士誉为“葡萄界的新新世界”。

Wine is made out of grapes, and so people always say to “plant good wine”. Most vineyards are limited to parts of the globe between the 30° and the 50° in latitude in both the Northern and Southern Hemispheres. Within this famous “golden latitude”, sunlight is plentiful enough for both growing and ripening. Mountains and highlands are grapes’ favourite places. Examples include Bordeaux, Burgundy in France; Toscana in Italy; and Napa Valley in the United States. The eastern slopes of Helan Mountains are also in this range. And to distinguish it from the New World and the Old World in wine terms, Ningxia has been called “the New New World” by wine critics.

摄影：吴宏林

那一抹红
Red

明代医药学家李时珍所著《本草纲目》记载“枸杞子甘平而润，性滋补……能补肾、润肺、生精、益气，此乃平补之药。全国入药杞子，皆宁产也。”宁夏的这抹红，聚焦中宁县。中宁的土壤和昼夜温差，加之黄河水和清水河水的混灌，使得中宁枸杞色艳皮薄、大小适中、肉厚籽少、品质超群，是唯一被载入新中国药典的枸杞品种，中宁县也被评为“中国枸杞之乡”。

The famous Ming dynasty herbologist Li Shizhen recorded in his *Compendium of Materia Medica,* “Goji berry is mild and nourishing… It can nourish kidneys and lungs, enhance a man’s virility, and increase one’s energy. It can be used as a very mild and safe medicine. All medical goji berries are produced in Ningxia.” Red goji berries are mainly grown in Zhongning County. With the right soil and right temperature difference between day and night, plus the mixed irrigation of the Yellow River and the Qingshui River, goji berries in Zhongning are full in shape, bright in colour, thin skinned, the right size, and have only little seeds. These features indicate it has very fine quality, and so it was the only goji berry variety recorded in the *Pharmacopoeia of the People’s Republic of China*. And Zhongning County is called the “China’s goji berry town”.

摄影：李国

供图：宁夏画报社

长在彭阳的“摇钱树”

Money Growing on Trees in Pengyang

人都说望梅止渴，可在宁夏，提杏会生津。由于彭阳的土壤含有大量的钾，种出来的杏子不仅富含钾元素，维生素 C 和硒也比普通的杏子要多，而且低糖、酸度适中，口感极佳。还可以加工成果干儿、果脯、果丹皮、果酱等，宁夏人最爱的甘草杏和蜜杏也是彭阳出产的味道最好。作为“国家地理标志产品”的红梅杏一斤卖到了 30 元，成了名符其实的“摇钱树”。

A Chinese idiom goes “The prospect of plums will quench thirst”. In Ningxia, however, the mere mention of apricots will serve the purpose. The soil in Pengyang abounds in potassium, so apricots here are not only rich in potassium, but also vitamins and selenium. In addition, they’re low on sugar but not too sour, and that’s why they’re so tasty. Apricots here can also be made into dried apricots, apricot rolls or marmalade. Some particular favourites among Ningxia natives are licorice apricots and sweetened apricots. Pengyang produces the best of these treats. Red apricots were picked as China Geographical Indication Agro-products and cost around 30 yuan for 500g. Money seems growing on these trees.

香水梨

Fragrant Pears

秋收入冬后，海原的果农用罐盆把香水梨储存于冷室，或在院内、房上用麦草盛装，食用时拿出置于冷水之中，浸泡30分钟，果外褪出一层厚厚的冰壳，打碎冰壳果子解冻即可食用。到春天冰雪融化之时，冻硬的香水梨开始融化，颜色转为棕黑色，果瓤全化成了果汁，喝一口，甘凉透心，润肺止咳、清胃泻火，亦能醒酒。

After the autumn harvest, fruit-growers put fragrant pears into jars and keep them in cold rooms, or cover them with wheat stalks in courtyards or on rooftops. When they want to eat some, they take them out and soak them in cold water for 30 minutes. A thick ice shell will form outside the pears. Then they will break the shell and enjoy the defrosted pears. For the rest, when spring comes and the snow melts, the pears will also melt into a brown juice. This pear juice is sweet and cool. It can nourish your lungs, clean your stomach and can even cure a hangover.

摄影：陶克图

供图：宁夏画报社

铺在人间的红地毯
A Red Carpet

9月的平罗黄渠桥，宽阔平整的林荫乡道，最惹人的是遮天蔽日的红辣椒，洋洋洒洒铺排着，就那么一点点消磨着时光，缓缓释放内心的火热与激情，最后留下艳丽的身体，来调剂人们平淡如水的日子。生活需要“辣”的佐料，只是此刻，只想在这人间的红地毯上走一走，享受火辣辣的快意。

Pingluo County’s Huangquqiao Town in September is a vibrant, colourful place. Boulevards provide shade, and what most catches your eye is those red chilies, laid out neatly on the vast ground. As time passes by, these dried chilies will exude their passion and through their flamboyant “bodies”, spicing up our otherwise monotomous life. Life needs a little bit of spice and one can almost feel the spiciness when seeing this chili-composed red carpet.

乡村赤脚医生金银花
Honeysuckle, the “Village Doctor”

宁夏农民给金银花起了一个洋气的外号叫“先生”。乡间地头，只要有土地就有金银花。它耐寒耐旱耐碱，刚开花的时候花是银色，那些银色的花渐渐地就变成了金黄色。金银花夏天就是宝贝，劳作的农民随手摘一些吃在嘴里，生津解渴，还能防蚊虫叮咬。偶尔有个头疼脑热，喝上一碗金银花泡的茶水，发一身汗，什么毛病都没了，基本不用去医院。

Local villagers call honeysuckle “Doctor”. As long as there’s soil, honeysuckle will grow. It endures cold weather and dry alkaline soil. When it first blooms, it’s silver in colour, but gradually its blossoms turn to gold. It’s vital to villagers’ life in summer. When farming in the field, they will grab some into their mouth, for it keeps insects away, helps produce saliva, and slakes thirst. When one doesn’t feel well, drinking some honeysuckle tea will make one sweat out the sickness. Since it can cure so many symptoms, local villagers don’t need to go to the hospital very often.

煤雕
Coal Carving

你可曾想过煤炭不仅能燃烧，还能作为艺术品收藏？当地的能工巧匠觉得“太西煤”漂亮又金贵，舍不得烧，就用浮雕圆雕等技法，将贺兰山岩画、黄河文化和宁夏地域文化特色，雕刻在煤块上，经过 12 道纯手工制作工序，将自然艺术的杰作与人类艺术创作融为一体，创作出一种新的艺术形式——煤雕，赋予了煤炭艺术生命。

Can you believe that not only can coal be used to burn, but it can also be made into art? Taixi Coal is very expensive and precious, so instead of simply burning it, craftsmen in Ningxia created a new form of art: coal carving. They make it into sculptures and reliefs, some of them imitating the rock art of Helan Mountains, some of them employing the regional art styles of the Yellow River and Ningxia province. Coal carving requires 12 manual procedures. It's a perfect combination of the art of nature and the art of mankind, and it brings new life to coal after thousands of years.

思乡情浓的大米
Nostalgic Rice

小时候，妈妈没有奶水，就把大米碾碎，用箩筐筛子过滤，打来井水熬米糊糊。长大后，无论到任何地方，一口就能吃出宁夏大米的味道。每次吃，眼前就出现临别桥头的妈妈，一边吃，一边淌眼泪，眼泪淌出来了，心情就晴朗了。吃到宁夏大米，无论什么时候，也不论在哪里，你都不会迷路，你都会找到回故乡的小路，你都能听到妈妈站在村头小桥上喊你回家吃饭的声音。

When I was a baby, my mother couldn't produce breast milk, and so she would crush rice and filter it with a sieve. Then she cooked it into congee with water from the well. After I grew up, no matter where I go, I can always tell the taste of Ningxia rice. Every time when I have Ningxia rice, the memory of that day when my mother sent me off from the bridge will come up. Also welling up are my tears, which blur my eyes but brighten up my heart. With this simple taste of rice, I'll never feel lost no matter where I go. I'll always find the way home and hear my mother standing on the bridge and asking me to come home for dinner.

一杯一世界
The World in a Glass of Wine

如果说赤霞珠是葡萄酒中的贵妇人，桃红酒则更像是一位隐匿深闺的清丽少女，非至情至好的知己不能相识。不管年轻人还是资深酒友都喜欢它绚丽多姿的色彩，樱桃粉、三文鱼肉红、浅桃红、杏桃色、浆果红……仅仅在视觉上就能让人胃口大开。一杯一世界，宁夏酒庄这么多，你要到哪一家呢？

If Sauvignon is a noble lady among wine, rosé is more like an innocent maiden in her chamber who is exclusively known to a few bosom friends. It is beloved by all wine lovers, veteran or rookie. It features a subtly different variety of colours: cherry pink, salmon pink, peach pink, apricot, berry red... The colour by itself looks appetizing. You can see a world in a glass of wine. There are so many vineyards in Ningxia, which will be your pick?

摄影：李旭竹

石头缝里蹦出来的西瓜
Watermelons Coming out of Rocks

每年七八月份来中卫旅游的人，都会被高速公路旁望不到边的瓜地所震撼，以至于有人说，“夏天到中卫，一为看风景，二为吃西瓜”。硒砂瓜，被称为“石头缝里长出的西瓜”，个大皮厚，甘甜爽口，富含人体必需的多种微量元素，被誉为“宁夏中部干旱带的精华，石头缝里蹦出来的珍品”。

Tourists who travel in July and August into Zhongwei City are sure to be shocked by the endless watermelon fields along the highways. Some people even say, “Visit Zhongwei in summer for the sightseeing and the melon eating.” Xisha melons have been dubbed “the melons that come from rocks”, because the soil is composed of a lot of limestone rocks, melons here are big and juicy with a thick skin. It also contains multiple micronutrients, and that’s why it’s been remarked that “the essence of the dry areas of mid-Ningxia is the treasure that pops out from the rocks”.

送给世界一份温暖
A Bit of Warmth Dedicated to the World

公元 1272 年，马可·波罗穿越西夏旧地，在贺兰山北部发现了一种黑色的“会燃烧的石头”，这就是“太西煤”。“太西煤”因产于太原以西的贺兰山而得名。这种煤具有低灰、低硫、低磷和高发热量等品质，俗称“太西乌金”。当地矿工的孩子提起父辈们，会很自豪地说，爸爸井下的工作很辛苦，可黑暗中掘出的却是送给世界的温暖和光亮。

In 1272, when Marco Polo was travelling across Ningxia, he found a kind of burning rock which came to be known as Taixi Coal, literally coal to the west of Taiyuan. The coal mine is in Helan Mountains, west of Taiyuan, thus the name Taixi. Being low in dust, sulfur and phosphorus but high in calorific value, it has been called “Taixi Black Gold”. When the younger generation talks about the stories of their fathers, they will proudly say the work was hard, but what they dug out is something that brings light and warmth to the world.

"闫家军"的五代紫色传承
The Yan Family's Unique Skills

贺兰石开采后，可以制砚，始于康熙年间宁夏府台及其随从张云亭。张云亭将其祖传制砚技术传于继子闫万庆和闫万年，自此开启了"闫家军"贺兰石守望者的征程。几世纪过去了，闫家传人出品了人民大会堂宁夏厅气势磅礴的大型挂屏、人物浮雕和作为1997年香港回归赠物的贺兰砚《牧归》等经典作品。贺兰砚制作技术列入了国家非物质文化遗产名录。

After Helan rock is mined, it can be made into inkstones. It was during the reign of the Kangxi emperor in the Qing dynasty when the governor and his follower Zhang Yunting started making inkstones from such rock. Zhang passed down his inkstone-making technique to his adopted sons, Yan Wanqing and Yan Wannian, who embarked the family's craftsmanship journey. More than a century later the descendants of the Yan family made a huge hanging panel and relief for the Ningxia Hall in the Great Hall of the People, as well as a classic inkstone called *Returning from Grazing* as a present at the Handover of Hong Kong in 1997. Helan inkstone-making is listed in the *Book of Chinese Intangible Cultural Heritage*.

摄影：陶克图

千金裘
Luxurious Fur Robe

"五花马，千金裘，呼儿将出换美酒，与尔同销万古愁。"滩羊裘皮不仅是李白笔下一带而过的一件大衣，更是上天铺洒在宁夏滩的一袭洁白如玉的袍子。在这里，人们不仅吃到了肥美鲜香的滩羊肉，还穿上了雪亮莹润、轻柔暖和的裘皮大衣。谁说宁夏人民不幸福，坐拥千金裘，万古愁思都消解。

"My treasured horse, my wool robe worth a thousand gold pieces! They are ready to be swapped for fine wine, and together with you I'll wipe out the worries of ten thousand ages." This wool robe is not merely something that Li Bai, the famous Poet of the Tang dynasty, mentioned in passing – it's also a robe laid in Ningxia, as pure as jade and as white as snow. Here, not only can one enjoy the delicious taste of local Tan lamb, but one can also try on the white, light and warm sheepskin coats made from their wool. Ningxia people are really lucky to have been granted this gift from nature. This luxurious sheepskin can wipe out all the worries.

摄影：左鸣远

土豆豆变成金蛋蛋
From Potato to Golden Egg

"土豆、洋芋、马铃薯"在西吉其实指的是同一种东西，是西吉人的宝贝，更多的时候称"洋芋"。"洋芋"是西吉人赖以生存的口粮之一，蒸洋芋、烤洋芋、煮洋芋、炖洋芋……一日三餐都离不开。"我一辈子也没见过五斤多的洋芋蛋。""洋芋王"成了村里的绿色食品明星，洋芋换了装束，土豆豆变成了金蛋蛋，为西吉捧回了"中国马铃薯之乡"的荣誉。

Tudou, Yangyu and Malingshu all refer to potatoes in Xiji, but they are most often called Yangyu, meaning "foreign sweet potato". They are the treasure of the Xiji people. Potatoes are a staple food for Xiji people. Steamed, roasted, boiled, poached… they are indispensable to every meal. "I never saw a potato that weighs more than 2.5 kilograms." The "Potato King" has become a bio-food celebrity in local villages. Potatoes here have transformed from ordinary food into "golden eggs" – and the town has won the title of "China's Potato Town".

与岩羊的一面之缘
A Glimpse of a Himalayan Blue Sheep

作家陈旭曾在贺兰山的汝箕沟遇到一只岩羊，跃过溪流和悬崖转眼间站在了公路上。“距离我的车 3 米远，它静静地看着我，大概 3 秒钟，一个助跑，后蹄一个弹跳，它重新跃上了石壁，沿着‘之’字形路线一直攀上了 30 多米高的峭壁顶端，停下来回望。”岩羊与人相遇会安静地对视，那一刻，你会惊觉人类的渺小，充满灵性的动物会洞察我们的心灵。

Writer Chen Xu once met a bharal (Himalayan blue sheep) in Rujigou in Helan Mountains. Jumping over brooks and cliffs, it suddenly stopped on a highway. “It was only 3 metres away from my car, and it just stared at me quietly. After about 3 seconds, with a bit of a run-up, it jumped back onto the cliff again. It jumped up for more than 30 metres following a zig-zag course, and after it reached the top, it turned back and looked at me again.” That moment of them staring at each other can help remind us that humans are but one species in this wide world, and these sagacious animals can read our minds.

摄影：陶克图

摄影：韩胜利

枸杞红了
Ripe Goji Berries

“采摘忙，歌飞扬，满坡的枸杞染夕阳，树树红果刺锋芒，小心翼翼竹篮装。”每年6月中下旬，枸杞红了，采摘是最热闹的事，枸杞园里多是女人和孩子，自然欢声笑语多，大家都比着摘，看谁家摘的多。枸杞果子虽然小，但你要吃20多粒就会流鼻血，只能尝尝。枸杞有特殊的强身健体的药用价值。宁夏人平时做菜、喝茶时都要放点儿枸杞，是与柴米油盐等一样的生活必需品。

“Busy with berry picking, the air is filled with joy and song. The whole slope is covered with goji berries as red as the sun. Beware of their thorns, and to my baskets they belong.” When goji berries ripen in late June, picking is the grandest time of year in these villages. The pickers are mainly women and children who laugh and chat while competing to see who can pick the most. Small in size, 20 goji berries would cause a nose-bleed. The key is to have the right amount, and then it will show its special medicinal effect. For Ningxia natives, they put it in dishes, in their tea, and so on. To them it is like salt or soy sauce, a necessary ingredient to their diet.

甘草，中药之国老

Chinese Liquorice, the Treasure of Traditional Chinese Medicine

甘草是中药中常用的药材之一，不少中药药方都会搭配甘草，可谓“十方九草”。诸药中甘草为君，治七十二种乳石毒，解一千二百般草木毒，调和众药有功，故有“国老”之号。清代赵瑾叔《本草诗》曾说，九土精英色正黄，药中甘草入诸方。部分上下俱无犯，性适寒温两不妨。宁夏甘草色红皮细、骨重粉足、条干顺直、口面新鲜，更合药理，有“西镇甘草”“西正草”之称。曾经有颗“甘草王”，长 1.4 米，重十多公斤。

Chinese liquorice is one of the most common herbs used in Chinese medicine. Most traditional prescriptions contain Chinese liquorice, almost 9 out of every 10. Chinese Liquorice is very mild, like a gentleman's manner. It can cure 72 kinds of symptoms and 1200 kinds of herbal poisons, and it can work well together with a lot of other herbs, earning its nickname “the treasure of traditional Chinese medicine”. In Zhao Jinshu's *Poem of Herbs* he commented that Chinese liquorice is top of all medicines, it's in yellow colour and can be used in most prescriptions, because it has a very mild effect. The skin of Chinese liquorice grown in Ningxia is red and very thin. The dried liquorice sticks are all large in size, and the cross-sections of liquorice chips are all very fresh, enhancing their medicinal value. It is also called the Liquorice of Xizhen or Xizheng Liquorice. One liquorice stick even grows as long as 1.4 metres and weighs more than 10 kilograms – making it truly the Liquorice King.

羊羔肉酒

Lamb-infused Alcohol

宁夏羊羔肉酒历史悠久，以灵武特有的地产羊羔肉、宁夏枸杞、灵武长红枣等为原料精酿而成，呈琥珀色，入口香甜，微辣，药用价值很高。常饮此酒可延年益寿。作为药酒，早在李时珍的《本草纲目》中就有记载。清雍正皇帝曾御批：“在宁夏出一种羊羔酒，……朕甚爱饮他，寻些送来，不必多进，不足用时再发旨意，不要过百瓶，特密谕。”绵长的酒体和浓厚的酒文化，是当地百姓的细腻生活和平和心态的体现。

Lamb-infused alcohol in Ningxia enjoys a long and storied history. The beverage is made with Lingwu lamb, goji berries and Lingwu jujube, among other ingredients. Amber in colour, the alcohol tastes fragrant and sweet with a bit of a spicy kick to it, and also has medical effect. Drinking on a frequent basis can do a person's health a world of good. It was recorded in the most famous Chinese herbology work, *Compendium of Materia Medica* as a medical alcohol as far back as the 16th century. Emperor Yongzheng of the Qing dynasty wrote a commentary, remarking “There's a lamb-infused alcohol in Ningxia, it's quietly lovely. Go and find some, bring back no more than 100 bottles and not in large quantity. Further command will be given in case of additional requirement. But keep this order a secret.” The region's good alcohol and drinking culture both show people's attitudes and their refined way of life.

长枣最长情
Lingwu Jujube

“一日吃三枣，青春不会老。”灵武农民芮玉瑞说，小时候，每年秋天父亲担着担子去卖枣，一天走到吴忠，两天走到银川，给我们换回上学的钱和日用品。68 岁的李银老汉说，我也说不清家里有多少树，反正一年收入几万元，光 8 株百年老树收入就 8000 元。收枣子那几天车水马龙，全国各地来的人，每天运走几千公斤。最好的枣送给最亲的人，灵武长枣最长情。

Three jujubes a day keeps a doctor away. Lingwu villager Rui Yurui said, “When I was little, my dad would load two baskets of jujubes on the carrying pole to sell in autumn. It took him a whole day to get to Wuzhong, and two days to Yinchuan. With the money he earned he was able to pay for our tuition fees and household necessities.” 68-year-old Li Yin said, “I don’t know how many trees there are in my orchard, but regardless, I have tens of thousands of yuan income every year. The 8 old trees which are all over a hundred years old alone bring me 8000 yuan. ”In the season of jujube picking, people come from all over the country and they take away several thousand kilos of jujubes every day. In China, people give jujubes to their families and close friends, and Lingwu jujube is no doubt the best in quality.

供图：宁夏画报社

盐池羊毛地毯
Yanchi Wool Rugs

滩羊毛是盐池特产，走进盐池人家会发现，他们身上穿的、炕上铺的、墙上挂的、柜子上摆的、身上背的大多是羊毛羊皮制成品。传统的地毯都是由人工捻成的，人们会在捻线的过程中唱出各种谣曲来，别有一种风情。欣赏一条地毯的制作过程，经纬纵横、飞梭传线，完全可以上升到美学的角度。盐池手工地毯是活着的文物，讲述着历史的传奇。

The wool of the native Tan sheep is a local specialty of Yanchi. If one visits local Yanchi people, one will immediately notice what they wear, what they put on their *kang* (bed-stove), what they hang on their walls, what they put over their cupboards, and what they are carrying on backs are mostly wool products. Traditional rugs are handmade. When workers are interweaving threads, they sing all kinds of folk songs. This working scene itself is like a painting. Watching the rug-making process is an artistic feast to the eye: warp and weft strands of the weave being interwoven, needles plying. The rug-making craft in Yinchi is a living antique and a vivid legend.

论斤卖的“黑金”
Black Gold Sold by the Kilo

宁夏有一种“罗加煤”，是论公斤卖的，一公斤就得一两千元，被称为煤中的“黑金”，全世界都在垂涎。“罗加”不是地名，而是用一个波兰人的名字来命名的煤样指标。这得感谢工程师江培林，数年中，无数次碰壁受挫，他坚持以严谨的研究态度和吃苦精神，最终得到国际的认可。罗加是“黑金”的标准，江培林是技术和学问人的标杆。

Roga Coal is produced in Ningxia. Sold for around 1000 – 2000 yuan per kilogram, Roga Coal has been dubbed a black gold among coals, and is popular worldwide. Roga is not a place name but a person’s name. It is named after the Roga Index, proposed by Polish chemist B. Roga in 1949. Chinese engineer Jiang Peilin did numerous experiments, went through uncountable failures with a strict and dedicated attitude and finally developed a Chinese anthracite. Because it’s the finest quality variety Jiang ever created, it was named Roga Coal. It’s as precious as black gold, and Jiang Peilin is a model for all researchers and technologists.

建设美丽新宁夏 共圆伟大中国梦
时代 · 行进
Amazing Achievements
1958
2018

建设美丽新宁夏，共圆伟大中国梦

Build a Beautiful New Ningxia, and Accomplish the Grand Chinese Dream.

2018年，宁夏回族自治区成立60周年之际，习近平总书记专门题写"建设美丽新宁夏，共圆伟大中国梦"的贺匾，贺匾中央部分以中国红为底色，衬托山水暗纹，体现天蓝、地绿、水美的美丽宁夏；边框由60朵高浮雕马兰花纹组成，象征宁夏回族自治区成立60周年的光辉历程；两个如意匾托表达了对宁夏人民万事顺意、吉祥美好的深切祝愿。贺匾凸显了党中央对建设美丽新宁夏的美好祝愿，为宁夏发展指明了前进方向，提供了基本遵循，激励着宁夏各族人民振奋精神、实干兴宁，为实现经济繁荣、民族团结、环境优美、人民富裕，确保与全国同步建成全面小康社会的目标，为建设美丽新宁夏、共圆伟大中国梦而努力奋斗。

In 2018, with the 60th anniversary of the Ningxia Hui Autonomous Prefecture, Chinese President Xi Jinping inscribed a congratulatory plaque with the words, "Build a beautiful new Ningxia, and accomplish the grand Chinese dream." The base colour on the central portion was China red, setting off dark langscape patterns in sky blue and deep green that evoke the landscape of Ningxia. The boarder is carved with the design of sixty Malan flowers, symbolising the glorious sixty-year history of the prefecture. The two supports, in a " ruyi " design, symbolise the high level of regard and care of the Central Communist Party, the path that they've provided to Ningxia for further development. Ningxia people are motivated to work hard with higher spirit for buoyant economy, ethnic solidarity, pleasant enviromment and well-off life, as well as ensure the accomplishment of a moderately prosperous society in all aspects in tandem with the rest of the country. All will strive to build a beautiful new Ningxia and together accomplish the glorious Chinese dream.

供图：《共产党人》杂志社

供图：宁夏画报社

铸造 3D 打印“领跑者”
A World Leader in 3D Printing

在中央电视台《大国重器》节目中，展示了一款由宁夏共享集团自主研发的砂芯 3D 打印机。它的体积比目前国外最大的机型还要大两倍，攻克了材料、工艺、软件、设备及集成等技术难题，被授权专利近 50 项，实现了国内首创，成为“领跑者”。铸造 3D 打印，展示了中国制造的实力。

The Pillars of a Great Power is a documentary made by China Central Television (CCTV) to showcase the great strides China has made in the equipment manufacturing industry. One episode shows a self-developed 3D printing device using sand mould, invested in and constructed by KOCEL Group Ltd. It is twice as big as the biggest 3D printer developed abroad, and has solved many technical difficulties in areas such as material, manufacturing technique, software and assembly etc., picking up more than 50 patents along the way. It is now a leading representative of domestic innovation and a leader in 3D printing. The 3D printer is a testimony to the technological and industrial power of China.

朋友圈越来越大
Expanding Circle of Friends

宁夏，既不沿边，也不靠海，一度被称为中国对外开放的“孤岛”。从被国家批准为内陆开放型经济试验区后，宁夏逐渐发展成为辐射西部、面向全国、融入全球的中阿合作先行区、内陆开放示范区、丝绸之路经济带战略支点。从内陆腹地走向丝路前沿，宁夏的全面开放已不再是传说，宁夏的“国际范儿”越来越足、“朋友圈”越来越大。

As an inland province, Ningxia has no national borders or coastlines. It was once called the “isolated island” during the process of China’s opening up. After being approved as an inland opening-up pilot economic zone by the State Council, Ningxia has gradually radiated its influence throughout Western China and been further connected to the rest of the country and the whole world. It has been a pilot area that witnessed the cooperation between China and the Middle-East. It has become a model area among inland open-up economic zones and a strategic pivot on the Silk Road Economic Belt.

摄影：左鸣远

社会主义是干出来的
Socialism Is Achieved Through Hard Work

在宁夏中东部有一片3484平方公里的国家能源化工基地，全球单体规模最大的煤制油项目在这里诞生。习近平总书记2016年7月19日视察宁东能源化工基地，工人们涌到高高的作业平台上，齐声向总书记问好，万千声音汇聚，像潮水般激荡。总书记深受感染："我的心情也很激动，看到了社会主义的大厦在一砖一瓦地建起来。在场的工人兄弟姐妹们，我对你们充满了敬意，社会主义是干出来的！"

In the central eastern parts of Ningxia lies an energy and chemical industry base some 3484 square kilometres in size. This base is home to the world's biggest coal-to-liquid project . On July 19th, 2016 when Chinese President Xi Jinping inspected the base, the researchers and workers all gathered at the working platform to welcome him. Their warm and delighted voice sounded like tide rising and falling. Xi Jinping was deeply touched, and said, "Comrades, today I feel a true sense of excitement, seeing our grand mansion of socialism being built brick by brick. Brothers and sisters, I have such deep respect for you! Socialism is achieved through hard work."

盐碱滩变成了花果园
Salt Marsh Turned into Orchard

孙家滩是一个移民开发区，以数万亩无污染、无公害的土地为媒，建设了万头奶牛场、万亩高酸苹果园、日光温室大棚、连栋智能温室育苗工厂、净菜生产厂、大枣种植资源园等项目。孙家滩已成为西北领先、示范全国的现代农业综合示范基地，是我国发展高酸苹果产业的首选之地。昔日的盐碱滩变成了花果园。

Sunjiatan is a migrant development zone. On around 10 square kilometres of uncontaminated, pollutant-free land there is a dairy farm with 10,000 cows, 6.7 square kilometres of orchards growing apples with high malic acid content, sunlight-supported greenhouses, an intelligent greenhouse seeding factory, a vegetable-processing factory, and multiple jujube orchards, among many other projects. Sunjiatan has become an advanced model agricultural base in North-western China. It's also the best place to plant high malic acid apples in China. Now this land, once a salt marsh, has become a bounteous orchard.

沙坡头，世界环保 500 佳
Shapotou, Global 500 Roll of Honour

地处腾格里沙漠边缘上的沙坡头治沙模式，超越了民族、语言和疆界，成为全人类共同的精神和物质财富。美国《国家地理杂志》说，沙坡头把扎麦草方格的技术介绍给了世界。国际上 60 多位专家说，这么大面积的流沙被固定，世界上还没有过，中国人了不起！这是世上绝无仅有的人工奇迹。沙坡头获得联合国授予的世界环境保护“全球 500 佳”金质奖章。

Shapotou, located at the edge of Tengger Desert, is a district of Zhongwei City. It is renowned for its unusual method of dune stabilization. Going beyond ethnicity, language and geography, it is a part of a material and spiritual commonwealth of humanity. In the 1980s, *National Geographic* first introduced Shapotou's grass-grid to the outside world. More than 60 foreign experts said, nowhere else has such a big area of flowing sand been stabilized, making this a true achievement of the Chinese people. It can be seen as a man-made miracle. Shapotou's desert ecological restoration program was listed on the Global 500 Roll of Honour by the United Nations Environment Programme.

中部干旱带上的奇迹
Miracle in Central Ningxia's Dry Zone

埃德加·斯诺在《西行漫记》中写道：“我骑马到红城子去，那是一个风景幽美的小镇，以盛产梨、苹果、葡萄的美丽果园著称。”这里所说的红城子，就是今天宁夏中部同心县罗山脚下的一个村庄。宁夏中部，历来以干旱闻名，但这样秀丽的村庄却非常多，就像一颗颗珍珠散落在宁夏大地上。这是宁夏人民与大自然抗衡的传奇与见证。

In Edgar Snow's *Red Star over China*, he wrote, "I rode out to Hongchengzi (Red City), a pretty little town famous for its beautiful fruit gardens of pears, apples, and grapes…" Hongchengzi here is a village on the foot of Luoshan Mountains in Tongxin County. Central Ningxia is renowned for its dryness, but it has never wanted for this kind of beautiful, charming villages and towns which litter the landscape of Ningxia like pearls. These beautifully built villages are a miracle achieved through Ningxia people's unceasing struggle against the hard climate here.

摄影：辛怡丽

黄河岸边升起璀璨明珠

A Pearl along the Yellow River

不少顾客在银川阅海湾中央商务区的"Y-BOX 无人智能超市"体验了智能购物。银川阅海湾中央商务区是宁夏首个高端、现代、国际化的商务区，创造了很多宁夏乃至西部第一。创新的发展理念、超高的人气指数、超前的发展定位以及多元化的产业布局使这里日渐繁荣，成为黄河岸边一颗正在升起的璀璨明珠。

A lot of customers have been lucky enough to experience shopping in the Y-Box AI-powered supermarket in Yinchuan Yuehaiwan Central Business District, which is the first high-end, modern and international business centre, having achieved a whole swathe of firsts or bests in Ningxia or even in the west of the country. Boasting innovative development ideas, skyrocketing popularity, an advanced development orientation and diverse industrial distributions, it is fast becoming a pearl rising from the waves along the Yellow River.

宁夏黄河大桥的密度

The Density of Ningxia Yellow River Bridges

自从 1970 年宁夏建成第一座黄河大桥——叶盛黄河公路桥开始，结束了被黄河阻隔、有渡无桥的历史，自此改渡为桥。在黄河流经宁夏 397 公里的重要渡口建设桥梁，使宁夏成为黄河上架桥密度最大的省份，平均 36.1 公里的河段就有一座公路大桥。黄河大桥是宁夏人民智慧的结晶，一座座桥梁就是一步步迈向新时代高质量发展的脚步。

Since the completion of the first Yellow River bridge in Ningxia in 1970 – the Yesheng Yellow River Roadway Bridge – the era of the Yellow River acting as a barrier was over, and now the ferries in this section of the river have become bridges. Ningxia is the province with the highest density of bridges on the Yellow River. On average there is a road bridge every 36.1 kilometres. Yellow River bridges are the crystallization of the wisdom of the local people. The bridges are a symbol of the step-by-step progress being made towards the high-quality development in the new era.

摄影：钟培源

摄影：陶克图

以新优势领跑国内新能源
A New Energy Role Model

宁夏是全国风能、太阳能资源最为丰富的地区之一，新能源装机位居全国第二位，新能源年发电量位居全国第三位……是全国新能源行业的领跑者，成为全国首个新能源综合示范区。新能源就是清洁能源、绿色能源，是提升生存环境的动力手。

Ningxia is one of the provinces that's most rich in wind power and solar energy in China. They have the second largest number of new energy equipment, and their total annual production of electrical energy via new energy ranks third in the country… Ningxia is a leader in new energy application and has become the first new energy demonstration zone in China. Clean and green, new energy is the key to improving our environment.

全国人进沙退第一省
The First Province to Push Back the Desert

宁夏地处毛乌素、腾格里以及乌兰布和沙漠边缘，荒漠化、沙化严重。防沙治沙，考验着人们生存的意志与智慧，彰显着人类和自然依存共生的过程。多年来，宁夏实施了三北防护林、退耕还林、天然林保护以及“六个百万亩”林业等生态工程，实现了“沙逼人退”向“人进沙退”的历史性转变，成为全国人进沙退第一省。

Ningxia is on the edge of the Mu Us Desert, Tengger Desert and Ulan Buh Desert, so desertification has always been an issue of paramount importance. Sand control and anti-desertification show the local people's willpower and wisdom, and provide insight into the processes by which humans coexist with nature. Through recent years, ecology projects like the Shelter Forest System in Three-North Regions of China, farmland-to-forest restoration, virgin forest protection, and the "Six Forests of One Million Mu"(667 square kilometres) have really made positive changes for the environment in Ningxia. Ningxia has thus become the first province to "push the desert back" in China.

有荒凉的沙漠，没有荒凉的人生

There Is Desolate Desert Here, but No Desolate Life.

银川 iBi 育成中心作为宁夏众多“双创”基地中的一家，如今已成为创业者的沃土。这里汇聚了近 500 家创业企业和 1 万名来自五湖四海的创业者，他们中有智能化技术专家、归国留学人员、沿海返乡创客、自主择业的军转干部……国务院总理李克强视察这里时，曾勉励他们说，这里有荒凉的沙漠，却没有荒凉的人生。

Yinchuan iBi Yucheng Centre (Information & Biology & Intellectual Property Industrialization) is one of the startup bases in the “Mass Entrepreneurship and Innovation” movement. It has already become a promised land for entrepreneurs. It’s home to around 500 startup enterprises and 10,000 entrepreneurs from all over the country. Some of them are experts in intelligentization, some of them are returnees from abroad, some of them once worked in coastline cities now decide to come back to their hometowns, and some are demobilized military officers... During Premier Li Keqiang’s inspection, he encouraged them, saying, “There is desolate desert here, but no desolate life.”

长征永远在路上

The Long March on the Way

2016 年 7 月 18 日，习近平总书记到宁夏考察，在将台堡参观三军会师纪念馆时说，红军长征创造了中外历史的奇迹。革命理想高于天，不怕牺牲、排除万难去争取胜利，面对形形色色的敌人决一死战、克敌制胜，这些都是长征精神的内涵。我们要继承和弘扬好伟大的长征精神。这次专程来这里，就是缅怀先烈、不忘初心，走新的长征路。今天是实现“两个一百年”奋斗目标的新长征。我们这一代人要走好我们这一代人的长征路。推进中国特色社会主义事业的新长征要持续接力、长期进行，我们每代人都要走好自己的长征路，长征永远在路上。

On July 18, 2016, Xi Jinping visited the Memorial Hall of Three Joined Forces in Jiangtaibu as part of his inspection tour of Ningxia Hui Autonomous Region, calling the Long March of the Red Army “a miracle of world history”. Xi Jinping summarized the spiritual core of the Long March: the revolutionary ideals of utter importance, the fervent wish for victory in spite of sacrifice and difficulties, the vigour and wisdom to face all kinds of enemies, fight fearlessly, and vanquish them at last. Xi said, we must inherit and promote this magnificent spirit. We make this special trip here to cherish the memory of the martyrs, remain true to our original aspiration, and set off on a new Long March. Today, we are starting the Long March of the Two Centennial Goals. Our generation must walk our own Long March. We must continuously carry out the new Long March of promoting socialism with Chinese characteristics for the long term. Every generation must walk their own Long March. The Long March is on the way forever.

摄影：李振虎

我和 CBD 打了个赌
I Bet on Yinchuan CBD

七年前银川阅海湾中央商务区筹建之初，全国记协 20 多名记者在宁夏采访，一位南方日报记者说，五年以后这里将成为一颗熠熠生辉的明珠。随之，他就和朋友一起在这里投资了地产。当时，有人对此表示怀疑。不到五年宁夏用时间应验了他的投资眼光。现在这里不但是金融中心，还成为旅游观光胜地。

When construction first began on Yinchuan Yuehaiwan Central Business District 7 years ago, more than 20 journalists from the Journalists Association reported this event, and one journalist from *Nanfang Daily* (Southern Daily) said that within 5 years it will have become a rising star. He himself along with his friends invested in the district. When he said Yinchuan is a promised land for investors, many people were sceptical. However, Ningxia proved him right within the 5 years he'd claimed. It is not only a bustling business centre but also an attractive tourist destination.

云轨
Skyrail

2017 年 8 月 31 日，全球第一条云轨在银川建成通车。相比较其他轨道交通，云轨具有投入成本低、建设工期短、噪音低、景观好、更智能、更安全等优势。比亚迪董事长兼总裁王传福表示："本次云轨通车为全球各城市云轨项目树立标杆，也对全球未来城市升级，应用创新科技解决城市拥堵顽疾带来极强的示范效应！"

On August 31, 2017, the world's first Skyrail line was opened to commuters in Yinchuan. Compared with other rail transit systems, Skyrail has the advantages of low input cost, a short construction timeframe, low noise, good aesthetics, smart technology integration and high safety standards. Wang Chuanfu, chairman and president of BYD said, "This Skyrail service has set a benchmark for other Skyrail projects in various cities around the world. It also has a strong demonstrative effect on the future of global urban upgrades and the application of innovative technologies to solve urban congestion problems!"

供图：宁夏大庆办

键盘敲出的西部“智谷”
The Silicon Valley in Western China

银川 iBi 育成中心主要为培育新兴产业、孵化中小科技企业提供全方位服务。积极开发云计算、大数据、物联网、卫星应用、生物科技等新兴业态。企业可以“拎包入园”，园区免费提供网络、公共服务设施、法律服务……键盘敲出智慧，网络带动经济，被称作是宁夏的“中关村”。

Yinchuan iBi Yucheng Centre primarily provides comprehensive services for cultivating the emerging industries and incubating small and medium-sized technology enterprises. The centre actively develops emerging technologies such as cloud computing, big data, the Internet of Things, satellite applications, and biotechnology. It's fully furnished and all set up for companies to move in hassle-free, and provides free Internet, public service facilities, and legal services. Keyboards knock out new wisdom, and networks drive the economy. It has been called the "Zhongguancun" (a technology hub in Beijing and is considered China's Silicon Valley) of Ningxia.

摄影：钟培源

互联网 + 医疗是健康平台
The Health Platform Combining Internet and Medical Care

银川市智慧互联网 + 医院覆盖了全区所有社区乡镇，实现了远程医疗诊断，成为我国规模最大的互联网 + 医疗产业聚集地，包括网上微医、好大夫在线、丁香园等在内的互联网 + 医疗，方便了老百姓就诊。“互联网 + 医疗”为宁夏乃至全国老百姓带来医疗便利，是健康平台。

A telemedicine system has been put in place, connecting hospitals at the regional, municipal and county levels, as well as medical care institutions at the township level – thus providing comprehensive coverage for the "Internet plus" healthcare demo zone. It has therefore become the most prominent "Internet plus" medical care industry base. With the help of online medical platforms such as We Doctor, Haodaifu and DXY, citizens can get treatment more quickly and easily. "Internet plus" medical care brings convenience for Ningxia and even for the whole country, proving itself to be a very helpful platform.

宁夏生态纺织园惊艳全国网络媒体
Ningxia Ecological Textile Industry Park Wows Chinese Media

位于贺兰县的宁夏生态纺织产业示范园区是集色纺色织、服装、家纺、装饰产品、产业用纺织品等为一体的新型现代化生态环保集约型纺织工业基地，并同步打造成企业、产业共同体、园区、景区多位一体的循环经济体系和国家级生态纺织产业示范园区。华丽的丝织品、精致的动物玩具等创意产品生动逼真，智能量体裁衣系统、智能吊挂等先进设备熠熠生辉，惊艳了全国网络媒体宁夏行采访团。

The Ningxia Ecological Textile Industry Park located in Helan County, Ningxia, is a modernized ecological intensive textile industry base combining products such as clothes, fabric, decorative products, and industrial fabrics. It also aims to be a nation-level ecological textile demo zone and a circulated economic system that integrates enterprises, business, industrial parks and tourist attractions. Innovative products such as delicate textiles and stuffed toys are all incredibly well-made. AI-powered tailoring system, auto-delivery system and other advanced facilities wowed the journalist delegation on their visit.

绿博园，新丝路上的绿飘带
The Green Expo Garden

绿博园是银川市内面积最大的恒温植物公园，仿佛一个巨大的天然氧吧。在这里，一天内看遍四季繁花。园区内还有阿拉伯国家展园、湿地净化园、防沙示范园、葡萄酒产业区等大大小小 60 多个主题展园。绿博园是银川与中阿绿博会成员国家、新丝路沿线地区以及国内各省区市友好交流的绿飘带。

The Green Expo Garden is the largest thermostatic botanical park in Yinchuan. It's like a huge natural oxygen bar. Here, you can see the flowers of all four seasons in a single day. There are also more than 60 themed exhibition parks and halls inside, including the Arab National Exhibition Garden, the Wetland Purification Garden, the Sand-control Demonstration Garden, and the Wine Industry Zone. The Green Expo Garden is a green ribbon symbolizing the friendly exchanges between Yinchuan and members of the China-Arab Green Expo, between areas along the New Silk Road and Chinese cities and provinces.

供图：宁夏画报社

供图：宁夏画报社

宁东能源化工基地

Ningdong Energy and Chemical Industry Base

在宁夏中东部地区，有一个南北长130公里、东西宽50公里、面积约为3500平方公里的煤炭富集区——宁东能源化工基地。这是全国罕见的储量大、煤质好、地质构造简单的整装煤田。基地重点以煤炭、电力、煤化工三大产业为支撑，是全国重要的火电基地、煤化工基地和煤炭基地。

Spread across the central and eastern parts of Ningxia is a coal-enrichment region with a length of 130 kilometres from north to south, 50 kilometres from east to west, and a total area of about 3,500 square kilometres: Ningdong Energy and Chemical Industry Base. This is a rare full-scale coalfield with large reserves, good coal quality and simple geological structure. The base is supported by three major industries: coal, electric power, and coal chemical. It is one of the country's most important thermal power, coal chemical, and coal bases.

让中国制造“在银川聚合，走向世界”

Gathering “Made-in-China” Products in Yinchuan to Meet the World

银川综合保税区以生物医药、黄金珠宝、牛羊肉进出口、航空服务等产业为主，积极引领宁夏外向型经济发展，打造宁夏对外开放新门户。一位落户银川综合保税区的企业经理说：“我们总公司在深圳，当初选择落户银川的一个重要原因就是看中了银川的航空物流优势以及综保区的政策优势，我们也想借此开拓海外市场。”

The main businesses in Yinchuan Free Trade Zone are biomedicine, gold and jewelry, exportation and importation of lamb and beef, and air services. The trade zone will actively lead the development of Ningxia's export-oriented economy and create a new portal for Ningxia to open up to the outside world. A company manager in the Yinchuan Free Trade Zone said, “Our headquarters is located in Shenzhen, and one of the main reasons we chose to set up shop in Yinchuan is its advantages in terms of air freight logistics and favourable policies. Leveraging these, we aim to extend our foreign market.”

干沙滩变成了金沙滩
A Deserted Beach Transformed into a Golden Beach

20 年前，习近平同志提议福建和宁夏共同建设生态移民点，于是就有了永宁县闽宁镇原隆移民村。生态移民点是对另一种生存方式的思考。20 年过去了，闽宁镇原隆移民村已经从当年只有 8000 人的贫困移民村发展成为拥有 60000 多人的“江南小镇”，从当年的干沙滩变成了今天的金沙滩。

Twenty years ago, Comrade Xi Jinping proposed that Fujian and Ningxia jointly build an ecological resettlement site, and so a project was put together that resulted in the building of Yuanlong Migrant Village in Minning Town, Yongning County. Ecological settlements are a reflection of another way of living. Twenty years later, Yuanlong has grown from a poor migrant village with only 8,000 people to a rich and beautiful town with more than 60,000 people, from a dry beach to a golden beach.

闽宁镇沟通闽宁
Mining Town Connects Fujian and Ningxia

20 年前，福建和宁夏启动了对口扶贫协作，闽宁镇从无到有，从弱到强，见证了闽宁两省区携手从单向扶贫到互利共赢。曾经生活在贫困山区的农民走出大山，通过移民搬迁走上了脱贫致富之路。闽宁镇，这个当年由习近平同志亲自命名的扶贫移民区，从曾经的戈壁荒滩发展为常住居民 60000 余人的特色小镇，成了现代化的移民示范镇。

Twenty years ago, Fujian and Ningxia launched a collaborative poverty alleviation project. Mining Town has grown from nothing to something notable, from poor to developed. It was the site of the two provinces working closely together, helping each other from one-way poverty alleviation to mutual benefit. Peasants once living in the impoverished mountainous areas moved onto a path of getting rid of poverty through migration. Mining Town, a poverty-stricken migrant area named by Comrade Xi Jinping, has emerged from a barren stretch of the Gobi desert to a town with its own special character and more than 60,000 permanent residents. It has become a modern migrant demonstration town.

供图：宁夏画报社

路是宁夏速度的见证官
Rail and Road are the Testaments to “Ningxia Speed”

1958 年，东南角的腾格里沙漠传出了第一声宁夏人自己的火车汽笛声，自此后，“路”一直是探寻宁夏的一杆指向标，是伴随宁夏奋进的见证官。从无到有、从稀疏到密致，从包兰铁路到宝中铁路，从大古铁路到银西高铁，从省省相连到即将开通的四条高铁路线，连接了陕甘宁，实现了宁夏人的高铁梦。

In 1958, in the southeast corner of the Tengger Desert blew the whistle of the Ningxia people’s first train. Since then, “Road” has been a target for Ningxia, and a testament to Ningxia’s endeavours. From nothing to something substantial, from sparse to dense, from the Bao-Lan Railway to the Bao-Zhong Railway, from the Da-Gu Railway to the Yin-Xi High-speed Railway, from provinces being connected together to the four high-speed railway lines that will be opened to connect Shaanxi, Gansu and Ningxia; rail and road have realized Ningxia people’s high-speed dreams.

供图：宁夏画报社

戈壁滩上甜美的创举
Sweetness in the Gobi Desert

硒砂瓜被称为“石头缝里长出的西瓜”，是宁夏中卫环香山地区农民在沙砾淤积丰富的香山冲击扇区域将大量碎砂石覆盖在山地表层，利用沙砾铺压对地表所具有的节水、增温、保墒效果种植西瓜和甜瓜的一种特色种瓜模式。站在茫茫戈壁滩上，手捧硒砂瓜，不能不感慨人类的伟大。为了改变沙漠，改变荒芜，在这片土地上生存，创造了奇迹。

Xisha melon is called the “watermelon grown from rocks”. This is due to a farming technique developed by peasants surrounding the Mount Xiangshan area of Zhongwei, Ningxia. The melon seeds are put in the ground in the gravel-filled alluvial fan area. A large amount of crushed sand covers the surface of the land, with which it can save on irrigation water, while warming and protecting watermelons and muskmelons. Standing on the Gobi desert, holding a ripe Xisha melon, one can’t help but feel the greatness of mankind. In order to change the desert, change the barrenness, and survive on this land, people here have created miracles.

只跑一次就好

Getting It All Done in One Go

银川市行政审批经历了七轮审批瘦身，从五证合一、审批改备案到网上审批、证照云等创新举措，只跑一次就办好。好多事只需要打个电话或者点下鼠标就可有效解决，引来美、英、法等世界各国考察团到银川政务大厅考察。印度、埃塞俄比亚、白俄罗斯已开始复制智慧政务的银川样本。行政审批其实是以敬民之心，行简政之道。

The administrative examination and approval of Yinchuan City has experienced seven rounds of approval "slimming", with certifications being reduced from five to one, the examination and approval of the record now being done online, certificates being saved in cloud databases, and other innovative measures. One now only needs to visit the bureau once and everything can be done in one go. A lot of things can be solved by merely making a phone call or with the click of a mouse. Delegations from all over the world, such as the United States, Britain and France, visited the Yinchuan Administration Hall. India, Ethiopia, and Belarus have begun to replicate the Yinchuan model of smart government. The spirit of the city's administrative examination and approval is to streamline administration and respect the people.

供图：宁夏画报社

供港蔬菜满足港人需求
Vegetables from Ningxia Meet the Needs of Hong-Kongese

宁夏生态环境好，粮食蔬菜日照时间长，宁夏供港蔬菜跨越 2500 多公里，以黄河水洗脸，以黄土地塑形，漂洋过海，以最新鲜最原生态的形象直奔香港。从最初通过深圳等口岸再中转到香港，到经宁夏出入境检验检疫局后直供香港，“寻爱之旅”从 45—50 小时缩短到了 12—24 小时，香港市民可以品尝到更为新鲜的供港蔬菜。

Ningxia has a good ecological environment, and it's got long stretches of sunshine each year that make it perfect for grain and vegetable farming. The vegetables are irrigated by the Yellow River, and nourished in the yellow land. Then, travelling across the sea for more than 2500 Kilometres, they are transported to Hong Kong in the freshest and most untouched state. From originally being transferred through Shenzhen and other ports, to nowadays being transported directly to Hong Kong after going through the Ningxia Entry-Exit Inspection and Quarantine Bureau, this "Journey of Love" has been shortened from 45–50 hours to just 12–24 hours. Hong Kong citizens can taste an even fresher supply of vegetables now.

摄影：钟培源

创造煤制油的新历史
Writing a New Chapter in the History of Coal-to-Liquid

1923 年，德国科学家发现了煤炭间接液化技术，但随着国内油田的依次发现，该项技术逐渐淡出中国人的视野。时隔近百年，2016 年，宁夏年产 400 万吨的煤制油工厂建成并试车成功，生产出了高品质的柴油、石脑油、蜡等产品，使中国进入少数掌握煤制油工业化技术的国家行列，并达到国际领先水平。

In 1923, German scientists first developed indirect coal liquefaction technology. It was a leading processing technique at a time. However, with the frequent discovery of domestic oil fields in last century, this technique became less and less commonly used in China. After almost 100 years, in 2016, a coal-to-liquid (CTL) plant has been put in use. It can make 4.05 million tonnes of oil products annually, including diesel, naphtha, and wax. This technique breakthrough shows that China is one of the few countries that turns coal into liquids and is considerably advanced in this area.

远看上去一片海
It looks like a Wide Ocean from Afar

太阳能光伏板连接成片，一眼望不到边，远远看上去像一片海。其实是宁夏盐池总规划为2000兆瓦，占地7万亩的新能源综合示范区，成为全球最大的单体光伏项目。每年可减少二氧化碳排放约261万吨，相当于143万棵树木一年吸收的二氧化碳量。

The solar photovoltaic panels are connected together so closely that the edge cannot be seen. From a distance, it looks like a wide ocean. In fact, the Ningxia Yanchi Master Plan is to build a new energy demonstration zone to produce 2,000 megawatts and covering an area of 47 square kilometres, with the aim of becoming the world's largest single photovoltaic project. After it's built, it can reduce carbon dioxide emissions by about 2.61 million tons per year, which is equivalent to the amount of carbon dioxide absorbed by 1.43 million trees a year.

大数据的郊区
Suburbs of Big Data

“未来的中卫一定会成为中国的凤凰城。”北京企业家苟小刚说。从中国最大云渲染基地数据中心项目落户，到阿里云计算有限公司服务节点落地，再到“一带一路”空间信息走廊数据中心中卫云基地合作建设协议签订，中卫成功引进了亚马逊、360等一批国内外互联网巨头。美国ZT、工信部信息中心、中国移动等140余家云计算及配套企业相继入驻，成为北京、上海、广州等城市的数据郊区。

“In future, Zhongwei will definitely become China's Phoenix City.” said Gou Xiaogang, an entrepreneur in Beijing. Zhongwei has successfully introduced a number of domestic and foreign Internet giants such as 360 and Amazon. More than 140 cloud computing and supporting enterprises and organizations such as ZT, the Ministry of Industry and Information Technology, and China Mobile have successively settled here, and have become data centre after Beijing, Shanghai and Guangzhou.

供图：宁夏画报社

供图：宁夏画报社

滩羊银行
Beach Sheep Bank

经济学家马光远说，参观宁夏盐池，除了欣赏独特的西部风情和品尝最鲜美肥嫩的羊肉外，印象最深刻的是把“滩羊”作为货币存入银行，并对存入银行的羊支付利息。这样把羊作为货币的方法其实自古就有。盐池滩羊，作为一种特殊的“货币”，还走上了二十国集团峰会和金砖峰会的餐桌，连对羊肉非常挑剔的俄罗斯总统普京也大加赞赏。

Economist Ma Guangyuan said that during his visit to Yanchi, in addition to enjoying the unique western style landscape and culture, and tasting the most delicious and tender lamb, what impressed him most was being able to deposit Tan sheep as a currency into the bank and pay off interest. This method of using sheep as a currency has existed since ancient times. As a special “currency”, meat dishes made from Yanchi Tan sheep were also served on the G20 summit and the table of the BRICS summit. Even the Russian President Putin, who is very picky about lamb, highly praised it.

反梯度的新经济
The New Economy

转过方向你就是唯一。宁夏以反梯度的思维快速发展新经济，从“招商引资”到“造商引资”，整合各方要素资源，建立起全产业链战略联盟，以大数据、云计算等新一代信息技术为核心，着力打造通航、电竞、智慧城市、光伏等众多全产业链。在新产业、新业态、新模式上率先发展，变“跟跑”为“领跑”。

Turning back, you will find oneself alone in this new direction. Ningxia has rapidly developed a new economy with anti-gradient thinking. From “inviting investment” to “creating enterprises to attract investment”, integrating all kinds of resources, establishing a strategic alliance along the entire industry chain, and focusing on next-generation information technology such as big data and cloud computing, Ningxia will focus on building a comprehensive number of full industrial chains such as navigation, e-sports, smart cities, and photovoltaics. In these new industries, Ningxia will take the lead in development and change from “catching-up” to “leading”.

摄影：陶克图

巨大的蜻蜓翅膀
Giant Dragonfly Wings

驱车从宁夏的荒漠戈壁穿过，往往会被远处高高矗立的像是巨大的蜻蜓翅膀的风机所震撼。塔架高六七十米，叶片长达七八十米，有的在加速转动，有的慢悠悠的。因良好的风场，宁夏成为风力发电的主战场。如果堂吉诃德看到这样的巨人，一定不会上去搏斗了。

Driving through the Gobi desert area in Ningxia, one is often shocked by the huge wind turbines. They stand tall and high in the distance like dragonfly wings. Each tower is sixty-seven metres high and the blades are seventy to eighty metres long. Some are turning at speed and some are slow. Due to its impressive wind field, Ningxia has become the main battlefield for wind power generation. If Don Quixote were to see such a giant, even he wouldn't dare tilt at such a windmill!

冷凉蔬菜成了“菜篮子”的主力军
Cold-season Veggies Become the Main Force of Local "Grocery Basket"

固原气温常年在17℃—25℃之间，不但适宜避暑，也适宜种植冷凉蔬菜，主要包括甘蓝、大白菜、胡萝卜、洋葱、马铃薯等。原州区彭堡镇姚磨村主要有西芹、蒜苗、西蓝花、娃娃菜、大白菜、红笋等。每年进入7、8、9月份，北京周边和中原以及南方大部分地区的蔬菜生产进入了淡季，冷凉蔬菜就成为“菜篮子”的主力军，暖了市民的胃。

The temperature in Guyuan City is between 17 °C and 25 °C. This climate is not only pleasant in summer, but also suitable for growing cold-season vegetables including kale, Chinese cabbage, carrots, onions and potatoes. Yaomo Village, in Pengbu Town, Yuanzhou District, mainly grows celery, garlic seedlings, broccoli, baby cabbage, Chinese cabbage, and red bamboo. Every year in July, August and September, vegetable production in Beijing and the Central Plains as well as most of the south has entered the off-season. Cold-season vegetables thus become the main force of the region's "grocery basket" and warm the stomachs of the local people.

动动手指问医三甲

Go to a Primary-ranked Hospital by Swiping on Your Phone

六个月大的天天患有血管瘤，他的爸爸通过互联网+智慧医疗平台，得到了上海交大医学院权威专家给出的诊疗方案。免去了长途颠簸周折，节省了各种费用一万多元。天天的爸爸说，现在给小天天看病，只用动动手指，就可以挂上外地三甲医院专家号，查看历史就诊记录，获取化验及检查结果，免去了挂号排队和等待报告的时间。

Tiantian is only six-month-old and he suffers from hemangioma. His father received the treatment plan given by authoritative experts at School of Medicine, Shanghai Jiaotong University through the "Internet plus" Smart Healthcare platform. It saved a long journey as well as more than 10,000 yuan. Tiantian's father said, "Now with just a swipe of my finger, I can make an appointment with experts in a primary-ranked hospital, check medical records, and collect the results of tests and checkups. In this way I can avoid the registration queue and the wait for information."

没有智慧就没有灵魂

There is no Soul without Wisdom.

一个城市只有自然山水没有智慧，如同一个人只有外表而没有灵魂一样。银川市主动联合全球 40 多个国家的 145 个城市参与创建智慧城市，从开蒙到智慧，从试点到获奖。创建智慧城市就是创建绿色、高端、和谐、宜居的城市，因为有趣的灵魂最长情。

A city has only natural landscapes without wisdom, just as a person without wisdom, has only their appearance and no depth to their soul. Yinchuan City actively participates in the creation of smart cities in cooperation with 145 cities in more than 40 countries around the world, aiming to go from enlightenment to wisdom, from first steps to winning awards. Creating a smart city is to create a green, high-end, harmonious, and livable city, because the interesting soul is the deepest love.

供图：宁夏画报社

跨越黄河送温暖

Sending Warmth across the Yellow River

华电银川“东热西送”集中供热项目是国内首家采用百万千瓦空冷机组供热的项目，输送距离约46公里，主支干线长约217公里，将穿越交通枢纽、水利设施53处，施工距离、作业难度等方面均开创了国内供热项目先河。其中，盾构机“穿黄”隧道施工是该项目的控制性节点工程，对实现银川集中供热目标具有决定性影响。

The China Huadian Corporation has an East-West Project in Yinchuan, “East-to-West Heat Project”. It is the first domestic heating project that uses a million kilowatt air-cooled unit for heating and supports long-distance, cross-Yellow River with the use of a large temperature-difference heat pump. The transportation distance is about 46 kilometres, and the main branch line is about 217 kilometres. It will cross 53 transportation hubs and water conservancy facilities in total. The construction distance and the difficulty of operation have created a new precedent for domestic heating projects. In particular, the construction of the shield tunnel “through the Yellow River” was the control node of the project, which has had a decisive influence on the realization of the central heating targets of Yinchuan.

摄影：陶克图

摄影：陶克图

借风飞翔
Drawing Power from the Wind

风很早就被人们利用，主要是通过风车来抽水、磨面……18 世纪初，横扫英法两国的一次狂暴大风，二十五万株大树被连根拔起。仅就拔树一事而论，风在数秒钟内就发出了一千万马力。目前全世界每年燃烧煤所获得的能量，只是风力在一年内所提供能量的三分之一。宁夏是全国首个新能源综合示范区。贺兰山、麻黄山、香山、南华山、西华山等大型风电厂，依据风能资源条件和市场消纳能力，借风飞翔。

The wind was harnessed by people from very early on in history, mainly for pumping water and powering mills. In the early eighteenth century, a violent wind swept across Britain and France, and 250,000 trees were uprooted. This wind sent out 10 million horsepower in a matter of seconds – the trees didn't stand a chance. At present, the energy that comes from burning coal every year in the world is only one-third of the energy provided by wind in one year. Ningxia is the country's first comprehensive new energy demonstration zone. Large-scale wind power plants such as Helan Mountains, Mount Mahuang, Mount Xiangshan, Mount Nanhua and Mount Xihua draw power from the wind according to the conditions of wind energy resources and market consumption.

首都带首府
National Capital Guides Regional Capital

“首都带首府，共同来创新”，由银川市与北京中关村共同建设、共同打造的协同创新示范区——银川中关村科技园从签订合作协议到正式挂牌运营，不到三个月时间。园区管委会一位负责人说，这充分体现了银川与中关村创新合作的务实高效，充分展现了银川所蕴含的巨大潜力与魅力。

“National capital guides regional capital, let's innovate together.” It took less than 3 months for the synergy demonstration zone jointly built by Yinchuan and Zhongguancun (a technology hub in Beijing considered to be China's Silicon Valley) – Yinchuan-Zhongguancun Innovation Centre – from having contracts written and signed to officially beginning operations. An official from the central administrative committee said that it shows how efficient the cooperation between Yinchuan and Zhongguancun is, and the potential and attraction Yinchuan holds in store for people across the province and wider country.

文化的碰撞很有意思
Interesting Cultural Collision

这里中午像个联合国的比萨店加咖啡馆，坐满了宁夏大学的各国留学生。墨西哥比萨、奶酪馅儿饼是美国李广哲的太太提供的配方，咖喱鸡肉比萨是来自新加坡陈龙的意见。来自罗马尼亚的米海兰笑着说，我们来自不同国家，带来的口味不一样，但我们爱这里的一切。银川很像我们的家乡，生活节奏不快，天，真的很蓝。三个不同国家的外国人，在银川开咖啡馆，把所有文化的碰撞，都融合在了一个小小咖啡馆里。

When sitting in the pizzeria cafe in Ningxia University at noon, one feels like being in the headquarters of the United Nations, because foreign students from all over the world gather to enjoy lunch here. The Mexican pizza and cheese pie recipes were provided by Tyler's wife (Tyler himself is American, and his Chinese name is Li Guangzhe), and curry chicken pizza was suggested by Chen Long from Singapore. Mi Hailan from Romania smiled and said, "Though we come from different countries and have different tastes, we love everything here. Yinchuan is like a hometown to us. The pace of life is unhurried, with a clear blue sky all the time." Three foreigners from three different countries opened a cafe in Yinchuan and integrated all these cultural collisions into a single humble cafe.

渔光共唱幸福歌
Synergy of Fishing and Photovoltaic Modules

贺兰县常信乡寇家湖在河网密布的区域架设光伏组件，把光伏电池板搭建在鱼池上，水中养殖名特优新水产。在提供绿色环保的新能源的同时，大量节约土地和不可再生能源，提升综合效益。渔光互补光伏发电，致富路上共唱幸福歌。

Changxin Township, Helan County, set up photovoltaic modules across the extensive network of local rivers, built photovoltaic panels on the fish ponds, and cultivated famous aquatic products in the water. By providing green and environmentally friendly new energy, it will save a lot of land and non-renewable energy, while enhancing other comprehensive benefits. The synergy of fishing and photovoltaic power generation has enriched the local people.

参考文献 | Reference

蔡国英《泾源史话》，宁夏人民出版社，2012 年。
蔡国英《宁夏新十景诗词集》，宁夏人民出版社，2016 年。
蔡国英、张进海《宁夏地方史话丛书》，宁夏人民出版社，2012 年。
陈旭《贺兰山，银川平原的守护神》，《中国国家地理》2010 年第 2 期。
丁明《宁夏小杂粮》，宁夏人民出版社，2008 年。
固原市委宣传部《固原名片——一座城池的记忆》，宁夏人民教育出版社，2016 年。
郭勤华《地域文化视阈下的民俗——以固原民俗为例》，《西夏研究》2013 年第 4 期。
郭永龙《你不知道的中国——塞上江南宁夏》，中国旅游出版社，2015 年。
海鹏飞《张承志　走不出乌托邦》，《南方人物周刊》2014 年第 22 期。
胡建东《水韵回乡——吴忠》，宁夏人民出版社，2012 年。
胡迅雷《宁夏掌故》，宁夏人民出版社，2008 年。
黄敬刚《“塞上江南”古乐觅踪——宁夏乐器乐种调查记》，《民族艺林》2017 年第 1 期。
贾长安《山水湖城——石嘴山》，宁夏人民出版社，2012 年。
李福祥、王晓华《浪漫沙都——中卫》，宁夏人民出版社，2012 年。
李进祥《清水河，一条流淌着人性与尊严的河》，《中国国家地理》2010 年第 2 期。
李进祥《女人的河》，宁夏人民出版社，2012 年。
李树江、吴忠礼《宁夏当代著名人物传略》，宁夏人民出版社，1999 年。
李文华《话说宁夏》，宁夏人民出版社，2008 年。
李祥石《发现岩画》，宁夏人民出版社，2005 年。
李祥石《解读岩画》，宁夏人民出版社，2012 年。
林涛《宁夏方言概要》，宁夏人民出版社，2012 年。
刘婷《“文化品牌”与“品牌频道”的市场探索——宁夏卫视频道“文化名家塞上行”系列活动》，《大市场·广告导报》2006 年第 11 期。
刘伟《食在宁夏》，宁夏人民出版社，2012 年。
刘喜林、陈世容《我们可爱的家乡——宁夏》，宁夏人民出版社，2010 年。
马世芳《音乐的生长——苏阳林生祥两岸民谣音乐对谈录》，《音乐时空》2013 年第 13 期。
马彦、张燕《宁夏旅游指南》，中国建筑工业出版社，2015 年。
孟秦《固原，曾为名城两千年》，《中国国家地理》2010 年第 2 期。
牛尔惠《余秋雨易中天北行记》，《文化交流》2007 年第 6 期。
秦川《一座巨大的“博物馆”——固原》，《中国国家地理》2010 年第 2 期。
孙凝异《贺兰山下艺如云》，《中华手工》2016 年第 12 期。
唐骥《诗话——宁夏旅游风光》，宁夏人民出版社，2003 年。
唐荣尧《水洞沟——见证东西方文化的远古碰撞》，《中国国家地理》2008 年第 4 期。

唐荣尧《中国有条贺兰山》，《中国国家地理》2008 年第 9 期。
唐荣尧《张贤亮眼中的宁夏》，《中国国家地理》2010 年第 2 期。
唐荣尧《宁夏之书》，宁夏人民出版社，2011 年。
王荣、何彤慧、吴宏岐《地名文化景观与地名资源开发、管理研究》，中国社会出版社，2016 年。
王晓华《神秘王陵》，宁夏人民出版社，2012 年。
王正儒《民间宁夏》，宁夏人民出版社，2012 年。
王正儒《文学固原（隆德卷）》，宁夏人民教育出版社，2015 年。
王正儒《文学固原丛书》，宁夏人民出版社，2015 年。
吴晓红《住在宁夏》，宁夏人民出版社，2012 年。
武宇林《中国花儿通论》，宁夏人民出版社，2008 年。
肖彭《宁夏景象》，中国言实出版社，2017 年。
薛青峰《沙湖奇景》，宁夏人民出版社，2012 年。
薛正昌《根脉与记忆——宁夏历史文化遗产》，中央编译出版社，2016 年。
杨宏峰《塞上江南神奇宁夏丛书》，宁夏人民出版社，2012 年。
杨弘章《宁夏石窟，刻在大山上的“战争与和平”》，《中国国家地理》2010 年第 2 期。
杨云、范晓儒《黄河金岸》，宁夏人民出版社，2012 年。
杨占武《宁夏城乡旅游》，宁夏人民出版社，2015 年。
叶长青《红绿六盘——固原》，宁夏人民出版社，2012 年。
银川晚报社编《发现宁夏》，宁夏人民出版社，2008 年。
于鹏亮《宁夏电影中的地域、民俗特点研究》，《长城》2009 年第 12 期。
于小龙、唐志军《百年银川》，宁夏人民出版社，2008 年。
张涛、郝峰《明珠凤城——银川》，宁夏人民出版社，2012 年。
张万静《游在宁夏》，宁夏人民出版社，2012 年。
张哲《宁夏民俗》，宁夏人民出版社，2012 年。
张哲《宁夏岩画》，宁夏人民出版社，2012 年。
张哲《宁夏长城》，宁夏人民出版社，2012 年。
张哲《远古水洞沟》，宁夏人民出版社，2012 年。
赵邵俊《固原东山的赎身习俗》，《宁夏师范学院学报》2015 年第 4 期。
郑晨阳《宁夏名人》，宁夏人民出版社，2012 年。
郑彦卿《塞上江南——宁夏》，宁夏人民出版社，2012 年。
周兴华、周晓宇《宁夏史地新证——神秘南长滩》，宁夏人民出版社，2013 年。
朱千华《九道村：饮一瓢水就是天堂》，《中国国家地理》2010 年第 1 期。
邹荣《六盘山传统文化探究》，文化艺术出版社，2004 年。
《走遍中国》编辑部《走遍中国——甘肃宁夏》，中国旅游出版社，2016 年。

索　引 | Index

A

B

C

D

E

F

G

H

J

M

N

P

Q

R

S

T

W

X

y

Z

图书在版编目(CIP)数据

微观宁夏:汉英对照/蒋文龄主编.—北京:商务印书馆,2019
(微观中国)
ISBN 978-7-100-16815-1

Ⅰ.①微… Ⅱ.①蒋… Ⅲ.①宁夏—概况—汉、英 Ⅳ.①K924.3

中国版本图书馆CIP数据核字(2018)第249005号

微观宁夏
(汉英版)
蒋文龄 主编

商务印书馆出版
(北京王府井大街36号 邮政编码100710)
商务印书馆发行
北京中科印刷有限公司印刷
ISBN 978-7-100-16815-1

2019年3月第1版 开本787×1092 1/16
2019年3月北京第1次印刷 印张16¼
定价:68.00元